THE PSYCHOLOGY OF GENOCIDE, MASSACRES, AND EXTREME VIOLENCE

THE PSYCHOLOGY OF GENOCIDE, MASSACRES, AND EXTREME VIOLENCE

Why "Normal" People Come to Commit Atrocities

Donald G. Dutton

PRAEGER SECURITY INTERNATIONAL
Westport, Connecticut · London

Library of Congress Cataloging-in-Publication Data

Dutton, Donald G., 1943–
    The psychology of genocide, massacres, and extreme violence : why "normal" people come to commit atrocities / Donald G. Dutton.
        p. cm.
    Includes bibliographical references and index.
    ISBN-13: 978–0–275–99000–8 (alk. paper)
    ISBN-10: 0–275–99000–1 (alk. paper)
1. Violence. 2. Social psychology. 3. Genocide—Psychological aspects. I. Title.
HM1116.D88 2007
304.6'63—dc22   2007005293

British Library Cataloguing in Publication Data is available.

Library of Congress Catalog Card Number: 2007005293
ISBN-13: 978–0–275–99000–8
ISBN-10: 0–275–99000–1

First published in 2007

Praeger Security International, 88 Post Road West, Westport, CT 06881
An imprint of Greenwood Publishing Group, Inc.
www.praeger.com

Printed in the United States of America

∞™

The paper used in this book complies with the
Permanent Paper Standard issued by the National
Information Standards Organization (Z39.48–1984).

10 9 8 7 6 5 4 3 2 1

Every reasonable effort has been made to trace the owners of copyright materials in this book, but in some instances this has proven impossible. The author and publisher will be glad to receive information leading to more complete acknowledgments in subsequent printings of the book and in the meantime extend their apologies for any omissions.

Understanding now the human condition,
I dedicate this book to my dog.
To Babar:
Would that all humans
Shared your beastliness

CONTENTS

PREFACE

Throughout film history men[1] have been transformed into mythical beasts—to vampires and werewolves, each with a terrible violence that supposedly transcended the human condition. In fact, this may be a metaphor for the transformation to brutality that we are capable of as humans. When we describe a kindhearted act, we call it "humane," and heinous acts are performed on "dehumanized" victims. Yet throughout human history humanity has been the most destructive species on the planet. Hopes that the Renaissance would produce a more enlightened, cultured, and nonviolent phase of humanity have long since been dashed. The twentieth century, just past, has been the bloodiest in human history.[2] Our capabilities to build more powerful weapons increase each year; our capacity to experience compassion for humanity as a whole does not. Indeed, as we will see in Chapter 1 of this book, the process of generating slaughter is no different in the twenty-first century than it was in the eleventh century: define an enemy, accuse that enemy of horrible actions or the potential for the same, generate fear and a sense of a just cause, and accuse those who do not fall into line of heresy or a lack of patriotism. A tribal passion ensues that generates the capacity for extreme rage and genocidal violence—the will to annihilate an entire people. The pathway to this tribal passion can occur through rapid societal change—the development of new norms defining violence as acceptable and targeting the victim group who are typically described as vermin or a virus. This view of the enemy group spreading generates rapid fear-based action to exterminate them as quickly as possible, even their infants.

The drive to kill is fueled by a societal sense of power and destiny—a sense of entitlement called narcissism in an individual but nationalism in a country. Sadakat Kadri,[3] in his wonderful history of the trial, recounts an apocryphal tale told by St. Augustine in the fifth century. A captured pirate, asked by Alexander the Great how he dared to plunder the high seas, responded, "Because I do it with a little ship I am called a pirate, because you do it with a great fleet you are an emperor."[4] Indeed, our moral judgments about murder are quite protean and are applied differentially in civilian and military contexts. Most Americans did not favor the punishment of Lt. William Calley for the rape and murder of Vietnamese women and children at My Lai.[5] Calley spent just a few days in prison. Recent revelations[6] indicate that his actions were not atypical. The U.S. 101st Airborne, nicknamed Tiger Force, cut a bloody swath through Viet Nam, torturing, raping, and collecting body parts. In a civilian context, just one person acting this way would generate heightened police surveillance, as with Gary Ridgway, the Green River Killer in Seattle. In war, it generates cover-up and indifference.

Although there are individual societal differences in aggression, these appear to ebb and flow within a culture and to be generated by a time-limited hubris[7] followed by decline. The capability for extreme cruelty seems not so much particular to any one culture but more to any culture when the "perfect storm" of conditions descends. For this transcultural reason, sociobiologists tend to view extreme violence as an inherited and vestigial remnant of our predator past, of the "pain-blood-death" complex, a set of associations with successful hunting.[8] Humans exhibit a greater capacity for cruelty than do other animals, leading some to think that a certain level of brain development, allowing for a "theory of mind" (i.e., how a victim would think), is essential for cruelty. Others wonder if our lack of success at contacting other forms of higher life, despite an array of satellites and detection equipment, could possibly mean that higher life forms destroy themselves and that extreme violence, a by-product of intelligence, has obliterated them.

In this book, which could be described as a marriage of social and forensic psychology with history, I try to explain the psychological mechanisms that generate extreme violence. I do not call it "savagery" because highly civilized groups are as violent as the "savages" they disdain. If there is a child of this marriage, it would be a new field of study, which I call forensic ethology.

I was inspired to write this book by reading Romeo Dallaire's *Shake Hands with the Devil*,[9] recounting the horror he lived through trying to save the Tutsi in Rwanda, as commander of the UN Forces there. I went to hear Dallaire speak and was moved by his courage and compassion—he is a remarkable man. I had earlier read Mark Danner's[10] recounting of the massacre at El Mozote in El Salvador and was stunned by the actions of the El Salvadoran army slaughtering civilians, including children. Now I know they were not atypical. Samantha Power's[11] amazing description of the problem of genocide in the twentieth century was very inspiring as well. I had a background in social psychology but with a taste for the great thinkers like Eric Fromm[12] and Ernest Becker.[13] Their insights on the generic basis of the problem of "evil" in humans is outlined in Chapter 2 and best describes the general motivational base of extreme violence. Some social psychological experimental research has supported the notions of Becker on out-group hatred as a response to one's own sense of mortality,[14] but generally laboratory research is not well suited to the issues raised here. In massacres, a spiraling feedback loop seems to occur that amplifies violence. Obviously this cannot be studied in a lab. My approach here is to mimic the naturalistic studies of animal behavior called ethology[15] that were performed before sociobiological theory swamped the field and forced all observations into the Procrustean bed of "proving" a theory. I argue that an ethology of human aggression should be obtained from descriptions of violence by perpetrators and eyewitnesses. Some such testimony is given in this book, by perpetrators of atrocities in Nanking, Rwanda, and Viet Nam.

I am indebted to the following people for help in writing this book. Michael Bond and Ehor Boyanowsky, both old friends and scholars, collaborated on the initial paper that led to this book, published in the journal *Aggression and Violent Behavior* in 2005. Both inspired me with ideas and material throughout the writing. My longtime colleague at the University of British Columbia, Peter Suedfeld helped direct my literature search. Christie Tetreault wrote the first draft of the chapter on the Holocaust as an undergraduate project and made substantial contributions to the revisions. Fortunately for me, she had obtained a history degree before "re-enlisting" in psychology. She did an enormous amount of research on this thoroughly researched event and, in the stretch, both she and Rene Lane helped immensely with final editing. Lindsey Korman also contributed to the chapter on lynchings—some of the most brutal acts we encountered in this most brutal of subjects. As Lindsey discovered, the preparatory arousal of prolonged agitation present with military massacres was not present for the most brutal lynchings—the killers had just come from church!

Let me issue a few words of warning about the contents of this book. This is not easy reading. The descriptions of violence are horrible but real. They are based on the best available historical evidence. The reason for this is that, as much as film portrayals of violence have become increasingly graphic and violent, they cannot approach what we describe here. People cannot watch realistic disembowelling or dismemberment or sadistic torture. They cannot watch the killing of children. The flashes of dismemberment of combat troops in the film *Saving Private Ryan* numbed many audience members. We resort to computer graphics to depict these acts in a way that does not produce revulsion (the "comic book" film, *Sin City,* is an example). This revulsion is a good thing, an emotional remnant of our conditioned revulsion at killing our own species. Unfortunately, we overcome it too easily. My purpose in writing this book was to describe human violence in all its horror, not the sanitized version studied in academic psychology labs, where the delivery of low level electric shocks or punching bags is as severe as it gets. My hope is that, fully apprised of what can occur, we can be more mindful as humans at preventing its recurrence.

Finally, a few words on the process of writing about the topics in this book. Victor Nell, in his provocative article on the sociobiology of cruelty (cited in Chapter 12) tells of paleontologist J. M. Coetzee saying that those who deal with evil become tainted by it—that evil is contagious. Iris Chang, overburdened by her topic in the *Rape of Nanking* and the *Bataan Death March,* committed suicide in the middle of writing the second book. My emotional reaction was a form of "psychic numbing," initial horror at what I was reading followed by a pervasive *Weltshmertz,* a German word that means a "world-weariness" and general disappointment in humanity. In effect, it is a flattening of affect that occurred for the killers, too, as I discuss in Chapter 9. I was walking with a neighbor who described being moved by a film (*Tuesdays with Morrie*) that we had both seen and asked my reaction to it. When I said it did not affect me much, he became agitated and accused me of lacking compassion. How could I tell him that, in the context of what I was then reading, the film paled by comparison. The man in the film (Morrie) was dying of cancer but had come to terms with his death. At the time, the image I was carrying was that given at the end of this book, the description by the Ukrainian engineer, Herman Graebe, of a Jewish family dying together with dignity that I found profoundly moving. This was the image last proffered by the prosecution at the Nuremberg trials and concludes Chapter 12 of this book.

What are the final lessons learned? I came to the conclusion that the most powerful human motive by far is the striving for attachment to loved ones in perpetuity. Humans will do anything for this, including blowing themselves (and others) to pieces. I learned that tribalism is universal. It may start with the attachment to another (typically, the mother and disinterest in those who are not her), and it may be furthered by the division of in-group as those we recognize and out-group as the rest, but our capacity for symbolism established in- and out-groups in us all, and we view their actions completely differently. We need, if we are to survive, a sense both of humanity as a tribe and of humanity's potential for radical violence. If we delude ourselves that we are the civilized entity we appear to be on the surface, we are doomed to repeat the mistakes of the past, only with more powerful and devastating weapons.

1 ———————————————————————————

A HISTORY OF VIOLENCE

> By the very fact that he forms part of an organized group, a man descends several rungs down the ladder of civilization. Isolated, he may be a cultivated individual, in a crowd, he is a barbarian—that is, a creature acting by instinct.
>
> —Gustave Le Bon, *Psychologie des Foules* (The Crowd)[1]

In the twelfth century, a terrible dilemma existed for knights and their followers. They were trained to kill and to lead relentlessly violent lives. At the same time, they believed in divine punishment for sins, including violence.[2] As Joan Acocella put it her *New Yorker* article on the Crusades,[3] "every church portal they gazed up at showed grinning devils hauling down the violent to Hell. So they were caught in a vise: the thing they were trained to do was also a thing that was going to cause them to burn for all eternity."[4] The cognitive dissonance[5] or psychological contradictions between these beliefs and practices was unbearable. A lifetime of killing surely meant that one would burn in hell forever, a thought too terrible to contemplate. The Catholic Church had problems of its own. Secular kings struggled for power with the church, and the church itself was divided between the center in Rome and the breakaway Greek Orthodox church in Constantinople, under the control of the Byzantine Empire. The process of buttressing the church's power began in earnest with Pope Gregory (1073–1085), described by Asbridge as "profoundly ambitious, wilful; and intransigent."[6] Gregory's solution to the interference of secular kings in Europe was to use the power of excommunication and, with it, the threat of being barred from heaven and from eternal peace. This strategy was first used successfully against King Henry IV of Germany, and we can gauge its power by what it was able to overcome, a claim of sole power over a country.

Gregory's successor, handpicked by Gregory himself, was Pope Urban II. Urban's initial time in office was problematic, since he had to contend with a rival Pope, Clement III, whom he eventually bribed to leave. It fell to Urban to devise an ingenious strategy to amplify the power of the church. He devised the concept of positive violence, a way that one could be violent and still get to heaven, a form of violence that would, in fact, guarantee admission to heaven. It was later called holy war.

The blueprint for holy war had been drawn out years before by St. Augustine (354–430 C.E.) in *Contra Faustum Manichaeum.*[7] The gist of the argument went like this: a "just war" is both legal and moral; it is one fought against enemies of God or of God's representative on earth (as the Catholic Church claimed to be). It must be proclaimed by a legitimate authority (a king, prince, bishop, pope), it must have a just cause (i.e., to avenge an injury, recover property, or defend against attack), and it must be fought with the right intention (without cruelty or excessive bloodshed). The just warrior restrained sinners from evil, acting against their will but in their own best interest. As quickly became evident, the criterion of right intention was rarely met. This new view sparked by Augustine meant that actions themselves, no matter how violent, were not evil in themselves (*mala in se*).[8] Only their intention made them so. The holy war, however, became seen as one that God actively supported, not merely tolerated. In a legal analogy, Augustine's concept is similar to freedom from punitive damages in law, whereas the prior concept (by Cicero) was commensurate with compensatory (rather than punitive) damages.[9] Augustine is given credit by Phillips for breaking "Latin Christian theology from the shackles of pacifism,"[10] and his resolution of the violence–eternal damnation dilemma quickly filtered down into European society.

As Phillips recounts, several attempts had been made by the Catholic Church to put the concept of holy war to practice before the year 1000,[11] including two attempts in the ninth century to rally military support by promising "heavenly reward" or "eternal life" for those who fought in defense of Rome. Subsequent brutal campaigns to convert the pagans of eastern Europe helped stimulate the idea that warfare might have a pious goal. By the eleventh century, the notion of the Christian soldier had progressed to the point where the Pope himself (Leo IX) fought in battle.[12] However, the notion was given great impetus by Gregory VII, who believed himself to be the living embodiment of St. Peter, that he should have unchecked control over the spiritual well-being of all humanity, and that his power took precedence over that of kings. Furthermore, Gregory instigated the notion of God as Lord or ruler to whom Christians owed obedience, as they would a mortal king.[13] Hence, the moral authority of God belonged with fealty to the Pope, and those who died in that service would be guaranteed a special place in heaven. Church sophists, in the manner of Augustine, began to "interpret" the scriptures in line with this Christian soldier view.

John of Mantua, for example, noted that, although Christ had ordered St. Peter to sheathe his sword in the Garden of Gethsemane, he had not told him to cast it aside. On this basis, John maintained that Jesus wanted his apostle to retain the weapon for use at a later date.[14] John concluded that God intended the pope to wield the laity in defense of Christendom. With loyalty thus secured and with promises of eternal life for just war, the cognitive groundwork for the Crusades had been laid.

The implementation of the just war concept was first successfully launched (Gregory had been unsuccessful in trying to launch a crusade) by Pope Urban II at Clermont, France, in 1095, claiming in a sermon "that a people from the king-dom of the Persians, a foreign race, a race absolutely alien to God, has invaded the land of those Christians and has reduced the people with sword, rapine and fire."[15] As Asbridge notes, Urban's sermon contained the three Augustinian prin-ciples of the just war as well as "denigration and dehumanization of Islam." An out-group was described that was "alien to God," savage and violent, and capable of incomprehensible levels of cruelty and brutality.[16] Urban falsely described the Muslims as using vivisection to search for money inside hapless captured victims (a practice later used by the Christians after the fall of Jerusalem). Furthermore, Muslim violence was directed at the in-group, the tribe, the Christians. This appeal, as we shall see in the chapters to follow, is a temporal and cultural univer-sal. It constitutes the original and the ultimate rallying cry.

As Asbridge put it, "Urban was activating one of the most potent impulses in human society: the definition of the 'other.'"[17] Further, his image of a captured Jerusalem was designed to be distressing to Christians, especially given the atroc-ities described as occurring there. It was also a popular belief at that time (as in 2006; see Phillips, *An American Theocracy*)[18] that the "Last Days" prophesied in the Bible—when all mankind would be judged and the "saved" would enter eternal paradise—could come only when the Holy City of Jerusalem was again in Christian hands.[19]

In the sermon Urban promised eternal reward for the new "Soldiers of Christ" who would fight a just war to reclaim lost land, and as a distinct class of warfare, prosecuted under controlled conditions. These conditions, though, had nothing to do with the degree of violence but were based solely on the "alien nature" of the enemy.[20] As Asbridge concludes, "this may, to some extent, help to explain why the First Crusaders proved capable of such extreme brutality."[21]

In this sermon, Urban redefined the ideological framework of sanctified vio-lence to produce a new model of sacred warfare that contained a recipe for salva-tion: one could now kill and go to heaven. In fact, heaven would be open to those who fought a holy war and who otherwise may not have been received in heaven. Fighting now became a means to purify one's soul and eternal peace the reward for earthly violence. The expedition preached at Clermont represented a new form of "super penance," a venture that could cancel out any sin through its sheer arduousness. As Asbridge puts it, "for the first time, fighting in the name of God and the pope brought with it a spiritual reward that was once readily conceivable and deeply compelling: a real chance to walk through the fires of battle and emerge unsullied by sin."[22] The foreshadowing of Muslim suicide bombers, guaranteed a place in heaven if they die fighting a jihad (or holy war), was laid a millennium ago, as was the definition of Christians and Muslims as sworn enemies. The fallacious attributes of the threatening target group (possessing weapons of mass destruction, performing vivisection on Christians) were as compelling in the twenty-first century as they were in the eleventh century.

Pope Urban's sermon had an electrifying effect on Europe, generating 60,000 to 100,000 crusaders drawn from all walks of life and fulfilling a varied set of motives. For the knights, it was an opportunity to live out life's calling with impunity and heavenly reward, and for the poorer serfs, a chance for adventure, as well as escape from starvation and tedium. Asbridge argues that the crusade was stage managed by having Adhemar de Le Puy attend the sermon at Clermont and then immediately (as the Pope stopped talking) step forward to "take the cross" and serve as the "primary instigator" to be modeled by the rest.[23] Another, Raymond of Toulouse, sent ambassadors the next day, suggesting advanced planning. Urban then engaged in an extended speaking tour that crisscrossed much of France, staging a number of mass rallies[24] (pp. 46–48). The result was "rapid spread of crusading fever"[25] now called a hysterical contagion that in some locations produced riots, as well as spin-off sermons by unofficial preachers and swarms of recruits—ecclesiastics, peasants, women, and children, a "diverse cross section of society."[26]

These diverse elements would gather into what became known as the People's Crusade led by a French monk called Peter the Hermit, which also included "adulterers, murderers, thieves, perjurers" as well as "pious folk."[27] In general, the First Crusade was made up of a cross section of society from France, Germany, and Italy (all called Franks by historians). Only a small subgroup included knights because only a small section of society could afford knighthood, which required the purchase and care of a fighting horse. At this time, the cavalry charge, designed to rip into the enemy at full gallop and shred them with lances, had not yet been perfected.[28] However, the knights that did come had been trained for combat and excelled at the type of fighting that did dominate the crusades: chaotic, close quarter combat. The knights were also well armed, carrying lances, spears, and swords, and were well trained in the use of weaponry (the training was labor intensive and required wealth in order to spare the time). Knights also had a five-man support crew who cared for their horse, weapons, and food and who themselves were armed and took part in combat. Typically, the choice of weapon for foot soldiers was a bow that was easy to make and could kill at up to 300 meters. Waves of arrows could pierce any kind of armor then developed. By 1095, the crossbow had also been developed. This weapon generated so much force that it could penetrate seven centimeters into solid wood. An early arms treaty in the twelfth century sought to have it banned.[29] However, the type of warfare required in the Crusades was siege warfare, with which the knights had considerable experience.

Siege warfare had become commonplace in Europe in the time preceding the Crusades. Medieval society depended on castles, and castles had to be fortified against attack. This fortification typically involved huge stone walls topped by parapets (from which boiling oil could be poured or arrows shot). Against these massive walls, the besieging force would use a variety of catapults (called by their Latin names *petraria* and *maganella*) capable of hurling boulders, flaming bundles, or human heads and bodies. The latter was used as a tactic of psychological warfare to spread terror and revulsion in the besieged. There is something archetypal about a siege; the two warring groups have antagonistic goals (defense and attack), and the siege typically lasts a long time during which both loathing and resolve increase on both sides. In the Crusades, psychological warfare was commonplace. Muslims hung dead Crusaders on top of their besieged walls and left them there so their friends could watch them rot. Christians beheaded Muslim prisoners in front of the walls so the enemy could watch and then catapulted the heads over the walls.[30] It was not unusual for the siege to be breeched by bribing someone from within to betray the fortifications. Needless to say, when the walls were finally breeched, the social conditions for atrocity (conflict, fear, and hatred) had been met.

In the First Crusade, two major sieges occurred, one in the city of Antioch and another in Jerusalem itself. They were preceded by a minor siege, in the city of Nicaea where the Nicaene Creed that defines modern Christianity was created in 325 by Constantine and 300 bishops. Before the siege of Nicaea began, several battles had already been fought between the crusaders and the "Saracens" or Turkish army. The People's Crusade had been badly routed, and many were killed. Hence, bad feelings had already developed. Nicaea was on the shore of the Sea of Marmara, so obtaining supplies for the besieging crusaders was logistically easy. The Muslims who met the crusaders were skilled warriors and were ferocious, the spread of Islam had been based on violence (Muhammad himself waged brutal campaigns while subjugating Mecca), and the concept of *jihad* or holy war was already legally enshrined in Islam by the eighth century.[31] However, the Muslims did not initially view themselves as being engaged in a grand struggle with Christianity. The focus of battle for Islam in the eleventh century was Sunnis against Shi'ites, and it took centuries of Christian crusades to redefine the enemy as Christianity.

The People's Crusade, led by Peter the Hermit, preceded the other armies. Made up of a ragtag group of civilians with no military training, they nevertheless slaughtered Jews in the Rhineland on their way to Asia Minor. The Turkish sultan there, Kilij Arslan, defeated the People's Crusade easily, virtually annihilating them and, for that reason, probably underestimated the following army of crusaders, led by Godfrey of Bouillon. For this reason, this army, which contained knights, was able to enter easily into Asia Minor and to push toward their first target city, Nicaea. According to Asbridge,[32] the arrival was piecemeal, composed of several existing armies under no central command and with no logistical plan for food and provisions. The crusaders were spared by Arslan's absence. Nicaea was south and close to Constantinople, the seat of the eastern Christian church led by Emperor Alexius I of Byzantium. Alexius bargained with the crusaders, promising supplies in return for liberated territories. Virtually from the beginning each side betrayed the other. Alexius also made what are now called "back channel" deals with Arslan, in case the siege of Nicaea failed.[33] While playing both sides, Alexius did establish logistical aid for the crusaders and sent 2,000 Byzantine troops to assist the siege.

Nicaea had a massive lake on one side and a 5 kilometer wall on the other three, 10 meters high, punctuated by 100 towers and reinforced by a double ditch.[34] When all their forces arrived, the crusaders encircled these three walls. It is estimated that this comprised an army of 100,000 with another half million in support. They spoke over 20 languages and had no clear leader. If Arslan had attacked at this point, the crusaders would have, in all probability, been routed. Starting around May 10, 1097, the crusaders isolated the city and built assault catapults, battering rams, and bombardment screens.

On May 15, through a captured spy who was threatened with torture, the crusaders found out that Arslan had finally gone on the offensive and was hiding his army to the south of them. Arslan attacked too late and was routed after more crusader reinforcements arrived. However, he fled with most of his army. The crusaders, in what was the first "threat display" of the engagement, decapitated the dead and vanquished, stuck some of the heads on their spears and paraded them before the city walls, and catapulted other heads into the city.[35] As Asbridge puts it, "any medieval army knew the profound significance of morale amid the slow grind of siege warfare and exchanges of horrific acts of brutality were commonplace."[36] The Turks hung the bodies of dead or captured crusaders from grappling hooks and left them to rot on the city walls. Several attempts to storm the walls took place, and all were repulsed. The defenders shot stones and arrows and poured burning oil and tar on the invaders who tried to defend themselves with shields constructed on the spot. These battles continued for over a month with many deaths on both sides. Finally, the crusaders decided to attack from the water side with the aid of an army of Greeks sent by Alexius. The city capitulated on June 18. The Greeks immediately took a policing role and prevented looting or carnage. There was much grumbling among the crusaders until Alexius, in effect, sufficiently bribed them. Diaries from the battle reflect the belief that those who died "entered Heaven in triumph."[37]

From this point, the crusaders moved slowly toward Antioch, their next target 100 kilometers away. The pace was determined by the size of the army (70,000 at this point) and their fear of breaking into smaller, more manageable groups because of the threat of counterattack by Arslan. The compromise was to keep two separate armies in close contact as they moved to Antioch. On June 30, the Turks attacked when the crusader army had been divided by a river crossing. Surviving eyewitness accounts described the Turkish army as huge and mobile (they were on horseback). The crusaders calmed themselves by forming a defensive circle and praying, repeating the phrase "Stand fast together, trusting in Christ and the victory of the Holy Cross. Today we may all gain much booty."[38] The fear amongst noncombatants was extreme; they huddled together and trembled. The Turks broke through and began a slaughter. Some women dressed up to appeal to "'love of beauty,' that the Turks might learn to pity their prisoners."[39] At last, the second crusader army arrived, and the Turks were routed.

About 3,000 Muslims and 4,000 Christians died. Asbridge attributes the success of the defense to Bohemond, a giant (over 7 feet tall), muscular legendary leader who, by force of his personality, kept the crusader army from breaking formation. The Turks lost hope and fled, using a scorched earth policy (destroying everything of possible use to the invaders) to deprive the crusader army.

Asbridge makes it clear that the crusaders were a heterogeneous group, composed of numerous nationalities from Europe and speaking over 20 languages (collectively called the "Franks" although not all of them were French). They had but one thing in common: they were Christian and had targeted a common foe, the infidel. However, as they were composed of several armies, each with its own leader, internecine squabbles were inevitable. These began in Tarsus, a town on the road between Nicaea and Antioch. The town was rather easily taken, but battles over the spoils of victory developed between two of the army leaders, Tancred and Godfrey. This was an omen of things to come. Christians killed Christians as greed triumphed.[40] Strategy came to be formed not so much on defeating a besieged Muslim force but on the postvictory division of spoils.

One of the knights, Baldwin of Boulogne, broke ranks with the others who were moving to Antioch to establish himself as Lord of a separate territory that he deemed conquerable, due in part to the fact that Armenian Christians who lived there welcomed the crusaders as liberators from Muslim rule. Baldwin became ruler of a town called Edessa (in what is today northern Syria) after the townspeople were let into the ruling leader's fortress by the crusaders who had sworn to protect him. They tore him apart with their bare hands and paraded his body parts around the city.[41]

When the crusaders entered Asia Minor in September 1097, they were only a month's march from Jerusalem, but their route was guarded by Antioch, then one of the greatest cities of the Orient and standing at the intersect of all major trade routes (today called Antakya in Turkey). Antioch had been founded in

300 B.C.E. and had been the third city of the Roman Empire (after Rome and Constantinople) with a population of 300,000. The Romans built a formidable defensive wall by 560 C.E., after 600 years of growth in the city. By the time of the crusaders' arrival, the city had been the subject of numerous invasions by Greeks and Turks, and its political composition was complicated by various political allegiances. Nevertheless, the strategic importance of Antioch was such that the crusade could not progress to Jerusalem without first securing Antioch. The siege was carefully planned to first conquer satellite cities around Antioch and cut off supplies. Antioch, however, was built at the foot of two craggy mountains, with a river on the other side and with a defensive wall, 5 kilometers long (that went up and through the mountains), 2 meters thick, and 20 meters high. The crusaders' first impression was that it was unconquerable.[42] The city had a 5,000 man Turkish garrison, plentiful supplies of food, and access to the river. The siege began on October 20, 1097, and lasted nine months. Seven armies surrounded the city with some jockeying for positions near gates and, hence, first access when the city fell. The rule for dividing the spoils was "right by conquest"; hence, first access was important. The attack strategy was based on a "pre-looting" model. Bohemond, in charge of the attacking armies, captured some of the Turkish garrison and "[those] whom we captured, were led before the city gate and there beheaded, to grieve the Turks who were in the city."[43]

Before the crusades had begun, Christians lived without repression in Antioch (and, for that matter, in most of the Muslim world). Once the siege began, the Greek Christian patriarch was regularly hung from the city walls and beaten on the soles of his feet. Any captured Latins were decapitated and their heads catapulted into the crusader camp. Captured women were raped, then killed. Asbridge warns his reader that "these acts may appear utterly barbaric by modern standards but they were a staple feature of mediaeval warfare," and that, "within the context of a holy war, in which the ranks were conditioned to see their enemy as sub-human, Christian piety prompted not clemency but, rather, an atmosphere of extreme brutality and heightened savagery."[44] As we shall see in the chapters to follow, this has not changed so much as Asbridge may think. In fact, the resemblance in the psychological structure of lethal conflict (dehumanized perceptions, rape of enemy women, displays of cruelty) are remarkably consistent, suggesting some form of universal template, occurring across time and place.

The siege at Antioch dragged on through the winter of 1097–98 with both sides scrounging for food and trying to stave off starvation. Battles and skirmishes occurred intermittently with deaths recorded on both sides. As Asbridge records, death by starvation, illness, or battle became a probability throughout the winter of 1098.[45] A black market developed whereby besieged Armenian Christians would scour the countryside for food and sell it to the crusaders. Asbridge's recounting of the siege depicts a spiraling conflict of starvation, occasional skirmishes, public torture, and killing of the other side as a threat.[46] In addition, Muslim reinforcements encountered the crusaders, and larger battles were fought. The grind of combat seemed to generate increasing anxiety, rage, and spiritual belief, all coexisting. The crusaders, for example, blamed their difficulties on God's punishing them for their sins.[47] Battles between the two sides took place almost daily,[48] including a decisive victory for the crusaders at a "Bridge Gate Battle." Despite these military campaigns and wars of attrition, the battle outcome came down to one of the besieged Muslims, Firuz, betraying the city in an act of treachery. Firuz commanded at least one tower and was possibly an Armenian (who had converted to Islam). He apparently had made contact with Bohemond, who bribed him with protection and promises of wealth in return for letting Bohemond get first entry into the city (and hence, first claim on booty) through the tower under Firuz's command. The crusaders successfully invaded at night on June 3, crying "God's Will!"[49] Native Christians still living in the city (Armenians generally) opened remaining gates and "what followed was a chaotic and bloody massacre, fuelled by eight months of suffering, starvation and stored aggression"[50] and "they were sparing no Muslim on the grounds of age or sex, the ground was covered with blood and corpses and some of these were Christian (from within the city)."[51] As Asbridge puts it, "repellent as it was, the appalling violence perpetrated by the Latins during the sack of Antioch did in fact improve the crusade's prospects of success. Their willingness to butcher the city's garrison gave them a reputation for absolute ruthlessness, and in the coming months other Muslim cities on the road to Jerusalem considered negotiating with the Latins rather than face wholesale destruction."[52] It was not clear who lived to spread the word. While the Christian armies were fighting amongst themselves over the spoils, a Muslim army arrived, making them the ones now besieged. Much has been written about this period, where the crusaders were hopelessly outnumbered and besieged for weeks but somehow engineered a victory on June 28, 1098, due largely, it seems, to the incompetence of the Muslim leader, Kerbogha, to gifted leadership amongst the crusaders, and to zealous conviction on their part.[53]

Antioch was secured, its inhabitants given the choice of converting or dying, its mosques turned into churches, and its possessions taken. In the months to come, this process was repeated in smaller towns on the road to Jerusalem. Marratt, for example, was conquered and plundered, and all its inhabitants were slain. As one participant recorded,

> Our men all entered the city and each seized his own share of whatever goods he found in the houses or cellars, and when it was dawn they killed everyone, man or woman, whom they met in any place whatsoever. No corner of the town was clear of Saracen corpses, and one could scarcely go about the streets except by treading over their dead bodies (from the *Gesta Francorum*, cited by Asbridge).[54]

Although Jerusalem was three days march down the road, it would take six months to set out on this final push because rival knights were fighting over the spoils in Antioch. The crusaders had now acquired a taste for slaughter, even of noncombatant women and children (what would now be considered a war crime). Although their violence was initially directed at "infidels," eventually it would be directed at any group that stood between them and booty.

As winter set in, the Christians in Marratt ripped apart Muslim bodies looking for coins with which to buy food. Failing that, they cut pieces of flesh from the bodies, which they cooked and ate.[55] Asbury notes that the historical sources recounting the holy war rarely showed signs of disgust. The cannibalism in Marratt was an exception. Again, these worst acts may have contributed to subsequent success, as tales of the cannibalism contributed to the myth that crusaders were bloodthirsty, invincible savages.

On June 7, 1099, the crusaders arrived at Jerusalem with 1,300 battle-hardened knights and 12,000 infantry.[56] Despite fierce battles, Jerusalem fell comparatively quickly. By July 15, after a final battle the Muslim defenders fled and chaos ensued. As Asbridge put it, "with their pious ambition realised, they unleashed an unholy wave of brutality throughout the city, surpassing all that had gone before."[57] One of the crusaders, Raymond of Aguilers reported,

> Some of the pagans were mercifully beheaded, others tortured for a long time and burned to death in searing flames. Piles of heads, hands and feet lay in the houses and streets...they were stabbing women who had fled into palaces and dwellings; seizing infants by the soles of their feet from their mothers' laps or cradles and dashing them against the walls and breaking their necks; they were slaughtering some with weapons, or striking them down with stones.[58]

The crusaders were wading ankle deep in blood.[59] Once this wave of slaughter subsided, looting began and involved cutting open Muslims who were believed to have swallowed money.[60] The city's Jews took refuge in their temple. The crusaders burned it down.

At this point, perhaps feeling some exhaustion from the acts of slaughter "they came, still covered in their enemies blood, weighed down with booty, rejoicing and weeping from excessive gladness to worship at the Sepulchre of our Saviour Jesus."[61] As Asbridge notes, "in the minds of the crusaders, religious fervour, barbaric [sic] warfare and a self-serving desire for material gain were not mutually exclusive experiences."[62]

The Turks had lost Jerusalem to the Egyptian Fatimids prior to the attack, so the crusaders took the city from the group they had been hoping to make their allies. Most of the wealth acquired was spent on the journey home, so most returned home penniless. The Eastern Christian sects (Armenian Christians and Copts) were expelled from the city. Pope Urban II never heard of the victory because he died two weeks after it occurred.[63]

Three more major crusades occurred in the next 200 years, since the Turks kept re-seizing the Holy City. Compared to the first crusade, they became progressively worse. The extreme violence continued (vivisections, cannibalism, infanticide, torture) but now was turned against other Christians (for example, the Christian city of Zara in Hungary) as well as other groups of infidels, such as the Jews.[64] The siege of Zara was purely for economic and political purposes and was opposed by the pope in Rome; in fact, he threatened excommunication. After some bickering amongst the leaders, the crusaders went ahead in 1203, apparently deciding they could buy the pope off later. Just in case though, they did not share the excommunication threat with the common soldiers. If there was a low point to the Fourth Crusade, commensurate with the First Crusade's sack of Jerusalem, it would be the sack of Constantinople, seat of the Eastern Christian Church and richer than any city in Europe. The invasion seems to have been motivated purely by politics and greed. The sack itself was reminiscent of the now established *modus operandi* of the crusaders: rape, massacre, and plunder (to this day, the four horses over the portal of St. Mark's Cathedral in Venice are booty from Constantinople). A crusader, Baldwin of Flanders, was crowned emperor of Byzantium but was killed within a year. The violence, as horrific as it had been in the First Crusade, reached worse levels, with both Muslims and Christians having their limbs hacked off and purposively being left to die a slow death.[65] In a letter to Emperor Baldwin on November 7, 1204, Pope Innocent expressed his joy at the capture of Constantinople, which he described as a "magnificent miracle" and attributed to "the Lord and is wondrous in our eyes."[66] Letters though the year 1205 show Pope Innocent's joy as unabated by the increase of power for the Roman Church. However, stories about the methods used to sack Constantinople eventually made their way back to Rome, including descriptions of merciless slaughter of Christians of all ages, men and women alike, "staining with blood Christian swords that should have been used on pagans." A returning crusader recited the atrocities "rape of matrons, virgins, nuns, the sack of churches and the violation of sacristies and crosses."[67] This caused the Pope to "express doubts as to the true motives of the crusaders."[68] However, this did not deter him from seeing the enormous benefit to the Church and the need to "reinforce and defend this land."[69]

Why start with the Crusades? There are several reasons. The first is practical; they were described in great detail by writers on both the Christian and Muslim sides. The sources available to modern historians such as Asbridge and Phillips were immense. Second, they represented simultaneously the horrors associated with siege warfare throughout the Middle Ages, a virtually inevitable massacre of the towns' inhabitants. Walled towns were commonplace throughout Europe and the Middle East for this very reason. The reader is invited to inspect the mammoth walls at Carcasonne, in southern France, for a sense of the importance of such protection. The Crusades represent the Middle Ages' form of violence, unbridled slaughter, in the service of an ideology—in this case a religious ideology, Christianity. As we shall see throughout this book, slaughter in the service of ideology is commonplace throughout history whether it be political or religious. Religious ideology has one great advantage over political ideology in generating violence. It can offer everlasting salvation, as Urban II did to launch the First Crusade. It was used with Japanese Kamikaze pilots and is used now to inspire Islamic suicide bombers (see Chapter 13). The belief that is central to this promise is the most powerful motivating belief in the human mind: that the martyrs will live, with their loved ones, in everlasting bliss. This notion of the promised future continues to generate extreme and self-destructive violence in the present. Both Christianity and Islam have done this, despite both the Bible and the Koran advocating peace and forgiveness. We have seen above how the theme of peace was twisted to fit the political necessities of church expansion.

A further power resides in religious ideology: the notion of Armageddon. Asbridge describes how the recapturing of Jerusalem was consistent with Christian belief that the "last days" before the Second Coming of Christ foretold in the Bible could only come to pass once Jerusalem was again in Christian hands.[70] Phillips' book, *American Theocracy,* points to the same belief amongst a sizable number of fundamentalist Americans (called "end-timers") and sees this belief as supportive of the 2003 invasion of Iraq, diminishing a threat to Israel and Jerusalem.[71] The weaponry has improved immensely in the millennium since the crusades; the ideological belief structure and psychological need to belong to a like-minded "tribe" still persists.

There are other reasons for examining the crusades. Although the knights involved had been trained for a life of violence, others were drawn from ordinary people. The People's Crusade, for example, contained "everyday people" who nonetheless slaughtered Jews in Germany on their way to the Holy Land. This raises another important question that we will attempt to answer: How can normally socialized people become murderous during politically sanctioned conflicts? Also, because of the wealth of information available, we can observe another thought process central to violence, that of projective identification. Through this process, motives or intentions that are unacceptable to the self are "projected" onto an outside group. Hence, extreme violence is described as "barbaric" (see the quote at the beginning) or as "non-human." In truth, "lower forms" of life are not nearly as violent as *Homo sapiens.* Only chimpanzees demonstrate sadistic behavior, which seems to require a certain level of complex brain organization.[72]

In this chapter, gruesome actions (such as vivisection) were attributed to the Muslims but eventually performed by the crusaders themselves. While visiting Rome once, I took a tour of the Roman Coliseum. The guide informed us that 1 million humans and 1 million animals had been put to death there "before the barbarians took over." The irony of the statement appeared lost on the guide.

One of the universals of intergroup savagery is that it is attributed to the enemy group and denied in the host group. The historical truth is that intergroup savagery is the rule, from Vlad (the Impaler) Tepes, to Genghis Khan, to the Conquistadors to World War II. In the latter, Iris Chang, author of the *Rape of Nanking*,[73] ascribed savagery to the Japanese for the atrocities visited on the Chinese at Nanking. This is a typical perception by a member of a victimized group, that there is something unique about the horrific perpetrators one focuses on. Only when one broadens the focus to all groups of perpetrators does this uniqueness disappear. In his autobiographical film, *The Fog of War,* former U.S. Foreign Affairs Minister Robert MacNamara, describes the U.S.-led firebombing of 60 Japanese cities (before the nuclear bombing of Hiroshima and Nagasaki), and in which over a million civilians were burned to death. If we'd lost the war, he intones, we'd be war criminals. It is rare for anyone to accept, as MacNamara did, in-group responsibility for savagery.

2 ───────────────────────────────

MASS VIOLENCE IN THE TWENTIETH CENTURY

...it is the disguise of panic that makes us live in ugliness and not the natural animal wallowing...this means that evil is now amenable to critical analysis and, conceivably, to the sway of reason.

—Ernest Becker, *Escape from Evil,* p. 169

We must, of practical necessity, limit our selection of examples of group violence. For this reason, amongst others, we jump from the Crusades in the eleventh century, chosen because of their extensive documentation and their seminal role in generating religious war, to the twentieth century. There are other reasons for this leap, which include the relatively superior documentation of twentieth century events (the Crusades are an exception) and the relevance of still recent events.

History, prior to the twentieth century, has been replete with the elimination of groups of people whether in biblical references to the elimination of the Philistines by the Israelites,[1] the destruction of Carthage by the Romans [including rubbing salt into the ground (so nothing new would grow) and an estimated 150,000 killed], and, later, the massacre of "infidels" by both sides during the Crusades of the eleventh to the thirteenth centuries[2] as we discussed in Chapter 1. Further incidents include the successful and bloody sieges of cities as disparate as Moscow, Kiev, Baghdad, Samarkand, and Beijing by Genghis Khan in the thirteenth century[3] and the extermination of the Huguenots by Louis XIV. Some would include in this lamentable litany the Spanish conquest of the Americas,[4] the state-inspired slaying of Jews in Tsarist Russia,[5] the bounty imposed on Apache scalps in the nineteenth century in Mexico,[6] and the annihilation of Beothuks in Newfoundland.[7] Hence, while the term "genocide" did not exist prior to

the twentieth century, there were historical incidents that were genocidal, including the treatment of natives in the United States[8] and the massacre of Europeans
during the Thirty Years War.[9] These in no way, of course, constitute a complete
list; for a more comprehensive review see Charney or Rummel.[10] We are unaware
of any prolonged period of human history that is not marked by ethnopolitical violence. However, the frequency of democide (murder by government of 1 million or
more people) and genocide increased dramatically in the twentieth century.

The twentieth century, far from representing advances in post-Renaissance
"civilization," witnessed the greatest number of separate large scale systematic
slaughters of human beings of any century in history.[11] One could argue that
prior centuries simply had poorer recording of events, especially in cultures with
oral traditions. Hence, both African and American native tribes existing before
the colonial powers arrived are frequently portrayed as living in an idyllic "state
of nature." Anthropological evidence suggests a different picture, that nonviolent
tribes are exceptions, usually because of isolation. In rare cases where an outside
observer was able to record observational data, a very different picture emerges.
For example, John Jewitt,[12] a British seaman taken captive by the Nootka, a tribe
on the west coast of Vancouver Island, British Columbia, described the constant
war raids, slaughters, and slave-taking that occurred during his stay. In 1803, his
boat had been attacked by the Nootka while anchored, and its crew was slain and
decapitated, with their heads arranged in a line.[13] Jewitt became one of the
Nootka chief's 50 slaves (the others were captured from adjacent tribes), kept
alive because of his skill with metal. Jewitt escaped 28 months later and wrote
his memoirs in a book originally known as *Jewitt's Narrative* and first published
in 1815. The factual descriptions of Jewitt about the Nootka tribe were largely
confirmed by Jose Mozino,[14] a Spanish scientist who visited the area even earlier
(1792). While native aggression toward the white man was historically justified
(given that on earlier visits the whites had been violent), the constant warring
with neighboring tribes may have been normative. Where literacy existed to
record events, constant war and slave-taking were reported as normative, as with
the Maya (who were literate and kept codices or written histories).[15]

DEMOCIDE

The twentieth century may become historically infamous for identifying new
and sinister types of aggression, namely democide[16] and genocide, a term that
did not exist in the lexicon of homicide until post World War II. The former
included routine killing as a form of political threat, such as the punitive killing
of workers in the Congo who failed to collect their quota of rubber for the plantations of King Leopold of Belgium.[17] As grim as these slaughters were, they are
beyond our current scope. Leopold's mass slaughter was not genocide. It was not
an attempt to exterminate the Congolese. Leopold, to the contrary, wanted to

keep them alive (albeit terrified) so they could work his rubber plantations. In order to keep control, Leopold ordered his militia to cut off hands, noses, and ears of the terrified workers.[18] This system was also used to reimburse the killers for their "work." (That is, they got paid by the body part.) A century later, in virtually the same geographic area, Hutu would slaughter Tutsi and refer to it as "the work." The traumas of Leopold's excesses persisted in the Congo via oral history for at least 50 years and were recorded by a Catholic priest sent to the area. In one oral report to the police, a man named Tswambe described one Belgian state official, named Leon Fievez, as follows:

> All the blacks saw this man as the Devil of the Equator...From all the bodies killed in the field, you had to cut off the hands. He wanted to see the number of hands cut off by each soldier, who had to bring them in baskets...A village which refused to provide rubber would be completely swept clean. As a young man, I saw Fievez's soldier Molili...take a big net, put the arrested natives in it, attach big stones to the net, and make it tumble into the river...Rubber caused these torments; that's why we no longer want to hear its name spoken. Soldiers made young men kill or rape their own mothers or sisters.[19]

The atrocities in the Congo were discovered and reported by whistle-blowers in much the same way as later genocides and were met with initial skepticism by a European (and later American) public who could not believe that civilized men could do such things. This pattern of denial, as we shall see, is still commonplace. Only the proliferation of portable video recorders has changed our ability to witness the violence. Leopold's public relations problems began when his state officers "dared to kill an Englishman"[20] and a series of writers and whistle-blowers began to alert the public about the nightmare in the "heart of darkness."

This nightmare was, simply put: slavery conducted by working the Congolese to death. A clerk, Edmund Morel, noticed discrepancies in the shipping lines records—that steamers going from Belgium to the Congo were not carrying trade items, as the government pretended, but instead were carrying only weapons. There was no compensation for the rubber and ivory being shipped back from the Congo. The Belgian "policy" in the Congo treated the Congolese as subhuman beasts of burden who were expendable unless they produced. This latter constraint stood between the Congolese and genocide; they were not hated, only dehumanized.

INCIDENCE

Rummel[21] put the number of victims murdered by democide (including genocide) at 169,198,000 for the twentieth century, ranking the "killed" as comparable to the sixth largest state in the world. The reader interested in body counts is referred to Rummel's numerous tables and figures documenting what he calls the "dekamegamurderers" (10 million or more—Stalin, Mao, Hitler, and Chiang Kai-shek) and the "lesser megamurderers" (1 to 10 million)—Japan's military, Cambodia under the Khmer Rouge, Turkey's purges, the Vietnamese War state, Poland's ethnic cleansing, Pakistan, and Yugoslavia under Tito. Finally, Rummel describes the "suspected megamurderers"—North Korea, Mexico, and Feudal Russia. The Mexican numbers included Maya killed under Porfirio Diaz as part of the national practice of slave labor. In 1910, one-third of the entire population (mostly indigenous people) were slaves and a mere 3,000 families owned half the property in the entire country—haciendas of up to 6 million acres each. During the Mexican revolution (1910–1920), both sides slaughtered at will, rape was commonplace, and entire local ethnic populations were eradicated. Pancho Villa, for example, killed all Chinese[22] in Torreon. Rummel puts the number of indigenous dead through slave labor and starvation at 825,000 —it was, in effect, an uncompleted genocide of the indigenous peoples.

In the twentieth century, the numbers of human victims of mass slaughter burgeoned. According to Gilbert,[23] in 1914, about 1 million Armenians were massacred or died from brutalities inflicted upon them by the Turks. This slaughter, along with the "death by labor" campaign in the Congo were the two first large scale atrocities of the twentieth century. In addition to 20 million eastern European war dead, the Nazis systematically murdered about 6 million Jews, as well as 5 million Slavs, Gypsies, and others, between 1933 and 1945;[24] Stalin masterminded the killing or starvation of up to 30 million "dissenters" in the Soviet Union;[25] Mao Zedong oversaw the killing of up to 20 million of the "bourgeoisie" in China;[26] and the Khmer Rouge led by Pol Pot killed 2.5 million "educated people" in Cambodia between 1974–1978.[27] In Rwanda, in 1994, in a mere three months, Hutus killed circa 800,000 people, most of them Tutsi.[28] Saddam Hussein orchestrated the killing of the Kurds and gassed others who are still suffering, while, in Bosnia, the Serbs under Slobodan Milosevic carried out "ethnic cleansing" of non-Serbs. Other mass slaughters fall short of the legal definition of genocide but share similarities in the psychology of the *genocidaires* (I will use the French term in this book, since English does not have a noun for those who commit genocide), e.g., massacres in El Salvador, Nanking, The Congo (currently), Somalia, Sierra Leone, Darfur, etc.

The focus of this book is on the psychological factors, both social and individual, used to explain this mass social violence. We examine massacres, political slaughter, and genocide. These three forms of political violence are by no means exhaustive. For a more complete taxonomy of ethnopolitical violence, the interested reader should see Suedfeld,[29] Rummel,[30] or Charney.[31] We do not review examples of various forms of terrorism, suppression, or retaliatory persecution described by Suedfeld. These are beyond our current scope: to understand the psychology of genocide and military massacre. Our focus is on sociopolitical violence generated in most cases by governments (as Rummel argues) and carried out by agents of the government, official or otherwise. For sake of comparison, two forms of spontaneous group violence will be examined: lynchings and prison riots. These will illuminate our argument that certain repeated structural forms involving perceived threat and a power differential can generate hideous violence.

The exacerbation of ethnopolitical violence in the twentieth century may have been due to crowding and increased contact,[32] globalization of the economy leading to increases in discrepancies between rich and poor,[33] increased availability of information (leading to greater resentment by the poor), increases in human rights (leading to rebelliousness amongst the politically oppressed), or rapid social change (leading to chaos, as well as a psychological need to assert the tribe). This change includes the withdrawal of colonial powers serving as superordinate authorities (e.g., Belgium—although the authority itself was, as we have seen, ruthless and violent). Also, the collapse of the Soviet Union has generated volatility and mass slaughter in numerous states from Yugoslavia to Somalia.[34] Wynne-Edwards proposed a homeostatic theory of population regulation in animals where species attempt to regulate population size.[35] As overpopulation increases relative to available food, warfare and violence increase. While he had animal behavior in mind, sociobiologists have reminded us that we are, amongst other things, animals, or, as Ernest Becker called us, "Gods with anuses."[36] Becker wanted to reconcile the earth bound–animal nature (anus) with the capacity for symbolic reasoning (gods).

The forms of politically motivated homicide include aggression against individuals (state execution, execution of dissidents, "disappearing" suspected dissidents, as in Argentina) and groups (war, with victims defined nationally or geographically; *pogrom or massacre,* the victims more specifically defined by any characteristic as a devalued out-group as occurred in the United States (at the Sand Creek massacre of the Cheyenne in 1864),[37] genocide, the victims defined by religious or ethnic group membership, as in Germany, and Rwanda; and systematic political slaughter (with victims defined by political ideology or expediency, as occurred in Cambodia and the Stalinist USSR). The use by familiar groups of massive aggression at its most extreme is well known (for example, the dropping of the atomic bomb on Hiroshima and Nagasaki, the firebombing of both German (Dresden) and Japanese (Tokyo) cities, and, hence, the wholesale slaughter of civilians),[38] but these actions are somehow regarded as less reprehensible in the context of war. In war, the justification for the massive taking of life is ultimately the saving of lives of the in-group (e.g., Hiroshima, Tokyo, Hamburg, Dresden), revenge for past injury (e.g., Hutu violence), or a policy decision regarding the greater good for the greater number (e.g., the systematic murder of millions of Jews in the Holocaust), and it is done in a series of massacres (Rwanda), or through indirect actions and remote operations as in aerial bombing, or in an "industrialized" form such as deportation, internment, and systematic execution, or by exportation of all foodstuffs (e.g., the forced starvation of several million Ukrainians by Stalinist Russia in 1932, now referred to as the Holodomor).[39] Hence our perception of murder as justified depends largely on whether it is murder committed to protect the in-group (or, symbolically, the in-group's central dogma or ideology). In a way, this is the symbolic extension of the "holy war" concept developed by Augustine where violence by the in-group is transmogrified. Our personal fear of death is assuaged by the empowerment of our in-group at the expense of and power over the out-group.[40] The ultimate power over the out-group is to hold life and death control of that group. Ernest Becker saw this action of exercising power as serving the "disguise of panic." In Stephen Spielberg's fine film, *Schindler's List*, Oskar Schindler (Liam Neeson) talks a sadistic Nazi officer (played by Ralph Fiennes) out of killing by convincing him that the ultimate power is to have the power to kill and choose not to exercise it.

The Perception of Culpability for Murder

In civilian circumstances, murder is exculpated only if the perpetrator suffered from a "mental defect," was acting in self-defense, or in some other way was not of "sound mind," so that he/she could not distinguish right from wrong. In the political arena, the distinction between right and wrong quickly blurs. An argument in criminal court against culpability for homicide is that someone "rightfully believed" he/she was in deadly danger and killed. In the civilian situation, it may be possible to establish the wrongfulness of this belief. In military situations, where there is some realistic threat of danger, it may be more difficult. We see this problem in the trial of defendants of the massacre at My Lai.

Military killing, including genocide and massacre, is routinely ignored or forgiven unless the offender belongs to an army that loses the war. In World War II, both sides committed what today would be considered war crimes, such as the deliberate mass murder of civilians who were not being used as shields by enemy combatants. In the biopic, *The Fog of War*, Robert MacNamara recounted how U.S. General Curtis LeMay directed the firebombing of Japanese cities and the incineration of civilians (including, of course, in this indiscriminate slaughter, women and children).[i] About 60 Japanese cities were firebombed, mostly during

---

[i]General Curtis LeMay was a belligerent Cold Warrior who was portrayed in the satirical film *Dr. Strangelove* as the trigger-happy General Jack D. Ripper. Ironically, LeMay was later decorated by the government of Japan. In 1961, during the Cuban missile crisis, LeMay advocated to U.S. President John F. Kennedy that he use the Strategic Air Command to bomb Cuba; "fry it" were his words. When the crisis ended peacefully, LeMay called it "the greatest defeat in our history." LeMay apparently had grown immune to the horror of killing. He had directed the gasoline-jelled firebombing of Japan—estimated to have killed "more persons in a six-hour period than at any time in the history of man" (see geocities.com/lemaycurtis). He said of war: "You've got to kill people, and when you've killed enough they stop fighting." He once said, "We killed off—what—twenty percent of the population of North Korea?" (see geocities.com/lemaycurtis).

1944–1945, using B-29 bombers flying from the Marianas and Iwo Jima. Napalm, a substance that sticks to the skin and burns, causing a horrific death, was first used in these firebombings, although it became more infamous in Viet Nam. On March 10, 1945, LeMay firebombed Tokyo, killing about 84,000 people and burning another 41,000. Sixteen thousand square miles of the city were reduced to ashes. Although the subsequent use of the atomic bomb against Japanese cities is well known, fewer people are aware of the firebombings. However, the phrase "firebombing of Japan" produces over 5 million hits on the Google Internet site. It seems that, with the possible exception of Germany, most countries dismiss their own violence. The government of Japan still denies the Rape of Nanking and Turkey still denies the slaughter of Armenians.

Virtually every Japanese city was firebombed except four: Nagasaki, Hiroshima, Niigata, and Kokura. They were being "saved" for something even worse (the atomic bombs killed 80,000 in Nagasaki and 150,000 in Hiroshima). According to the film, LeMay, although a man of few words, disclosed to MacNamara that "if we lose the war, we'll be tried as war criminals." The ensuing debate would turn on the military necessity of the firebombing to ensure Japan's capitulation. It was argued, as with the firebombing of Dresden and other German cities, that the mass slaughter of civilians lowered enemy morale. Although the Nuremberg Convention prohibits the killing of civilians, exceptions are made (see also wikipedia.org).

In later chapters, we review several military massacres in which the target was women and children. We are not referring to circumstances where they are killed as collateral damage because of guerilla deployment using them as shields. We are talking about their deliberate massacre. No one in the U.S. Army has yet done prison time for any war related killing (although at the time of writing rape and murder charges were laid and a conviction obtained against a U.S. Marine based in Iraq). William Calley, who raped and killed civilians in My Lai, did a few days in jail before being put under "house arrest" at his girlfriend's apartment.[41] When asked to kill noncombatant civilians, especially "by hand," most soldiers balk initially. Bombing and firebombing, however, represent a type of killing where the target is made more remote and impersonal. In his famous experiment on obedience, where experimental subjects were asked to give what they believed were electric shocks to fellow subjects, Stanley Milgram[42] found that making the recipient more remote (by putting the subjects in another room) increased obedience to the order to shock. While there may be some discussion of the war crimes aspect of the actions in the military decision making group, they are inevitably justified as necessary for victory. Since discussion of military options occurs at a top level conference, collateral damage is inevitably regarded as an unpleasant cost of doing war. The "groupthink" aspects (see Chapter 8) drive the military decision outcome inevitably towards annihilation of the target group. One of the few exceptions was the decision by John F. Kennedy to negotiate rather than use deadly force during the Cuban Missile Crisis. Perhaps for this reason, Irving Janis provides this positive example of a group avoiding groupthink in his book on policy decision making.[43] While the numbers of victims of firebombing are impressive, the social process of destruction is relatively simple, due to the immense firepower involved, allowing a few perpetrators to destroy a huge number of victims. We focus here on violence made more difficult by the enormity of its target (i.e., an entire people), carried out over an extended period of time, and involving the more difficult act of killing by hand, where the victim is visible to the perpetrator and, hence, where more prohibitions against killing exist in civilian circumstances.

Genocide

The term genocide was coined by Rafael Lemkin, a Polish Jew who escaped the Holocaust and lobbied tirelessly for recognition of a form of mass killing defined by the United Nations Convention on the Prevention and Punishment of the Crime of Genocide, 1948, as acts committed with the intent to destroy, in whole or in part, a national, ethnical, racial, or religious group.[44]

Genocide itself is a special case of a more general campaign of persecution and elimination of any identifiable group. The UN Resolution of 1948 called for genocide to be defined as follows: Article 2: (UN Convention on the Prevention and Punishment of the Crime of Genocide, 1948): acts committed with the intent to destroy, in whole or in part, a national, ethnical [sic], racial, or religious group, as such: a) killing members of the group, b) causing serious bodily harm or mental harm to members of the group, c) deliberately inflicting on the group conditions of life to bring about its destruction in whole or in part, d) imposing measures intended to prevent births within the group, e) forcibly transferring children of the group to another group. Our focus in this paper is on components a), b), and, to a lesser extent, c).

In addition to genocides and "classicide" or political slaughter, I include examples of three "massacres." One is the "Rape of Nanking"[45] because of its enormity (250,000 killed) and the particularly hideous atrocities committed (rape, killing contests, bayoneting of infants), contemporaneous quality (it occurred in 1937), documentation[46] (Iris Chang, author of The Rape of Nanking, interviewed perpetrators), and potential comparison to genocide. Another is My Lai, where, in 1968, Vietnamese civilians were raped and killed by a Company C, 11th Light Infantry Brigade, American Division of the U.S. Army. There is extensive documentation of this event, including the trial of the second in command, Lt. William Calley.[47] Finally, I include El Mozote, a town in El Salvador where the army raped and slaughtered unarmed women and children, again with living witnesses.[48] Other historical examples of massacres are too numerous to mention but would include, as a short list, Angola, East Timor, Chechnya, the

Sudan, Sri Lanka, Sand Creek (Colorado), and Sierra Leone (see Charney). All of those slaughters occurred during war conditions, and all involved unarmed and helpless civilians. While the genocides appear to constitute controlled or "dispassionate" or instrumental violence (serving a political objective), the massacres, although based on military orders, typically involve "overkill"[49] or violence beyond what is required for military purposes: rape, torture, mutilation, and the killing of harmless civilians, including infants. Finally, mixes of massacre and genocide occur. In Rwanda, a government policy of genocide toward the Tutsi minority was enacted largely through a series of massacres or *pogroms*[50] and, hence, represents a blend of the two forms of political killing.

For genocide, sociopolitical explanations may suffice to explain the choice of a target group and the social induction to killing. In those processes, the "dispassionate" individual killer can be only a cog in the machine and has a very circumscribed role, from signing death warrants (e.g., Adolph Eichmann) to pressing a button to open a bomb bay door, or to release poisonous gas or, under gunpoint, to remove food from starving people. The perpetrator is a specialist who does not usually have to repeatedly engage in the individual infliction of pain, mutilation, and death, or confront the horrific consequences in terms of piles of corpses. Hence, denial, minimizing of the consequences, and the use of euphemism to describe the acts serve to sanitize the actions. In massacres, however, the actions of military, regardless of degree of training, become cruel and violent, limited only by the human imagination. As we shall see, this is not much of a limitation.

Finally, both genocide and massacres involve international complicity, an active *decision by outside countries to disregard the slaughter, a willful ignorance* of what is occurring. In nine genocides in the twentieth century, no outside party intervened until the violence had played itself out, if at all. Power describes the admixture of willful ignorance and disbelief accompanying the Holocaust, the Cambodian genocide, and both the Serbian and Rwandan genocides.[51] Power argues that the world's powers and the United Nations had current information on the progress of all genocides and constructed a rationale for inaction based on national self-interest. Such behavior appears to go far beyond the failure to detect the harm that has been observed in bystander intervention studies of individuals or small groups[52] and to involve political decisions to willfully ignore and remain unconnected from the event and any obligations under international law to intervene. All massacres reviewed here involved extensive obfuscation by the perpetrators. Genocides were denied and "sanitized" language developed to describe events euphemistically (e.g., "the work" used in Rwanda for the slaughter of Tutsi).

In this book, we describe the following genocides: the Turkish slaughter of Armenians in 1915, the starvation of Ukrainians by Stalin in the 1930s known as the Holodomor, the slaughter of Serbian Muslims in Bosnia by Milosevic, Tutsi by Hutu in Rwanda in 1994, and the Holocaust. This is not an exhaustive list. We have not included the mass murders by Mao Zedong, for example, nor the current slaughter in the Darfur region of Sudan (which may be the first genocide recognized as such worldwide and while still in progress). In addition, we include one example of mass political slaughter, that of Cambodians by the Khmer Rouge in 1979–1988 (Suedfeld[53] has termed this *classicide*), as well as examples of massacres: the rape and massacre of the Chinese by the Japanese Army in Nanking in 1937[54] and the massacres at My Lai and El Mozote. To broaden our scope and to serve as comparison situations we also examine two other forms of extreme social violence, lynchings and prison riots.

In each case, I have extracted key historical elements relevant to the perception of an out-group as threatening, to the decision to take violent or genocidal action, and to the acting out of that decision against that group. I should point out that conflicting accounts exist for virtually all examples set out below, typically one (of denial) by the perpetrator group and one by the victim group. For example, Japan still denies the "Rape of Nanking" described below (see Takemoto and Ohara[55]). Wherever possible, I have relied on third party reports by groups such as Human Rights Watch or historians or witnesses from disinterested countries. In Nanking, a member of the Nazi party, John Rabe, gave sanctuary to besieged Chinese civilians and later wrote to Hitler cautioning against any pact with the savage Japanese.[56] Rabe's diary, translated into English by John Woods, makes for chilling reading. When a Nazi is the hero of a piece, one senses that the situation is far removed from normalcy. In some cases (El Mozote and Iraq), forensic evidence supported the victims' version of events. In El Mozote, a forensic anthropology team from the University of Buenos Aires unearthed skeletons of women and children, just as frightened survivors had claimed to skeptical U.S. government officials.[57] In other cases (Nanking and Rwanda), rights tribunals have provided corroboration, and third party witnesses existed to bear testimony (see, for example, Dallaire[58]).

THE PSYCHOLOGY OF THE CROWD: GUSTAVE LE BON

The questions posed by this book are the following: How can people who appear normal be transformed to the point of killing, torturing, and enjoying the pain of other humans? Is this a potential in us all, an inherited wellspring of violence hinted at by the philosopher Thomas Hobbes? If so, what are its mechanisms? How is it that people we view as pathological in everyday life—the rapists, serial killers, sadists—emerge with such frequency during wars? What can we learn abut the human condition from the careful analysis of violence generating situations and the responses people make to them? In a social psychological classic called *The Psychology of the Crowds* (Psychologie des Foules, 1895), Gustave Le Bon described the behavior of revolutionary mobs in the French revolution as indicative of what he called the "group mind."[59] This form of collective unconscious was shared by all men, even those who were civilized. In crowds or "psychological groups" where everyone had one common goal, the behavior of men descended several steps down the evolutionary ladder to the position of "primitive people." As Le Bon put it, "by the very fact that he forms part of an organized group, a man descends several rungs down the ladder of civilization. Isolated, he may be a cultivated individual, in a crowd, he is a barbarian —that is, a creature acting by instinct."[60]

In this group situation, the individual gains "a sentiment of invincible power which allows him to yield to instincts, which, had he been alone, he would have kept under constraint."[61] This occurred, Le Bon suggested, because of the anonymity and consequent loss of personal responsibility in crowds coupled with a form of contagion, where normally proscribed acts would be mimicked and enacted. The suggestibility of the individual in the crowd led to his control by the group mind, a form of racial consciousness causing him to do things and perform actions that contradicted his moral beliefs. This group mind was similar to that of primitive people and led to acts that were impulsive, irritable, changeable, and driven by the unconscious. It also had a thirst for obedience and sought a strong leader. The crowd, Le Bon claimed, acted on "image-like ideas"—visual impressions lacking reason.

Group Psychology and the Analysis of the Ego

Le Bon's work stimulated Sigmund Freud's venture into social psychology, *Group Psychology and the Analysis of the Ego.* To Freud, this crowd produced both leaders who were dangerous fanatics, with attachment to anyone except themselves, and followers who were bound to these leaders because they represented a form of ideal self. Hence, the followers were also bound to other followers through their common connection to the idealized leader.[62]

This "common ego ideal," as Freud called it, held the group together and allowed freedom from social anxiety, the emotional response that acted to direct normative rule—following behavior in everyday life. Since all societies generated rules against aggression within the group (as a way of ensuring group survival), social anxiety served to inhibit in-group aggression. The resulting liberation from social anxiety was a regression to violence, the behaviors of what Freud called the "primal horde," a hypothetical group that slew its father figure and erected totems in his place.[63] Freud viewed the followers as presenting slavishly to the leader, coming with a thirst for obedience that made the leader-follower combination a natural and bidirectional synergy.

Ernest Becker later provided a much more powerful motive than "freedom from social anxiety" as the basis for the leader-follower relationship.[64] More than social anxiety, binding oneself to the tribe served as a symbolic panacea for avoiding the terror of death.

The felt power of immersion in the tribe transcended the mortal and feeble self and generated a sense of immorality. Becker, who was an anthropologist, was far better informed about research on early man than was Freud (especially the extensive writings of A.M. Hocart, written from 1933 to 1969 after Freud had died), and argued that primitive man "raised himself" above his animal nature through his superior left hemisphere capacity for reasoning. This was also his downfall. As Becker put it, "it was man's ingenuity, rather than his animal nature, that has given his fellow creatures such a bitter earthly fate."[65] The "ingenuity" was man's ability to contemplate his own mortality and seek, through his actions, to symbolically avoid it. This avoidance took the form of control of one's environment in the illusion that, by so doing, death could be avoided. This was the basis, as Becker saw it, for religion and the creation of the primal out-group. To the extent that we gain control over the out-group, we feel powerful and, hence, immortal.

Man finds it unpleasant to entertain the notion that accidents or chance determines human affairs. We need to invent a "cause" to replace the notion of chaos in human affairs. Hence, for early man, when evil befell people, it must have been caused by dead spirits. For his early history, man invented ritual as a way of controlling these spirits. The dead were, in effect, the first "out-group" and different from the living. Eventually the out-group became other tribes, and their function became to strengthen the in-group tribes' sense of power and immortality. As Becker put it, "for man, maximum excitement is the confrontation of death and the skilful defiance of it by watching others fed to it as he survives transfixed with rapture."[66] It is to this motive that Becker ascribes the "scorched earth policies" of retreating armies that takes the form of a heightened aggression when in retreat such as the frenzied "final solution" (and in-group violence with the SS shooting the Army) of the Nazis began when they began to sense they were losing the war. This extreme aggression was Becker's "disguise of panic" played to the ultimate.

Post-Renaissance man, according to Becker, replaced ritual with technology, but the purpose was still the same, to create an illusion of a controllable universe and hence to cheat death. Becker's ideas suggest that in-group–out-group thinking has a deep and unshakable source in the human mind, that it serves as one line of defense against death terror, the unbearable dread of our demise. As a relatively weak animal, man had to become acutely aware of sources of power in order to survive. As Becker puts it, "this is one way to understand the greater aggressiveness of man than of other animals: he was the only one conscious of death and decay,[ii] and so he engaged in a heightened search for powers of self-perpetuation."[67] Early man performed ritual sacrifice to his gods to earn their

---

[ii]There is some evidence that other animals also have sense of death. Masson and McCarthy describe elephants appearing to anticipate their death, leaving their herd, and going off to die.[69]

goodwill. He believed he could transfer life from one thing to another, hence, taking a scalp, or eating a heart or liver transferred life force or power from the victim to the conqueror. In modern times, cannibalism still is practiced (e.g., in both Cambodia and the Congo), and these beliefs persist.

At the time Le Bon and Freud wrote their theories of the group mind and the primal horde, no method existed to assess whether some neural mechanism might contain the racial unconscious or the group mind. We now have that means. Functional Magnetic Resonance Imaging indicates "brain behavioral systems" on connected neurons that fire together and produce complex behaviors including violence.[68] Are these neural networks a form of the group mind? Do they indicate an inherited set of behaviors common to all humans and restricted by social convention? When these conventions are weakened by social circumstances such as war, are we all prone to terrible violence? Are we all candidates to join the primal horde? Finally, what diabolical glue serves to make us need the group so strongly and to be willing to surrender our critical faculties in order to belong?

3

GENOCIDES

> The core of sadism, common to all its manifestations, is the passion to have
> absolute and unrestricted control over a living being...It is transformation of
> impotence into omnipotence.
>
> —E. Fromm, *The Anatomy of Human Destructiveness,* p. 323

The annihilation of an entire group of people occurred repeatedly in the twentieth century. While the Holocaust is the best known example, it is not the only example nor even the one claiming the most victims. It is estimated that 6 million Jews died in the Holocaust. About 8–10 million Ukrainians died in the Holomodor. The reader wishing a more detailed version of these events is referred to Samantha Power's excellent book[1] or that of Niall Ferguson.[2]

ARMENIA

According to Power, in 1914 Russia declared war on Turkey and invited Armenians living within Turkey to rise up against the rule of the Ottoman Empire.[3] A small minority did so. The majority of Armenians, however, expressed loyalty to Constantinople. When Turkey, ruled by a group called the Young Turks, entered World War I (on the side of the Germans and Austrians) in 1915, they declared that they would target Christian subjects (the Armenians were Christians) as enemies of the state. Until this time, the Armenians had status as *"infidel dhimmis"* (non-Muslim citizens).[4] In January 1915, the leader of the Young Turks, Mehmed Talaat, declared that there was no room for Christians in Turkey and that they should leave. Ferguson points out that, like the Jews, the Armenians tended to be wealthy,[5] implying that envy was part of an elaborate mixed motive for the coming violence. By March, Armenian men serving in the Ottoman army were disarmed. When the Allies (Britain, France, and Russia) invaded Turkey on April 25, 1915, Talaat ordered the roundup and execution of 250 leading Armenian intellectuals in Constantinople. Prominent Armenians in other provinces met the same fate. Disarmed Armenians were enlisted as pack animals to transport supplies, churches were desecrated, schools were closed, teachers who refused to convert to Islam were killed, and Armenians were "deported" through the Syrian desert without food or water, virtually all dying en route. Many women were raped and killed by their Turkish guards. All boys over the age of ten and all men were shot in batches of 15–20.[6] By proclamation, they had to leave their homes at once and could not take their property. Their houses were stripped of valuables. These actions were justified by the Young Turks as "necessary to suppress an Armenian revolt." Talaat excused his generalizing from a few to the entire group as follows:

> We have been reproached for making no distinction between innocent Armenians and the guilty, but that was utterly impossible, *in view of the fact that those who were innocent today might be guilty tomorrow* (italics added).[7]

By December 1915, about eight months after the Turkish slaughter had begun, the *New York Times* reported that about 800,000 Armenians had been killed. By 1916, the number was put at 1 million and was, at that time, unparalleled in modern history.[8] Estimates of the death toll range from 200,000 (by Turkish historians) to 1 million (by British historians).[9] The slaughter was described by the American consul at Smyrna as follows: "it surpassed in deliberate and long-protracted horror anything that has hitherto happened in the history of the world."[10]

Britain and France were at war with the Ottoman Empire and publicized the atrocities. The British press published photos of the massacre victims, and the Allies (Britain and France) published a declaration condemning "crimes against humanity and civilization."[11] The United States remained neutral and Woodrow Wilson wanted to stay out of World War I, so, with the exception of the *New York Times* (which published numerous stories), there was no coverage of the massacre. The U.S. Ambassador to the Ottoman Empire, Henry Morgenthau, received daily reports of atrocities and became convinced that the Turkish assurance that this was simply random "mob violence" was a lie. He became convinced that "race murder" was occurring, and on July 10, 1915, he cabled Washington as follows:

> Persecution of Armenians assuming unprecedented proportions. Reports from widely scattered districts indicate systematic attempt to uproot peaceful Armenian populations and through arbitrary arrests, terrible tortures, whole-sale expulsions,

and deportations from one end of the Empire to the other accompanied by frequent instances of rape, pillage and murder, turning into massacre, to bring destruction and destitution on them. These measures...are purely arbitrary and directed from Constantinople in the name of military necessity, often in districts where no military operations are likely to take place.[12]

Morgenthau continued to send blistering cables back to the United States (as Romeo Dallaire did to the United Nations when the Rwandan genocide was unfolding). At one point Morgenthau confronted Talaat, then the interior minister of Turkey, and Talaat snapped at him, "why are you so interested in the Armenians anyway? You are a Jew, these people are Christians." When Morgenthau responded that he was not there as a Jew but as the American ambassador, Talaat seemed perplexed. "We treat the Americans alright too," he protested.[13] The Turkish Army surrendered to the British on October 30, 1918. However, four years later, and with a new leader, the Turkish Army renewed the genocide in the seaside city of Smyrna, slaughtering all the remaining Armenians and some Greeks by shooting them en masse or driving them into the sea.[14] The London *Daily Mail* described it as follows: "The sea glows a deep copper-red, and, worst of all, from the densely packed mob of thousands of refugees huddled on the narrow quay, between the advancing fiery death behind and the deep water in front, comes continuously such a frantic screaming of sheer terror as can be heard miles away."[15]

To this day, the Turkish government refuses to acknowledge the Armenian genocide, despite evidence from numerous neutral sources, including the Americans, the United Kingdom, Catholic bishops, and independent mercenaries and Europeans living in Turkey.[16] The British initially tried to set up a war crimes tribunal but eventually gave up.

THE UKRAINIAN TERROR STARVATION OR HOLODOMOR

Ten paces away and our voices cannot be heard. The only one heard is the Kremlin mountaineer, the destroyer of life and the slayer of peasants.

—Osip Mendalstaum, poet, executed for writing that verse about Stalin

Although the Ukraine has been a free country for only a brief period in history, when the Russian revolution occurred the farmers, many of whom were "Cossack-farmers"[17] and used to independence, were given the opportunity to develop semi-independence in return for the obligation to turn over part of their crop to the government for a fixed price. According to Ulam,[18] there followed a remarkable recovery in the fecundity of the Ukrainian countryside. According to Conquest,[19] however, the Ukrainian farmer (who was not a true "peasant" in that he owned his modest acreage rather than working land as a tenant) was regarded with suspicion by Marxist zealots for his individual success and the fact that, in an election, 50 percent of the Ukraine had voted for Ukrainian parties instead of the Bolsheviks.[20] The Marxists were largely urban and dogmatically chose to replace the farmer with a proletariat in the countryside. Their first efforts at forced collectivization were greeted with resistance by farmers who chose to kill their livestock rather than completely turn them over to the state. For a time, the Soviets relented, but then they redoubled their efforts to force the farmers into line, lowering the fixed price and increasing the quota demanded by the state. Those measures were enforced at first by tens of thousands of armed fanatical party members who were indoctrinated to view the farmers as "petty capitalists and class enemies" and sent into the countryside, and then by police and troops. By 1932, ever-increasing government quotas finally exceeded production, and a furious Stalin ordered that not only all the harvest be removed but forbade, by force of arms, the country people from either traveling to find food or importing food. The results were calamitous. According to Conquest,[21] this produced the greatest genocide of the twentieth century, outnumbering all the war dead on both sides of World War I, and eventually reaching approximately 7–10 million deaths in the Ukraine, Kazakhstan, and neighboring Byelorussia. Twenty percent of the world population of Ukrainians died, as well as Kazhaks and Kuban Cossacks.[22] One survivor described it as follows:

> The first deaths from hunger began to occur...there was always some ceremony in the village cemetery. One could see strange funeral processions: children pulling homemade handwagons with the bodies of their dead parents in them or the parents carting the bodies of their children. There were no coffins; no burial ceremonies performed by priests. The bodies of the starved were just deposited in a large common grave, one upon the other; that was all there was to it. Individual graves were not allowed, even if someone were still physically able to dig one...Looking back to those events now, it seems to me that I lived in some kind of a wicked fantasy world ...All the events which I witnessed and experienced then and which I am now describing, seem unreal to me because of their cruelty and unspeakable horror.[23]
>
> To safeguard the 1932 crop against the starving farmers, the Party and government passed several strict laws...watchtowers were erected in and around the wheat, potato and vegetable fields...the same kind of towers that can be seen in prisons. They were manned by guards armed with shotguns. Many a starving farmer who was seen foraging for food near or inside the fields, fell victim to trigger-happy youthful vigilantes and guards.[24]

Those who were not starved were shot. There was a capricious aspect to the killing, set by Stalin's paranoid logic. Stalin ordered all Ukrainian folksingers to be shot,[25] and the Cossacks were deported to Siberia. The Russians went to great pains to keep the extreme human carnage a secret, even in the Soviet Union, though many Western intellectuals including H. G. Wells, George Bernard Shaw, and Pulitzer Prize winner Walter Duranty of the *New York Times* knew but chose to look the other way and even to deny the horror for ideological reasons. Others such as Malcolm Muggeridge and George Orwell sounded the alarm and were dismissed as anticommunist. Apparently even Stalin admitted the numbers in private to Winston Churchill.[26] English government documents now confirm that the United Kingdom knew of the "Holodomor" or Great Hunger. However, no one wished to risk Stalin's wrath by raising a protest. As it turned out, removing food from a whole, unarmed population was a much more efficient means of genocide than gas ovens, deportation, firing squads, or even nuclear weapons. Ferguson makes the point that Stalin was as ruthless as Hitler and did his killing of non-Russians in the midst of an imaginary civil war.[27] As Ferguson puts it,

> we can now see how many of the things that were done in German concentration camps were anticipated in the Gulag: the transportation in cattle trucks, the selection into different categories of prisoner, the shaving of heads, the dehumanizing living conditions, the humiliating clothing, the interminable roll-calling, the brutal and arbitrary punishments, the differentiation between the determined and the doomed.[28]

CAMBODIA

In Cambodia, the symbolic aspect of target selection was emphasized. Cambodian Buddhists killed Cambodian Buddhists who were quintessentially identical to them, except for a manufactured political distinction: to create a "higher" ideal of total political equality, those "educated people" who had participated in an unjust system that had favored them had to be dispatched. All Cambodians with above a grade 7 education were killed, along with people who wore glasses. Some debate exists over whether Cambodia can be termed a genocide, since, on the basis of race or ethnicity alone, genocide in Cambodia would have logically extended to in-group slaughter. For present purposes, we term Cambodia a *systematic political slaughter* as opposed to a true genocide. Rummel calls this a "democide,"[29] which he defines as a government directed mass slaughter that can be based on politics or on "actions in opposition to social policy (in addition to race, religion, ethnicity, etc.) and which causes death by virtue of a depraved disregard for life."[30] The distinction is that while both mass slaughters are government-driven, a democide can include annihilation of a group because of its symbolic political meaning. The Maoist revolution preferred people who were "blank slates," not those who were educated and capable of dissent. Because the violence in Cambodia was directed at Cambodians who were racially identical to the perpetrators, it was not a true genocide (which would logically imply autoextinction). Apart from the basis for the in-group/out-group distinction, the democide in Cambodia was implemented like a genocide. This distinction is important. It suggests that, although religious, racial, or ethnic categories often serve as the basis for mass slaughter, artificial distinctions, based on political ideology, can supplant these categories.

Two communist countries backed by the USSR (Viet Nam) and China (Cambodia) were involved in the struggle for Cambodia. After the Vietnamese had invaded Cambodia, the United States had sided with the Khmer Rouge. The rise of the Khmer Rouge intersected with the American war in Viet Nam, intended to prevent a "domino effect" of Chinese Communism spilling into Cambodia's neighbor, South Viet Nam. U.S. President Richard Nixon expanded that war into Cambodia because North Vietnamese units were taking sanctuary there, and he ordered carpet bombing and then an invasion by ground troops. As the U.S. war against communism spilled into Cambodia, a civil war broke out in Cambodia in 1970 between the forces of Lon Nol, the U.S.-backed leader in Cambodia, and the Khmer Rouge, a radical, Maoist-inspired rebel force, led by Sorbonne educated Saloth Sar, who went by the name of Pol Pot. In 1975, the victorious Khmer Rouge (KR) entered Phnom Penh, the capital of Cambodia, and began to transform Cambodia into a "pre-industrial, pre-capitalist utopia."[31] As early as 1973, the U.S. consul in Cambodia had been notified that villages were being razed by the KR, and this information was relayed to Washington in 1974. In that report, Kenneth Quinn, a U.S. foreign service officer, described the KR's programs as having "much in common with those of totalitarian regimes in Nazi Germany and the Soviet Union."[32]

Those events were described as "infighting" by the U.S. press. Little was known about the KR, or Pol Pot, although reports of genocidal acts began to filter out with Cambodian refugees in Viet Nam and from Francois Ponchaud, a French Jesuit priest who lived among the Cambodians. Ponchaud reported that the KR took no prisoners, instead killing all soldiers and their entire families. Cannibalism had become a common practice during the civil war, as the Cambodians believed (as do some African tribes in The Congo and Burundi[33] and the Japanese Army[34]) that eating an enemy's liver gave them more physical strength. Reports of depravities by the KR were met with incredulity, even in Phnom Penh before it fell. When the last foreign journalists left Cambodia, a cloak of secrecy enveloped the country.

Refugee reports were made to Charles Twining of the U.S. Embassy in Thailand by refugees at the Cambodia-Thai border. The refugees reported mass executions of people killed mechanically by a blow to the back of the head with a garden hoe. The killers were teenage boys. Children had been starved, and Buddhist monks asphyxiated. The KR were killing all ethnic Vietnamese, ethnic Chinese, Muslim Chams, Buddhist monks, and "enemies of the state" (all deemed to be "intellectuals"). One of the "crimes" punishable by death was reminiscing. Memories of the past life were banned (at least their public expression). Libraries were burned. Other prohibited activities included praying, flirting, expressing joy, contacting the outside world, and owning private property. Maoism proclaimed that the revolution should proceed with people who were a "blank slate" and that "to keep you is no gain, to kill you is no loss."[35] Michael Radford's terrifying film version of George Orwell's novel *1984* had nothing on the dystopia created by the Khmer Rouge.

This ideology and a clinically paranoid leader drove the genocide. Like Stalin, Pol Pot believed that he was surrounded by enemies of the revolution. As a witness against him later said, he saw "enemies surrounding, enemies to the front, enemies behind, enemies in all eight directions, enemies coming from all nine directions, closing in, leaving no room to breathe."[36] Pol Pot was able to generate his own paranoia as a world view of the Khmer Rouge, so that the paranoia fed on itself, becoming the new reality. Anybody who might challenge that view would have been regarded as an enemy of the revolution and in turn dispatched, so there was no countervailing voice to moderate the leader's suspicions of other groups. Paranoia spiraled to the extreme of extreme: anyone suspected of even momentary disloyalty was dispatched. In such psychotic groups, a frenzy ensues as to who can demonstrate the most extreme "loyalty." This consequence of terror characterizes all despotic regimes (Stalin was famously paranoid), making them closed systems (described in Irving Janis's concept of groupthink)[37] where opposition to violence is voiced at risk of death. The initial meaning of the word "paranoia," literally "against knowledge," becomes painfully clear in such groups.

Estimates of deaths rose to 800,000 in the first year the KR took power, and a total of about 2.5 million were buried in the "killing fields." Sixteen thousand people had been tortured to death in a prison camp called Tuol Sleng.[38] Typical methods included hanging prisoners by their feet and applying electric currents to their genitals, submerging their heads in jars of water. More prolonged torture was reserved for former officials.[39] Many were publicly disembowelled, and their livers were cooked and eaten by the executioners.[40] To save bullets, killing was done using pickaxes and garden hoes, and children selected for death had their heads smashed against banyan trees.[41]

One problem that war crimes tribunals face is estimating the number of perpetrators. One former KR official came forward in Paris claiming to have personally executed 5,000 people with a pickaxe.[42] As with the Nazis who used euphemisms such as "resettlement, removal or special action" for genocide, the KR used the terms "sweep, sweep out, and discard."[43] Such euphemistic language served the function of helping the perpetrators dissociate from the horrific acts and obfuscated the slaughter for any outsiders who may have heard rumors about so-called "infighting." As of 2002, the KR had still not "officially" admitted any responsibility for the atrocities, and Cambodians born after Pol Pot's reign know more about the atrocities from the American movie *The Killing Fields* than through anything learned at home.[44] Before he died in 1988, Pol Pot denied any knowledge of Tuol Sleng and blamed the Cambodian deaths on "Vietnamese agents."[45]

Whereas the Nazis disguised their crimes with euphemisms such as "resettlement," "removal," and "special action," and the Rwandan Hutus called mass slaughter "the work," the Khmer Rouge used terms synonymous with "sweep, throw out or discard" but never used Khmer words for "kill, assassinate, execute."[46] The Cambodian democide was enacted in the service of an ideal: political purity. The Nazi genocide was enacted also in the service of an ideal: racial purity. What finally destroyed the maniacal regime was the war it had launched against North Viet Nam.

RWANDA

A background condition for genocide appears, with some exceptions (e.g., Sudan), to be the presence of a war. In Cambodia, genocide developed from a brutal civil war that had killed 1 million people. Even the Nazi genocide of Jews developed from long simmering resentments over the settlements imposed for World War I.

Power argues that, "War legitimates such extreme violence that it can make aggrieved or opportunistic citizens feel licensed to target their neighbors."[47] War also generates an ambient terror of extinction that can be displaced into rage,[48] identifies the target for crystallizing that rage,[49] and provides the camouflage and informational vacuum for the genocide.

When, in 1962, Belgium withdrew from its colony, Rwanda, two tribal groups with a history of friction existed in the country. The majority Hutu numbered about 6.5 million, the minority Tutsi about 1 million. The Tutsi were taller, were lighter skinned, and, in the Hutu view, had been favored for political posts by the Belgians. When the Belgians left, 30 years of Hutu rule ensued during which the Tutsi were systematically discriminated against and subjected to periodic bouts of killing and "ethnic cleansing."[50]

Despite the tribal animosity, Hutu and Tutsi lived together and intermarried, attended the same schools, and drank at the same bars. By 1990, the political tensions generated a group of armed Tutsi exiles called the Rwandan Patriotic Front (RPF). In 1993, the Arusha Accords were signed by the RPF and the Rwandan Government,[51] stipulating a peace arrangement between Hutu and Tutsi and calling for a UN force to keep the peace. Canadian General Romeo Dallaire headed that UN force and arrived in Rwanda soon after. For at least a year before his arrival, Hutu extremists had been stockpiling guns, grenades (85 tons), and over a half million machetes. Hutu-dominated newspapers and radio called for an extermination of the minority Tutsi.[52] The Tutsi were depicted by the Hutu power elite as arrogant, privileged immigrants and devils who were "enemies of the people." Anti-Tutsi propaganda was broadcast around the clock by the government-owned radio station.

In April 1994, the governing president of Rwanda was killed in a plane crash. In the ensuing months 800,000 Tutsi and moderate Hutu (those who believed in peaceful coexistence with the Tutsi) were raped, mutilated, and slaughtered by Hutus armed with grenades and machetes. In many cases, they were herded into churches and hacked to death. Davenport and Stam (genodynamics.org) put the number of Tutsi slaughtered at 500,000 and claim that 300,000 Hutu were slaughtered as well by other Hutus in a killing frenzy that took both political and personal victims. Whether political or personal/political, the slaughter was primarily genocidal and succeeded in exterminating 77 percent of the Tutsi population. It could also be described as "ultra genocidal" in that it was extended to those moderate Hutu who believed in living harmoniously with the Tutsi.[53]

Human Rights Watch[54] reported that, once the killing began, the killers could not stop and turned to killing suspect Hutu once all local Tutsi were killed. Women, men, and children (the Hutu militia had boys as young as age nine)[55] took part in the killing and even killed their former neighbors. Dallaire, in his testimony[56] before the ensuing tribunal in Tanzania, reported that Tutsi women had been raped, mutilated, and murdered, and had objects inserted in their vaginas and their corpses "posed" in what forensic psychologists would view as the *modus operandi* of a sexual sadist.[57] Such "posing" of rape/murder victims also occurred in Nanking.[58] This behavior raises questions about sadism in general and, more specifically, sexual sadism. This "perversion" is usually attributed to trait pathologies by forensic psychologists or psychiatrists in civilian circumstances, but it appears in both wars and genocides as a form of sadism that is generated by a short term psychological state and by the toxic environment produced. We examine this issue in Chapter 10.

There were daily warnings and reports of genocide made by Dallaire to Kofi Annan at the United Nations and to U.S. Foreign Secretary Madeleine Albright, but they were ignored. France, Belgium, and the United States sent troops to Rwanda to extricate their own citizens. All forces refused aid to the beseeching Tutsi survivors, walking past them even though their imminent death was obvious.[59] These inactions coupled with his own inability to save the situation drove Dallaire to a bout of post-traumatic stress disorder that was highly publicized in Canada (as was his heroic tour after he recovered, in an attempt to generate aid for Rwanda and generally raise public awareness about genocide).

BOSNIA

Before 1991, Yugoslavia comprised six republics. But when Serb president Slobodan Milosevic began to promote Serb dominance, Slovenia and Croatia seceded. Serb citizens boycotted the vote. A country cobbled together under the 45-year iron-fisted rule of the communist, Marshal Tito, was about to come apart. In Bosnia, the Serbs began the practice of what they called "ethnic

cleansing" that involved a plan to partition Bosnia, hatched by Serb leader Slobodan Milosevic. Although Muslims constituted 40 percent of the Bosnian population, the partition had no section assigned to Muslims.[60] Ethnic cleansing
initially entailed limits on jobs for non-Serb Bosnians, as well as limits to their
free assembly, travel, and communication. Serbs controlled and limited their
use of space.[61] Then the term was extended to include the systematic, sanctioned
elimination of targeted ethnic groups who were "deported" on forced marches.
The hygienic implications of the word "cleansing" gave those actions a salutary
spin.

Power quotes Holocaust historian Raul Hilberg as saying,

> The key to the entire operation from the psychological viewpoint was to never utter
> the words that would be appropriate to the action. Say nothing, do these things, do
> not describe them.[62]

Soon the deportations were accompanied by rape and murder by Serb paramilitary death squads. Some victims were dismembered with chain saws.[63i] Four-
teen Muslim captives were decapitated in Eastern Bosnia in a town called
Visegrad.[64] Within the next few months, about 1,600 Muslims were killed.
Croats and Muslims alike were put in concentration camps and starved to death.
In the first seven months, about 70,000 Bosnians were killed, and within a year,
the total was 100,000.[65] Unlike events in Cambodia, there was extensive and
graphic coverage of the violence in the West. Despite worldwide awareness of
the atrocities perpetrated in Bosnia, nothing was done. Eventually, a weak UN
force was put in place in Bosnia to, amongst other things, protect non-Serbian
Bosnians. In 1995, the UN force was overrun and 7,000 Muslims were slaughtered in Srebrenica—raped and bayoneted, throats cut, and shot.[66] The killings
were systematic, men were separated from women: the men killed; the women
were raped and then killed. Estimates of the number of rapes are between
20,000 and 50,000,[67] and many of these women were subsequently murdered.
The exact number murdered is not known.

On October 2, 1992, 100,000 people marched through the streets of Sarajevo
to demonstrate for peace. The next day, Milosevic's Yugoslavian National Army
began mortar shelling of the city, killing 12,000 people in a siege that lasted four
years. Soccer fields had to be dug up to bury the dead.

Eventually a peace accord was signed in Dayton, Ohio. The Dayton Accord
did not stop the violence, however, as it did not order arrests for those perpetrat-
ing war crimes. The site for violence then shifted to Kosovo in the south, where
the target now was Albanians, 3,000 of whom were killed. The motto used by

---

[i] It is not known whether the victims were dismembered while alive or dead. Catholic attacks on "infidels"
during the Fourth Crusade involved dismembering fallen foes and leaving them to bleed to death, which
took about three days.[71]

Serb forces was, "A massacre a day helps keep NATO away."[68] NATO (North Atlantic Treaty Organization) eventually bombed Serbia, and Serbia retaliated by driving 1.3 million Kosovars from their homes in an act of ethnic cleansing. The NATO bombing and subsequent deployment of 60,000 NATO troops eventually brought a fragile peace to Bosnia.

The initial world view explanation for the Bosnian genocide was that "ancient hatreds" had surfaced after Tito died and the superordinate authority imposed on Yugoslavia was lifted. Ferguson, however, disputes this view, arguing that there was no evidence for "ancient hatreds" before 1989. In fact, there was some inter-marriage among Bosnia's main groups (Croats, Muslims, and Serbs), but demographic trends were not favoring Serbs, whose numbers were static while the other populations grew[69] and whose economy was stagnant. Milosevic began to portray the Serbs as "endangered." After the hostilities were stopped and forensic tests done on the victims, DNA testing failed to find any genetic differences between Muslims, Serbs, and Croats.[70] The differences we construct amongst groups of human beings are largely symbolic.

4

THE HOLOCAUST

The Holocaust disturbs us so deeply because it demonstrates that none of the things we associate with the advancement of civilization—peace, prosperity, industrialization, education, technological achievement—free us from the dark side of the human soul. Just as there is evil in the heart of every man, there is evil at the heart of even the most "civilized" human society. It is a humbling recognition. Man and society are both capable of the most appallingly depraved behavior. Only in the case of society, it occurs on an industrial scale.

—Mark Bowden, *New York Times,* October 4, 2006

In his review of conflicts in the twentieth century, Niall Ferguson makes the point that someone in 1901 trying to predict a future Holocaust would have been unlikely to have picked Germany.[1] The Jewish population there was less that 1 percent and had been declining for two decades—Western Russia, Hungary, and the United States all had larger Jewish populations. Furthermore, the Jewish population in Germany was integrated, even intermarried—around 20 percent intermarried in the early 1900s. Jews had been loyal and long-standing citizens of Germany dating back 2000 years to Roman times.[2] Twelve thousand Jews had died fighting for Germany in World War I.[3] Nevertheless, the Nazi Party, as early as 1920 and prior to its coming to power had issued a manifesto that was explicitly anti-Semitic and focused on notions of a superior "Aryan" race that excluded Jews (amongst other non-Aryan groups).[4] Daniel Goldhagen dates the origins of European anti-Semitism to Christianity, specifically to the period in the fourth century where Christianity became the official state religion of Rome under Constantine. Goldhagen viewed this as a "psychological and theological need impelling Christians to differentiate themselves from the bearers of the religion from which their own had broken off,"[5] in other words, a social psychological phenomenon involving tribalism (religious in-groupism) and power (a newly powerful religion that had been previously power-less in pre-Constantine Rome). Furthermore, since Jews rejected the revelation of Jesus, they unwittingly challenged the Christians' certitude in that revelation. As we saw in Chapter 1, any challenge to that certitude, whether from Jews or Mus-lims, became the focus of violence in medieval Europe. Social psychological experiments performed in sanitized laboratory settings in the 1950s essentially replicated the tendency of groups to reject any threat to an absolute group dogma.[6] In theological terms, it indicated that if the Jews, the people of God, shunned the Messiah that God had promised them, then either that Messiah was false or the people had gone astray, perhaps tempted by the Devil himself. The former was too troubling to contemplate, so the latter explanation was pref-erable. The second branch of this theological view was that as Christianity had superseded Judaism, the Jews ought to disappear from the earth unless they became Christians, which they refused to do.[7] Jews and Christians had a common heritage, what we now call the Judeo-Christian ethic, and the under-standing of the sacred and the secular moral order depended on a clear view of Gods' words (and hence, attachment in perpetuity might not exist). If Jews were right, Christians were wrong. Christian clerics in the fourth century portrayed Jews as adversaries of the church and as a threat to good Christians.[8] Jews were depicted as "Christ-killers," not only the Jews of Christ's time but contemporary Jews who rejected Jesus as the Messiah. As John Chrystotom, a pivotal and influ-ential Christian theologian put it,

> Where Christ-killers gather, the cross is ridiculed, God blasphemed, the father unac-knowledged, the son insulted, the grace of the spirit rejected. . . . If the Jewish rites are holy and venerable, our way of life must be false. But if our way is true, as indeed it is, theirs is fraudulent.[9]

Hence, the Christian concept of Jews was woven into the moral order of the cos-mos and society. To be Christian meant to have a visceral hostility to Jews, just as it did to evil and the Devil. In the medieval Christian mind, evil, the Devil, and Jews became conflated as a vague but interrelated concept, personified by the notion of the Antichrist (see Falwell quote above).

During the nineteenth century the German anti-Semitic concept of Jews changed. Framed originally with the religious terms described above, it broad-ened into a sociopolitical view where the Jews now became viewed as fundamen-tally amoral, asocial, and bent on undermining the social order (i.e., as a threat to the status quo).[10] Occasionally, this sociopolitical view included ascribing com-munist sympathies to the Jews while simultaneously blaming them for being too successful as capitalists.[11] Thirty-one percent of the richest families in Ger-many were Jewish, as well as 22 percent of all Prussian millionaires.[12] In a sense they were both envied and resented as well as viewed as a threat to the existing social order. As Ferguson put it, "Anti-Semitism, then, was sometimes nothing more than the envy of under achievers."[13] Hence, the Jews became a lightening-rod scapegoat group as did the African Americans in the U.S. South or, later, the Tutsi to the Rwandan Hutu. Jews came to be viewed not just as different but as malevolent and corrosive.[14] The power of this view extended to seeing the Jew as the cause of everything that was wrong in German society, an identification of Jews with social dysfunction. As Goldhagen put it, "The Jew was everything that was awry, and he was intentionally so."[15] Hence, according to Goldhagen, there was a profound and ubiquitous hatred of Jews in Germany as it emerged into modern times. Goldhagen's argument that anti-Semitism pre-Nazi was normative cannot account for the lack of legislative discrimination as well as the fact that there were no physical assaults being reported prior to the Nazi rise to power.[16] Geoff Eley points out Goldhagen's argument that anti-Semitism was rampant from 1871–1945 is fundamentally flawed because of its circularity.[17] Goldhagen essentially argued that since there was no evidence disproving there was no prejudice against Jews, then that was an indication that hatred for Jewry existed during that time.[18]

Of course, anti-Semitism existed in France, Russia, and Spain as well. Anti-Semitism in Russia took the form of pogroms or massacres directed at Jewish ghettoes.[19] Russian anti-Semitism was based not on the Nazi idea of racial purity but on "blood libel; the belief that Jews murdered Christian children to mix their blood in unleavened bread. This belief had persisted throughout Christian Europe since its origin in England in the twelfth century.[20] The flare-up of pogroms in Russia coincided with a sudden rapid increase in the Jewish urban population, the extraordinary economic success of Russian Jews, and the involvement of Jews in revolutionary politics.[21] Ferguson sees the Russian pogroms as a "largely spontaneous phenomenon, eruptions of violence in economically volatile, multi-ethnic communities."[22] In contrast to this spontaneous violence, in Germany it seemed that imperial aspirations and the initial failure during World War I (WWI) added the ingredients to the "perfect storm" that was to generate the Holocaust. In fact, while Goldhagen traces the roots of anti-Semitism to medieval Christianity, others point out that Nazism rejected Christianity as well as Judaism. Initially the response to Christianity was muted. In 1920, the German Workers' Party (later the Nazis) manifesto read, "We demand that the Roman Law, which serves the materialistic world order, shall be replaced by a legal system for all Germany." Also, "We demand liberty for all religious denominations in the state, so far as they are not a danger to it and do not militate against the moral feelings of the German race. The party, as such, stands for positive Christianity, but does not bind itself in the matter of creed to any particular confession. It combats the Jewish-materialist spirit within us and without [around] us...." At this point, any religion that did not "militate against the moral feelings of the German state" was acceptable. This "clause" later became the pretext for denouncing all religion, as all were "deviated" in some way from the "moral feelings of the German state" as defined by Nazism.[23] As Nazi power increased, Hitler began to denounce Christianity. "He [Hitler] denounced Christianity, claiming that (1) it was a religion that sided with everything weak and low; (2) it was purely Jewish and Oriental in origin; (3) it began among sick, exhausted, and despairing men who had lost their belief in life; (4) Christian ideas of forgiveness and sin, resurrection, and salvation were just nonsense; (5) the Christian idea of mercy was altogether dangerous; (6) Christian love was silly because 'love paralyzes'; and (7) the Christian idea of equality of all human beings meant that the inferior, the ill, the crippled, the criminal, and the weak are to be protected."[24] "Christianity, said Hitler, just as much as Judaism, was opposed to the healthy Nordic pagan ideals he had for Germany. He would not destroy Christianity, but he would redefine it and use its more positive principles—such as 'Render unto Caesar what is Caesars' and 'drive the money-changers out of the temple.'"[25] Hence, while anti-Semitism may have existed in medieval Christian thought, it coexisted with Christian values that may have served as buffers against malignant expression. Hitler rejected those values and any safeguards against their malignant expression.

The Nazi rise to power in Germany in the 1920s gave them enough political power to implement policies that could create the genocide to which all others would be compared. As soon as Adolf Hitler seized control of the government, he, along with fellow party members, created policies that had enormous popularity because they appeared to be aimed at eliminating the severe problems in Germany created, in large part, by the German loss of World War I and the reparations it was forced to pay by the Treaty of Versailles.[26] The social consequences of these reparations included an economic depression, a rising crime rate, and a sense that Germany's exalted place in history was being frustrated. However, the vaguely worded policies were later used against self-proclaimed problems, including political opponents and any group defined as being "non-Aryan" (and obviously including Jews). For instance, any "public" remark against the regime was a crime.[27] This type of law is so subjective that it can be all encompassing. As each year passed, the laws targeted more and more groups simply because they were not a part of the "master Aryan race." The "out-groups" were primarily legislatively and then physically put into isolation where they were further stripped of basic human rights and of life itself. Through the years, the Nazis began to physically eliminate their "enemies" with systematic and carefully calculated murders, first by beatings and shooting and then by shooting, hanging, and gassing. Even when defeat was forthcoming, the Nazis pressed forward and tried to complete their plans of total physical decimation of European Jewry. Nazi Germany from 1933 until its collapse in 1945 saw a progression of violent events that incrementally escalated, leading to unparalleled genocide.

In order to fully comprehend how the Nazis gained so much public support, one must look back to the end of World War I and the Treaty of Versailles that ended it. The Treaty of Versailles was finally signed on June 28, 1919.[28] According to Michael Burleigh, the Treaty was not responsible for the Nazi's rise to power because several terms of the Treaty such as the reparation and military inspections dissolved prior to the Nazi movement beginning.[29] However, Louis Snyder states that the Treaty "paved his [Hitler's] way to power" because he used it to gain political momentum.[30] It is clear the "negotiations" at Versailles appeared vindictive to Germans and geared towards punishing Germany more than trying to compensate for losses.[31] The Treaty greatly decreased German controlled land by forcing them to return Polish territory as well as relinquish any overseas territories.[32] The Treaty further diminished the once great German military by limiting the number of naval vessels in operation at any one time.[33] Despite all that damage, perhaps one of the most detrimental and vengeful articles, from the German perspective, was the article known as the "guilt" clause.[34] This article stated that Germany was entirely responsible for all "the loss and damage" of WWI.[35] The Nazis would later use the guilt clause to rally the German people against this perceived miscarriage of justice.[36] Regardless of how the German people initially felt about the Treaty, Hitler used it in speeches, proclaiming that it was unbearable and enslaved the Germans to the Allied forces.[37] Furthermore, he declared such severe conditions brought on by the Treaty would do nothing but force Germany to revolt.[38]

After WWI, the Weimar Republic tried to implement democracy in Germany by creating a constitution based on those of Britain, the United States, France, and Switzerland.[39] Unfortunately, the Weimar Republic faced problems immediately since it had neither public nor Allied support. The German economy began to falter almost immediately following the end of WWI, and the Weimar regime was blamed.[40,41] Ironically, the Weimar Constitution would be of later assistance to the Nazis. In 1920, Hitler and the German Workers' Party, which would become the National Socialist Workers' Party (Nazis), had created a manifesto with anti-Semitic and Aryan superiority rhetoric.[42] Throughout the 1920s, Hitler and his party steadily gained more exposure and support. On April 10, 1932, the German presidential election results were tallied: 49.6 percent to Paul von Hindenburg. 30.1 percent to Hitler, 13 percent to Communists, and 6.8 percent to Nationalists.[43] Since a majority government was not elected, second ballots were needed. Hitler still did not get elected.[44,45] Von Hindenburg gave the chancellorship to Kurt von Schlicher, who found it challenging to maintain power in light of the ever-growing Nazi movement; hence, he asked von Hindenburg to dissolve the Reichstag (German Parliament) and subsequently resigned.[46,47] This opened the door for Hitler to seize power. Just two days later, Hitler took the oath of office as chancellor.[48] Hence, although not elected by a majority, Hitler came to power in a democratic system. On this date too, Hitler began his move to remove all political opponents and to end democracy in Germany.[49] On February 27, 1933, the infamous "Reichstag Fire" occurred, which many later felt the Nazis had done themselves.[50] The Nazi propaganda machine used the event to their advantage by claiming it was a sign of a Communists revolt.[51] Hitler then suspended freedom of the press in addition to freedom of speech by declaring a national emergency.[52] This event and the propaganda that followed led Hitler to finally receive a majority vote in the 1933 elections.[53] He responded by legally abolishing all other political parties with the Law Concerning the Formation of New Parties.[54] Just one year after becoming chancellor, Hitler made his dictatorship "legal" in the Law for Reorganization of the Reich.[55]

Hitler told Heinrich Himmler, the head of the SS[56] (*Schutzstaffel*—Hitler's personal guard unit) that if any problems arose at home while Germany was involved in a war, all "opponents" in camps would be executed to avoid a similar fate as that Germany had suffered in WWI.[57] Hitler felt that Germany lost WWI because the fatherland was not unanimous in supporting the troops, and ethnic minorities were to blame for that.[58] This came mainly from the shock that the great German army had been defeated, which could only be explained by some Germans having become traitors.[59] Since the end of WWI and the Treaty of Versailles, there had been strained relations between Poland and Germany, at least on the Germans' behalf.[60] Under the Nazis, this tension was emphasized because Hitler played on the fact that Poland received part of its land at the expense of Germany due again to an article of the Treaty of Versailles.[61] Thus, Hitler wanted to reinstate the land to its rightful owner, Germany, putting Poles directly in his genocidal sights.[62] This became evident through his orders to cleanse Poland of anything Polish and then return the land to Germany.[63]

The ideological background of Hitler's plans resonated and had support by many who wished to be a part of "German racial imperialism."[64] This support would be the firm base upon which genocide of the Jews and other ethnics would materialize. "It was the feeling that Hitler had a historical mandate which made a large part of the nation ignore the horrors of the Nazi take-over."[65] In *Mein Kampf,* written nearly a decade prior to the Nazi rise to power, Hitler had made it clear that "racial mixing" was to blame for the collapses of the great previous civilizations, including the German defeat in World War I.[66] Needless to say, Hitler's historical scholarship was self-serving and biased.

Nazi policies were designed to segregate good "pure" Germans from those they felt were degenerates and unworthy of life in a pure community. According to Goldhagen, there were ten steps with increasing mental devastation the Nazis went through to solve the Jewish "problem" between 1933 and the end of World War II (WWII) in 1945:

1. Verbal assault.
2. Physical assault.

3. Legal and administrative measures to isolate Jews from non-Jews.

4. Driving them to emigrate.

5. Forced deportation and "resettlement."

6. Physical separation in ghettos.

7. Killing through starvation, debilitation, and disease (prior to the formal genocidal program).

8. Slave labor as a surrogate for death.

9. Genocide, primarily by means of mass shooting, calculated starvation, and gassing.

10. Death marches.[67]

The incremental nature of these steps contributes to acceptable normative shifts (see Chapter 8) that would meet resistance if enacted all at once. Despite beliefs that Hitler formed all policies with help from his central authorities exclusively, there were many contributions from local and regional authorities as well as from individual party members.[68] Hitler was not solely responsible for all the decisions being made that sealed the fate of millions of Jews.[69] Locals at work camps and ghettos contributed to the ever-escalating death toll by implementing their own death sentences to the Jews and the others under their control.[70] Neither local initiatives nor central orders were more important than the other.[71] According to Christopher Browning, local initiatives gave the central part of the regime ideas on how to solve the "Jewish problem."[72] For instance, in Bialystok in Russia, a massacre occurred in 1941, prior to any orders from Heinrich Himmler, Waffen-SS (Hitler's elite "bodyguard").[73] Moreover, Browning indicates that some local "authorities" seemed to interpret the upper echelon Nazis' intentions more accurately than the laws themselves actually stated.[74] The top leaders most definitely had a plan, but in some cases the Nazi guidelines were initiated fullheartedly and to the extreme by local authorities.[75] Once the initiatives were deemed successful, they were implemented into other regions of the Third Reich.[76]

Because of Germany's economic downward spiral between 1927 and 1933, crime had increased to such an astounding level that citizens were desperate for any resolution.[77] The Nazi regime gave the people what they wanted with their extreme answer to crime by declaring war upon it.[78] Concentration camps sprung up immediately after Hitler's appointment initially to handle all the arrested criminals.[79] The public was told the camps were to retain order and "re-educate" prisoners through honest hard work.[80] However, in 1933, the war on crime clearly began to be abused, and its true intentions became transparent.[81] The Nazis created a new slogan, "no crime without a punishment," and it started to be abused by punishing even petty crimes to the extreme of being sent to concentration camps without ever having been convicted in court.[82] The police demonstrated their new strength by killing about 100 SA members including their leader, Ernst Röhm.[83] Unlike governments that try to censor news like this, the Nazis spun it in the press that their deaths were a result of a failed coup attempt by the SA, *Sturmabteilung,* who were storm troopers used to defeat the Communists when the Nazis were trying to gain control of the government.[84] This benefited Hitler because "it gave many citizens the opportunity to accept the new 'normality' and the coercive side of the dictatorship."[85] That is, the social norms shifted again toward the extreme. How could people suddenly reject a policy they had previously supported that was ultimately effective at eliminating crime? Hence, the incremental nature of the normative shifts also played a role in acceptance of emerging "new realities." This same principle has been used to explain the conformity obtained in the infamous experiment by Stanley Milgram on obedience to authority, where ordinary everyday subjects were "ordered" to give electric shocks of increasing intensity to recipients demographically like themselves.[86]

THE LAW AS A WEAPON

Beginning as far back as 1933, Hitler started to take strides towards making a pure "community of people."[87] The Nazis were "anti-Semitic, anti-Marxist, anti-Bolshevik, anti-Catholic, antiliberal, anti-democratic, anti-Masonic and most of all anti-Treaty of Versailles."[88] Hitler's anti-everything gave him tremendous public support.[89] Even in the beginning stages, media played a major role in the Nazi party gaining support for their endeavors. Originally the crackdown was solely used against criminals.[90] Later it was used for even minor crimes such as panhandling.[91] Again the media were vital in portraying the police as the best solution to crime, hence gaining more vital support.[92]

Moreover, the press was used as a tool to "stigmatize enemies" such as Jews, Communists, and Catholic priests.[93] They aggressively targeted the Jews in the press by connecting them not only to Communism but also to criminality.[94] The Nazis believed that there were clear racial and biological predispositions to criminality.[95] The German press stated "in the case of the Jews there are not merely a few criminals (as in every other people), but all of the Jewry rose from criminal roots, and in its very nature it is criminal."[96] Incessant anti-Semitic propaganda fed to German people definitely played a part in altering the minds of those who at one time lived peacefully with Jews.[97] This attitude and belief contributed to the complete physical annihilation of Jews, whereas other ethnicities were considered able to be "Germanized" and therefore "save-able."[98]

The Nazis were in power less than a week when boycotting of Jewish businesses began.[99,100] Nonetheless, in the beginning years, the businesses could not be targeted too tenaciously because of fears the precarious economy might be disrupted and subsequently collapse.[101] Despite that, excesses did happen almost immediately.[102] The number of signs in villages denouncing or showing

Jewish patrons were not welcome were exponentially increasing as early as 1934.[103] This forced many originally unwilling business owners to place Jew unwelcome signs for protection against being accused of socializing with Jews regardless of their true personal beliefs and even though there was no official policy requiring it.[104] On the other hand, many had no qualms or reservations in partaking in these actions.[105] Most of these actions happened due to local authority initiatives and not from official policies from the central government.[106] Additionally, the regime began to restrict certain groups' movements and services they could receive, which were already disliked by "German" citizens.[107] While underlying currents of anti-Semitism were clearly in the regime's ideology, they were not blatantly in the forefront during the early years.[108] The anti-Semitism progression can be seen through "semi legal steps to begin the reversal of Jewish emancipation."[109] Then, once Jews lost their legal rights, their lives would be devalued by others. However, initially if there were any backlash or resistance, the regime would "retreat" slightly, at least temporarily.[110] According to Goldhagen, another intent of the racial propaganda was to terrorize the Jews, and it was ultimately responsible for killing them socially.[111] It was essential first to murder Jews socially, economically, culturally, and politically in order to enforce more drastic measures upon them: emigration, ghettoization, and death camps.[112] Had the Nazis not removed the Jews from every aspect of society, "Germans" may have posed more resistance to Hitler's treatment of Jewry because their lives would still have been interwoven into the fabric of society.

Deaths due to police confrontations were always presented in the newspapers after they occurred in such a way that the result was unavoidable even if it were for petty crimes.[113] In spite of the carefully orchestrated media stories, some Germans did see through the "justifications" for the executions.[114,115] In 1933, approximately 100,000 people were arrested by the police throughout the nation in the attempt to rid the cities of criminals and decrease the crime rate.[116] During this time, even smaller crimes were punished to the extreme.[117] In 1934, Himmler won over the public by having a "Day of the German Police" where the police were collecting money, showing their humanity, and demonstrating their willingness to assist those in need.[118] It was essential that the police were seen as a beneficent agency because they had an enormous amount of power and were abusing it. Therefore, the public needed to be reassured that all their actions were purely for the good of society even though it was a façade.

At first, a new criminal code was sought, but eventually the Nazis wanted "police justice" where the police both created and enforced the laws.[119] This ultimately decreased trial lengths, rights of the accused, and equality under the law.[120] One example of police justice occurred when the police decided certain criminals were repeat offenders, and they could send them to concentration camps even if they had not committed a crime recently.[121] Another method instituted besides killing those who defiled the race was widespread sterilization. Approximately 400,000 men and women were forced to undergo the medical procedure regardless of whether they had a mental disorder or a physical impairment. Even those with illegitimate children who were considered habitual criminals were sterilized.[122]

At the beginning of 1933, German police were given powers to arrest Communists to "protect" them.[123,124] The Gestapo could now arrest and detain any "Communist" who would then wind up in a concentration camp indefinitely without receiving a trial.[125] The once targeted Communists had been replaced in the camps with "race defilers, rapists, sexual degenerates and habitual criminals,"[126,127] in other words, Jews, homosexuals, and anyone who disagreed with the government. The "typical" prisoners at that time were portrayed as alcoholics, criminals, and Jews.

The Law for the Restoration of the Professional Civil Service initiated on April 7, 1933, started excluding Jews from receiving certain services. This law implied incorrectly that numerous civil service workers and judges received their positions based on political appointment.[128] Furthermore, the law included a racist clause that resulted in over 100 judges and prosecutors in Prussia alone losing their positions.[129] For example, the law stipulated that any civil servants with one Jewish grandparent must "retire" unless they were either veterans or descendants of WWI veterans.[130]

The Nazis in April/May 1933 took aim additionally at Jehovah's Witnesses.[131] State by state they were banned, and by April 1, 1935, they were banned everywhere in Germany for refusing to serve in the military and refusing to use the Nazi salute.[132] To the Nazis this demonstrated they were "unGerman" because they would not support a war, and Hitler thought this lack in unanimity on the home front would lead to another German defeat like WWI.[133] Yet another reason they were targeted was due to the fact that they were accused of using religion to further their political aspirations to create a kingdom where Jews would rule.[134] With a link to Judaism in the Nazis' minds, of course, the Jehovah's Witnesses caught the attention and persecution of the Nazi regime. Out of a total of 25,000–30,000 Jehovah's Witnesses, 10,000 were arrested, and 2,000 were sent to camps where 1,200 were murdered.[135]

THE ATTACK ON HOMOSEXUALS

Another group considered "asocials" were homosexuals. Germany was not unique at that time for discriminating against homosexuals.[136] Homophobia predated the Nazi regime; however, once the Nazis took power, they exacerbated it.[137] Prior to the Nazis, homosexuality was not accepted, but the Nazis actually criminalized it.[138] According to Nazi rhetoric, homosexuality was caused by

Asians and spread to Aryans via the Catholic Church,[139] which also explains in part the Nazi contempt for the Catholic church.[140] Moreover, homosexuals may have been despised based on the fact that they performed openly in the Weimar Republic (which seemed to celebrate decadence to the Nazi sensibility), and the Nazis were trying to eradicate anything reminiscent of the Weimar era.[141] Sexual outsiders or "deviants" like prostitutes as well as homosexuals were targeted and received harsh treatments including sterilization and concentration camp sentences.[142] Gay males were targeted because the Nazis thought homosexuality would decrease the ever-important birthrate, therefore making it difficult to increase the population of Aryans.[143] From 1934 to 1938, convictions for being gay steadily increased from 948 to 8,562.[144] The start of WWII affected the number by further increasing the number of those convicted of homosexuality because the war made Hitler more paranoid about eliminating all potential dangerous obstacles at home.[145] Once again, ordinary people turned against one another and reported those they suspected of being gay to police.[146] In some cities like Düsseldorf, where a flourishing gay subculture existed, police were able to raid the known hangouts.[147] In just eight months in 1936, the *Kriminalpolizeior* (Kripo), Criminal Police, arrested 6,260 men accused of performing homosexual acts.[148] One year later during the same eight months, that number had escalated to 12,356 due to the Kripo's zealous pursuit.[149] Since Germany was then in a police "justice" state, being investigated for homosexuality had dire consequences. If a man happened to be homosexual and Jewish, the police harassment was unrelenting until his death, usually in a concentration camp.[150] Himmler, on May 20, 1939, told the Kripo that castration could be offered as a means of possible release from "protective" custody.[151] Still, 5,000–15,000 homosexuals perished in concentration camps.[152] The goal of the concentration camps was always portrayed by the Nazi party as the reeducation of all criminals including homosexuals, while for the Jews, the Nazis wanted complete annihilation because Jews were deemed "un-reeducate-able" based on their genetic predisposition for criminality and inferior being.[153,154]

In 1934, Hitler granted amnesty to some of those imprisoned.[155] Many concentration camps closed temporarily.[156] "Public" criticism against the government became a crime, often resulting in a sentence of death by order of a new special court.[157] Even the onset of the war did not decrease those "tried" before the special courts.[158] In fact, the war caused even minor offenses to be seen as antigovernment, thus ensuring a sentence of death.[159] This included things that were previously outside the "norm" like homosexuality and petty crime.[160] Less than one year later, Hitler allowed Himmler to construct more concentration camps after the Nuremberg party rally in September 1935 where more laws against Jews and "enemies of the nation" were announced.[161] Hitler gave a speech where he proclaimed something would be done to the "internal enemies of the nation."[162,163]

The Nuremberg Laws were passed in 1935 and were the legislative beginning for the Jews being made a clear target and an "out-group." The Nuremberg Laws consisted of two distinct laws: The Reich Citizenship Law and the Law for the Protection of German Blood and Honour.[164,165] The laws were passed for two purposes: first to decrease Jews' social status and to "protect" the Jews from being harmed by other citizens.[166] These laws sealed the fate for many by defining who was Jewish solely through bloodlines regardless of their religious affiliation.[167] Moreover, the laws removed citizenship from the Jews and even went a step further to eliminate the possibility of any more Jews in Germany by prohibiting further marriages and making sexual relations between Jews and "pure" Germans illegal under the term "race defilement."[168] To ensure "pure" bloodlines, Jews could not have German women as domestic help, therefore preventing male Jews from seducing or taking advantage of vulnerable women.[169] In fact, they were now even denied basic German affiliation by being prohibited from raising the national flag.[170] Once the Nuremberg Laws were passed, many non-Jews who had had long term relationships with Jews immediately broke them off or were discrete enough to avoid detection.[171] Since the Nuremberg Laws prohibited any relationship between Jews and "Germans," any gesture indicating sympathy could be misconstrued as being sexual, resulting in an investigation.[172] Despite race defilement laws not being passed officially until September 1935, as early as 1933 "relationships between Jews and non-Jews were already being policed."[173] These laws were also wide open to abuse for personal revenge against Jews.[174] Accusations were often unsubstantiated and not corroborated even after Gestapo investigations.[175] In fact, the number of false accusations was debilitating to the Gestapo at times.[176] This was one of the problems the Gestapo was never able to rectify completely, probably because denunciations were an essential component of the terror the regime spread throughout Germany.[177] Many citizens took it upon themselves to report others to the Gestapo for further investigation.[178] Denunciations began immediately following Hitler's appointment and continued to be a vital aspect for the Gestapo and other "policing" agencies.[179]

In spite of the harshness of the Nuremberg Laws, the laws that followed became increasingly more restrictive and segregating. For instance, in 1935, the Gestapo's list of enemies and criminals was increased.[180] Despite a steady decrease in the number of concentration camp prisoners in "protective custody" since mid-1933, Hitler's proclamation led to a drastic increase.[181] In 1935, Hitler officially denied those in the concentration camps legal representation.[182] This is an example of how each law the Nazis passed was incremental in establishing more extreme laws. The Gestapo subsequently had rule of the land, and no provisions existed to oversee their actions.[183] Germany was for all intents and purposes under martial law.[184] Officially any person arrested had to be told why he was arrested and could be detained for only three months when the

Gestapo had to apply in writing for renewal to continue holding him.[185] Although this was the official procedure to follow, reality was quite different.[186] The Gestapo themselves were responsible for these decisions, and the "accused" were not allowed any representation.[187] They were not even permitted to appear on their own behalf.[188] After serving a sentence, "undesirables" would be rearrested or, if they were found not guilty, the Gestapo would impose their own "verdict" of death, usually meaning it was spun in the press that "a violent criminal had been shot while resisting arrest."[189] Everything was made public through newspapers.

The Gestapo had changed from fighting communism to fighting any and all opponents of the Nazi regime[190] and fought "enemies of the state," whereas the Kripo fought the "asocial elements" in society.[191] Both tried to prevent crimes, not deal with them retroactively, which led to innocent people being detained or killed so they would not have the opportunity to commit crimes.[192] The police justified their racist policies by stating that "criminals frequently develop out of inherited predispositions," thus allowing them to predict who would become criminals.[193] Additionally in 1939, Jews "were not allowed on the streets after 8pm" because the Nazis claimed they used the darkened streets as a mask for molesting Aryan women.[194] Through this measure, it is possible to see the continuous link the Nazis made between Jews and criminality.[195] Jews were not the only group targeted. The Poles were forced to wear a "P" in 1940 before the Jews were forced to wear a yellow Star of David in 1941.[196] However, since being Jewish was an irreversible "flaw," wearing the yellow star segregated the Jews from the non-Jews, which led to an abrupt and nearly instantaneous increase in both verbal and physical assault.[197] Poles were not as despised as Jews due to their not being perceived as inherently predisposed to become criminals, and they were considered as capable of benefiting from reeducation.[198] In 1941, it officially became a crime for a non-Jewish citizen to be "friendly" with a Jew even with something as simple as a public greeting recognizing the Jews' presence.[199] The punishment for breaking this law was either an indefinite time in a concentration camp for the Jew who only received the greeting or a three month term in protective custody for the non-Jew in order to be educated on Nazi policy.[200]

The prospect of another world war intensified Nazi prosecution and persecution. Hence, once Britain officially declared war on Germany, the political climate shifted, allowing Hitler and the Nazis to "secure" the home front, ensuring there would be unified support within Germany and German occupied land for the war.[201] Thus, ordinary citizens turned on one another and reported people to the Gestapo for everything and anything.[202] However, ultimately it led to the arrests of "anyone who voiced doubts about victory or questioned the justification for the war," and they were dealt with harshly.[203] Again it is possible to see the war radicalizing the behavior of citizens especially with a law in 1938, which made any "defamatory" remark against the regime criminal.[204] This, of course, would have been "unpoliceable" had "ordinary" citizens not been willing to denounce friends, neighbors, and even family members if necessary.[205] Those put into protective custody officially were not to be released during the war because they posed a great risk since they could not be watched carefully due to the focus on the war.[206]

The Gypsies, or Sinti and Roma, were targeted by the Nazis from the very beginning of the regime because they, like the Jews, were viewed as criminals.[207] The Nazis equated mixed race with criminality; therefore, Gypsies were targeted because they were mostly mixed races and thus an inferior race.[208] Moreover, Gypsies led nomadic lives, so they would have been seen as having no loyalty to any government, making them a security risk in the Nazis' eyes. Those of pure Gypsy race were eventually seen by Himmler as worth keeping, unlike Jews of pure blood because Jewish blood was genetically coded with criminality.[209] Initially the Gypsies were deported, which led to their physical decimation due to the depravity.[210] Beginning in 1940, Gypsies were deported to Polish camps.[211] There are clear parallels between the Gypsies and the Jews in their treatments and the escalation of destruction thrust upon them.[212]

With the progression of the war, more groups became susceptible to Nazi plans. June 22, 1941, was the day Hitler officially declared war on the former USSR.[213] Starting at the beginning of the war, the line between crimes under the criminal code and political crimes all vanished, thus mostly resulting in death by shooting.[214] Also, the Gestapo could take any action they deemed necessary even if it went against the courts' wishes.[215]

In 1942, Himmler pointed out the need for workers, so camp personnel were to take this into consideration prior to terminating their prisoners' lives.[216] In 1943, Himmler "restricted the killing further to those who were either mentally ill or could not work."[217] This policy that was labeled euthanasia raised very little opposition even by many of the relatives of those euthanized.[218] This lack of opposition may have "created the psychological conditions for the genocidal policies" because no one would object to the persecution of the Russians, Poles, Gypsies, or Jews if they had approved it for their own family members.[219] It is evident that legislative maneuvers created the path the Nazis took en route to genocide.

Because of the unbearable and still deteriorating atmosphere within Germany, Jews felt forced to emigrate, resulting in 278,000 leaving between 1933 to the end of WWII in 1945.[220] Between 1933 and 1938, 46.8 percent emigrated, another 42.4 percent from 1938 to 1939, and only 10.8 percent after the war started in September 1939.[221] This is another clear example of how the onset of war altered the situation within Germany. During one of Hitler's speeches in January 1939, he stated a world war would destroy the Jews mainly because he would initiate mass death upon them.[222]

CONCENTRATION CAMPS

The documentation for the beginning of the concentration camps is scarce, but from 1933, 26,789 were in protective custody.[223] Throughout the entire year of 1933, 100,000 people had been in concentration camps, but only 500–600 were killed while in custody.[224] In the early stages, it is not likely that many Jews were in "protective" custody, and those who were imprisoned were not segregated from the other detainees.[225] In 1934, Himmler appointed Theodor Eicke as "Inspector of Concentration Camps and SS guards."[226] Eicke made several changes to the camps and their operations. One change was amalgamating all the existing camps into four main ones by August 1937.[227] He also developed the code of conduct for the guards, which included the exact physical punishments that should be dealt out for disobedience or other "infractions."[228]

Ordinary citizens also instigated violence and destruction onto the Jews as their hatred became clearly apparent. The 1938 pogrom, *Kristallnacht,* resulted in retaliation for a young Polish Jew who murdered the "third secretary of the German embassy in Paris."[229] As soon as the news of the death reached Germany, violence against Jews erupted.[230] Throughout Germany, "ordinary" citizens, the SS, *Schutzstaffel* who became the elite corps for the Nazis, and SA members vandalized Jewish property and sacred religious artifacts like Torah scrolls and prayer books.[231] In 1938, wealthy Jews' property and Jewish synagogues' wealth were confiscated and 20,000–30,000 wealthy Jews were arrested and sent to concentration camps for "protective custody."[232] The SA went through synagogues, smashing them with axes and then setting them ablaze so long as no other adjacent buildings were endangered.[233] The SA and the SS were not the only destructive forces. Citizens came together in a volatile atmosphere and threatened Jews.[234] This decimated many small Jewish communities, especially those in rural settings.[235] This pogrom spread from one neighboring city to the next.[236] No town where Jews resided was left untouched by this horrific display of anti-Semitism.[237] After the vandalism ended, on November 10, 1938, Jews were rounded up and marched to the synagogues still standing to read passages from *Mein Kampf.*[238] Following the "ceremony" the synagogues were torched.[239] The pogrom's total effect throughout Germany was 91 murdered immediately, 30,000 sent to concentration camps, 267 synagogues destroyed, and 7,500 businesses and cemeteries vandalized.[240] To add insult to injury, all Jews had 20 percent of their assets confiscated as a fine for the damage of *Kristallnacht.*[241] Although many Germans physically destroyed the Jewish way of life and property in this incident, others were more shrewd and business oriented and tried to buy Jewish businesses once confiscated by the Nazis.[242] There was some resistance to *Kristallnacht,* but it was on pragmatic not ethical or moral grounds due to the absolute waste from the plundering and vandalism.[243] All of the steps to this point were to force Jewish emigration from the German "empire," but *Kristallnacht* was the dividing line to the future violence that would be inflicted on the Jews.[244] By September 1939, German authorities were reporting that "tens of thousands" in Poland had already been murdered even before war was declared.[245]

The onset of WWII intensified the regime and their methods of implementing their racist agenda.[246] Even as early as 1939 there were plans under way to isolate and relocate the Jews east.[247] However, the actuality of this would be far from simple.[248] In 1939, Heydrich informed his division heads that Germany would become larger by dividing Poland and occupying some of its land.[249] Among historians there is a consensus that it was not until 1941 that a plan to annihilate the Jews physically came about instead of the original plans to relocate them to an undetermined location partially due to the complexity of how not only to move physically so many but also where to relocate them. There were serious pragmatic concerns relocating all European Jewry. Thus, physical decimation may have become a more viable solution as well; now that the United States had entered the war, there was no reason to maintain the façade that no genocide was occurring. The Nazis had not wanted the Americans to enter the war; therefore, they had previously attempted to mask their genocidal actions.[250]

In the beginning summer months of 1939, Hitler began to euthanize adults with incurable illnesses, including mental illnesses and physical impairments deemed "unfit" to live.[251] Patients initially were taken and shot by the SS.[252] This program became known as the T-4 operation because of the street address.[253] Since individual shooting took a significant amount of time and an estimated 65,000–70,000 people fell into this category, gas soon became the preferred method of choice for efficiency of time and money.[254] Under this program, 70,273 were killed by mid-1941,[255] which marked a temporary stop partially due to some public criticism from the victims' families.[256] After the T-4 program was officially "ended," it was implemented once again in a manner in which the public was obscured from knowing about its existence due to previous outrage and opposition to it.[257] By the end of the war, an estimated 200,000 perished as a consequence.[258] Seeing how this program was so successful in 1941, Himmler wanted to use the T-4 facilities to decrease the number of asocials, criminals, and Jews in concentration camps because shooting was just not feasible any longer due to the sheer number of people in "protective" custody.[259]

In the midst of the T-4 program, on September 21, 1939, Heydrich ordered Polish Jews to be ghettoized.[260] This ghettoization made the next step, deportation, simpler. Adolf Eichman was more than eager to get the collection and deportation of the Jews under way. In 1939, he ordered the head of the Gestapo to begin deporting 70,000–80,000 Jews from East Upper Silesia.[261] Eichman then increased the program, and by 1939, Hitler had ordered 300,000 Reich Jews deported and all Jews in Vienna would suffer the same fate in the subsequent nine months.[262] In approximately one month, mid-September to mid-October 1939, the genocide of Jews and "Gypsies" was under way.[263]

The former Soviet Union was the first area to feel the wrath of the Nazi ideology beginning in 1941.[264] Hitler declared war because the Soviet government tried to undermine Germany by creating anti-German policies and by breaking treaties with Germany by positioning their forces along the German border.[265,266] The plan was to see complete Russian destruction because they were "inferior" and communists were a political threat.[267,268] For the Soviet Union, there were two verbal orders given to the "soldiers" by their commanding officers in speeches. One denied POW status to anyone suspected of being anti-German.[269] This gave the German battalions in the USSR the ability to execute anyone immediately (today called a "kill zone").[270] The second, "Barbarossa decree," absolved German soldiers of any wrong doing and prevented them from being prosecuted in court for any of their actions while in the USSR.[271] Thus, the two orders meant all Jews including men, women, and children of all ages were to be slaughtered.[272] The plan to decimate Jews in the Soviet Union would overshadow what the Nazi's initial plans were for Poland.[273] This plan, Operation Barbarossa, demonstrates a shift in German treatment of Jews.[274] Prior to entering the USSR, no more than 2 to 3 percent of any Jewish community had been killed.[275] This was about to change because Operation Barbarossa eliminated entire Jewish communities starting on the first day of its operation, creating the foundation for the Final Solution.[276] To carry out Operation Barbarossa, Himmler created four mobile armed forces, *Einsatzgruppen,* which were to follow behind the army in order to secure the area they had just "conquered."[277] Consequently, they had to slaughter any communist leaders to prevent them from being able to regroup and raise a counterattack.[278]

One German group sent to the USSR was the Reserve Police Battalion 101, a group of Order Police (*Ordnungpolizei*) of approximately 500 men deemed unfit for front line combat due to their age.[279] The actions of this Battalion are described in Chapter 9 and constitute an example of how the average man, untrained to kill, reacts when forced to kill. Many more men joined the Order Police to avoid conscription into the army.[280] In Bialystok, Russia, in 1941, Operation Barbarossa started like a pogrom: "beating, humiliation, beard burning, and shooting at will."[281] It then turned into a systematic murder.[282] Jews were lined up against a wall and shot,[283] and burned in a synagogue.[284] Anyone who managed to break through the fire was shot.[285] A total of 2,000–2,200 Jews died that night.[286] The next massacre was systematically carried out by "the highest echelons of the SS."[287] An execution order was given to kill all male Jews in Russia between the ages of 17 and 45.[288] They were to make sure there was no evidence, no pictures, and no sign of the mass grave after it.[289] All the Jews were rounded up and brought to a stadium.[290] Once the stadium reached full capacity, they were all shot.[291] The only records of the deaths are from the German courts saying about 3,000 Jews died, which in all probability is a huge underestimate.[292] In mid-1941, some 37,253 Russian Jews were shot by different battalions, which is taken from incomplete reports again indicating that the number may, in fact, be much higher.[293]

Efforts in the Ukraine were just as destructive with a mass shooting of 33,000 near Kiev in the Babi Yar Ravine in two days.[294,295] "Smaller" executions varying from hundreds to thousands continued as the German battalion moved through the USSR.[296] In October 1941, a police battalion along with Lithuanian auxiliary police went to Minsk.[297] En route together they massacred all the Jews in Smolevichi, a village east of Minsk.[298] This massacre was justified as a deterrent or warning to prevent other civilians from helping partisans resist and organizing a counterattack.[299] Subsequently, the group was given orders to move onto Slutsk and decimate the Jews there as well.[300]

These murders by no means were done "humanely." There was massive brutality such as beatings as well as any other acts that might inflict humiliation and degradation preceding the slaughter, and then the Jews were trucked out of the city to be shot.[301] One commander, Otto Ohlendorf, had the foresight that the men in the armed forces might be unable to carry out such psychologically damaging and demoralizing acts.[302] Hence, he enlisted men from auxiliary units of non-German groups like the Lithuanians or Ukrainians in order to spare the Germans.[303] Having local auxiliary units do the killings had another advantage. This was spun as locals getting revenge against terrorist communists, so the killings seemed justified to the German soldiers, decreasing the psychological trauma of such outrageous and inhuman acts.[304] Lithuanians and Ukrainians killed hundreds and thousands of Jews under the "guidance" of the German armed forces including those at Kovno and Lvov.[305] This by no means meant the armed forces were going to be exempt from partaking in the genocide.[306] In fact, they would kill Jews "through a stepwise escalation."[307]

An estimate of 25 million died either through starvation or direct murderous methods in Russia.[308]

Another massacre of Jews in the Soviet Union was Brest. There were three phases for the Jews in Brest. The first saw 15 percent of the population slaughtered in only the two opening months of Operation Barbarossa.[309] This chaos was followed by almost 14 months of relative "stability."[310] However, this stability was more precarious than locals probably imagined for it came to an abrupt end on October 15–16, 1942, when all the Jews were massacred.[311] The Jews were killed by firing squad outside the city of Brest where the Jews had unknowingly dug what was to be their own mass grave.[312] A total of 20,000 were shot, including 9,000 who were employed and 2,000 of those who were highly skilled and irreplaceable workers.[313] According to Browning, "Most historians agree that there is no 'big bang' theory for the origins of the Final Solution, predicated on a single moment in time."[314] The Wannsee Conference, generally thought to have been the origin of the Final Solution blueprint, is now generally believed to have been a formality.[315] More recent historians see the prewar years as leading to more radical and escalating steps, which landed the Nazi regime on the doorstep of the Final Solution.[316] The Nazis shifted policies mid-step not only to accommodate initiatives but also to inflict as much violence as could be tolerated by both citizens and the "police." Moreover, most believe that total decimation in the former USSR was not decided upon until after the invasion had already begun when it became a feasible prospect.[317] The murders in the former USSR sparked an increase in killings throughout German occupied land as well perhaps in part due to the increased confidence and excitement stemming from the victories.[318] The power fed on itself and led to increased atrocities.

By the fall of 1941, the massacres finally started to subside.[319] However, instead of shooting Jews, there would now be transportations sending them to the east.[320] Browning states that this was a result of "local and regional authorities" trying to solve the crisis of housing shortages due to ghettoization.[321] Goldhagen lists numerous Jewish massacres numbering from 19,000 to 33,000 victims each.[322]

THE DEATH CAMPS

The year 1941 was a critical turning point. It was the year, according to Browning, when the Nazis crossed the line into the Final Solution and the Holocaust as it is recognized today.[323] In 1941, the Final Solution would be carried out by both firing squad and gassing. Following victories on the eastern front in 1941, Hitler gave his approval for Jews to be deported to "killing centres."[324] Gassing was implemented for efficiency as well as because it was less psychologically traumatizing to the perpetrators since it required less direct involvement than shooting in a firing squad.[325] According to Martin Gilbert, Auschwitz was in operation as early as June 1940.[326,327,328] While gassing was under way, shootings were still happening. In fact, by the end of 1941, there were orders that any Jew found outside a ghetto was to be shot immediately.[329] This was initially implemented due to fear that typhus, which was rampant in the ghettos, would spread.[330] Therefore, "search" parties were formed. Jews were found in bunkers in forests.[331] When they were discovered, they were shot through the back of the neck with the bayonet as a guide to bring about instantaneous death without a lot of carnage to the bodies.[332] The year 1941 also shows the shift in Nazi policy from forced emigration to systematic destruction.[333] The gas chambers became increasingly more active in 1941.[334] The initial gas chambers were tested on Soviet POWs.[335]

Prior to going to the camps, Jews were placed in ghettos, which caused massive death due to starvation and rampant disease from lack of sanitary facilities and medical attention.[336] Ghettoization had another appeal. It segregated the Jews.[337] The Warsaw ghetto housed 445,000 Jews by spring 1941.[338] That is not to say their conditions were even slightly tolerable, but they were at least seen as temporarily valuable, so their lives were spared for the time being. In spite of their valuable work, in the summer of 1942, deportation to the death camps of both working and nonworking Jews was rampant.[339] This decision destroyed any economy and productivity the ghettos had, raising concerns by some local German authorities as to why Jews were not being utilized to their full capability.[340] "Discussion" about this was to occur at the Wannsee Conference.

The Wannsee Conference took place on January 20, 1942.[341] The Conference, despite its severity of topics, lasted merely one to two hours.[342] Although this Conference cannot reveal when Hitler made his decision to execute all Jews, it does mark the time when his senior civil servants were informed about it.[343] The main purpose of the Conference was to proactively eliminate foreseeable challenges between agencies that may have arisen as the Final Solution was carried out completely.[344] The proposed number of Jews to be decimated under the Final Solution was a staggering 11 million.[345] Heydrich made it clear that the Jewish "problem" would be rectified through the use of gas chambers and by ignoring the Jews as a resource of "free" labor.[346] The Conference iterated there was to be mass deportation to death camps for gassing.[347] The interested reader is directed to the film *Conspiracy*, based on recorded dialogue from the actual conference.

Within just a four year period, 1941–1945, more than 710 deportation trains transported Jews to either ghettos or death camps.[348] This number does not include the transports within Poland.[349] There was no air circulation, no food, and no water provided despite the lengthy trips.[350] The train cars were originally built for cattle, and anyone who attempted to escape was shot on the spot or the following day upon arrival at the destination.[351] During the journey, Jews who were deemed no longer worth transporting due to illness, old age, or frailty were shot.[352] In some cases on transportations when ammunition had run out, the guards resorted to using stones and bayonets to prevent escape.[353] About 25 percent of those being transported perished, excluding those shot during escape attempts.[354]

Despite the enormous number of those already dead, the time period between March 1942 and February 1943 was the deadliest time.[355] Up until the middle of March 1942, 75 to 80 percent of Holocaust victims still clung to life.[356] However, in the following 11 months, only 20 percent would still be alive.[357]

When the Reich Jews' deportation began again in March 1942, they were not immediately sent to gas chambers but to "work" camps in order to "preserve appearances to the outside" that a genocide was not in progress.[358] However, these appearances would not be maintained long.

Starting in the summer of 1942 there was an acute increase in mass murder, which coincided with the regime's food shortage.[359] Since Germany was involved in a war and had ghettoized thousands and thousands of people, the government took on the responsibility of "feeding" them all. The price of food throughout Germany and German-occupied territory rose anywhere from 6- to 70-fold during the war years.[360] This meant the Nazis would try to reserve all the food for the army and "citizens" even though by now even less food was going to those incarcerated. In May 1942, the systematic genocide of the Jews was in full swing as per Hitler's decision almost a year earlier.[361]

After the "resettlement" into the larger ghettos, police battalions searched nearby towns and woods to find those who had escaped.[362] Before being shot, they were forced to strip and then searched for any valuables.[363]

In October 1942, deportations had ceased for the time being. Many Jews who had escaped decided to return to the ghettos because winter made it nearly impossible not to leave traces and thus be tracked down and shot.[364] However, this action did not guarantee their safety in the ghettos despite the hiatus of deportations.[365] There were still mass shootings of up to 500–600 people regularly.[366] Between the fall of 1942 and the spring of 1943, the camp commandant of Treblinka, Willi Althoff, would kill some Jews almost every night, and many of these killings were carried out like theatrical productions for both his and invited guests' enjoyment.[367] The sadistic guard, Amon Goethe, played by Ralph Fiennes in the film, *Schindler's List,* closely resembled Althoff.

In 1943, Jews began to "revolt" against their captures. The fear of further uprising in the ghettos led to the *Erntefest* or Harvest Festival Massacre.[368] Prior to the camps' liquidations, work Jews dug trenches in a zigzag pattern, which was realistically explained as protection from air strikes.[369] Yet once again, Jews were unwittingly digging their own graves. In 1943, both male and female Jews totaling 16,500–18,000 were marched to Majdanek from small adjacent work camps surrounding Lublin.[370] When they reached the inner camp, they had to remove all clothing, walk with their fingers interlocked behind their heads, lay down, and be shot with the now infamous neck shot.[371]

As the war dragged on, the Final Solution escalated, and ghettos were cleared at an alarming rate. Clearing most ghettos usually went uneventfully, but some did not. Many hundreds were shot en route to the train station because they were unable to continue.[372] The typical procedure for clearing the ghettos was to round the prisoners up and bring them to a marketplace or another central location, where those who were too young, old, or ill were shot on the spot.[373,374,375] Worker Jews were selected to dig mass graves.[376] After the graves were dug, the Jews at the marketplace were taken into the woods in groups; the men were taken first followed by the women and children, were stripped to some degree, made to lay down on their stomachs, and shot in the back of the head with the bayonet as a guide.[377]

While the ghettos were being cleared, some Jews were able to escape. The regime wanted Jew-free areas, so "Jew hunts" were performed to recapture and murder those who had previously escaped. In the fall of 1942, the Reserve Police Battalion 101 (see Chapter 9) encountered little to no resistance.[378] However, come spring 1943, Russian POWs and Jews had united and made camps together.[379] The typical style for the "Jew hunts" was to go into the forest to eliminate a bunker about which they had been informed.[380] The battalion had Polish informers and trackers whose sole purpose was to search for bunkers.[381] Once at the bunkers, the battalion members would toss in grenades, and anyone who survived that blast had to lie down and got shot with the typical neck shot.[382] In the Lublin district, from May to October 1943, 1,695 Jews were hunted down and executed.[383] The "hunts" played an essential role in the Final Solution and genocide by completely creating Jew-free areas and consistently adding to the death count.[384]

Despite the astronomical number of dead, not all the ghettos had been liquidated.[385] The surviving camps became more stable and slightly less torturous because of pragmatic economic concerns of a huge labor shortage in combination with the prospect of imminent defeat of the war.[386] For instance, at Flossenbürg in northeastern Bavaria, there were approximately 4,000 prisoners mostly consisting of Polish, Russians, and German ethnics.[387] At the end of its collapse in 1945, 52,000 were detained there.[388] Flossenbürg had neither the infamous gas chambers nor "assembly line killing."[389] However, throughout its existence, at least 100,000 were held there and 30,000 expired.[390] The death toll includes both direct killings by shooting and indirect by disease or malnutrition brought on by the incarceration and deplorable conditions.[391]

Hungarian Jews were the last to be attacked by the Nazis.[392] From the middle of May to early July 1944, 437,000 Hungarian Jews were shipped to Auschwitz.[393] Upon arrival, most were greeted with gas.[394] Most of those who were not immediately liquidated died subsequently either in the camp or during the death marches.[395] Anyone found attempting to escape was shot immediately.[396] Prior to their arrival at Auschwitz, hundreds of Jews perished due to the lack of ventilation, food, and water during the strenuous trip.[397]

When the Nazis could no longer stave off defeat, they forced debilitated prisoners to march in hopes of fulfilling the goal of the Final Solution. Death marches near the end of the war were initiated due to the proximity of approaching armies, Allied or Soviet.[398] On the death marches, 250,000–375,000 died as the Germans tried to keep one step ahead.[399] Jews were not the only ones who died on the marches since there were other groups confined in the camps.[400] However, Jews were in poorer condition than non-Jews, so it is presumable that the Jews would perish at a faster rate than those who left the camp in questionably "better" condition.[401] While marching, anyone unable to go on was shot by the soldiers forcing them to march.[402] Based on survivor testimony, only around 30 percent survived the marches.[403] Either they died from exhaustion or they were shot before exhaustion could take their lives.[404] Additionally, guards would regularly beat the marchers with rods if they were too slow, but this made them slower, for which they would then be murdered.[405] Moreover, prisoners were inexplicably shot randomly at will under no orders from above to do so.[406]

There is no consensus as to how many Gypsies perished under Nazi hands.[407] There is a range from 100,000 to 500,000.[408] Regardless of the exact number of dead, the Nazi policies, actions, and intentions were genocidal. An "estimated number of Jews murdered during the Holocaust" as of 1945 borders was, according to Goldhagen, about 6 million, including 3 million in Poland alone.[409,410]

The Nazis' unique rise to power in Germany played a vital role in their gaining public support and momentum. From the beginning of the Nazi power, they brutalized any and all groups that opposed them or did not "fit" into their Aryan racist vision of the "pure" community they desperately wanted. The torment began with legislation designed to draw clear distinctions between "Germans" and non-Germans. The policies ultimately led to emotional, psychological, economic, and physical attacks by ordinary citizens on the Nazi adversaries. As time progressed, the policy changes became increasingly more restrictive and detrimental to the "out-groups'" survival until finally the policies became genocidal with the ultimate goal of complete physical decimation. Although 1941 marked this shift to physical annihilation in policies, systematic and premeditated mass murders were already taking place prior to that. Physical destruction and obliteration were top priority even though it significantly hampered the German war efforts. Despite the end result for prisoners being death, the men who performed the genocide still emotionally and psychologically tortured their helpless victims prior to executing them or while in transport to their deaths. To prevent the German men from becoming demoralized as well as to provide efficiency, gas chambers were constructed and implemented to handle the vast majority of the murders.[411] However, mass and individual shootings continued even while the gas chambers were in full operation. Nearing the end of the war, when defeat was looming, the prisoners clinging to life were forced to march, and for many who had survived unimaginable torture this would be too much. If there is one commonality linking the early and the end years of the Nazis, it is systematic psychological, emotional, and physical torture of any and all who were deemed outside the "norm." If there is one feature that makes the Holocaust distinct, it is the use of "efficient" technological applications to mass murder. If there is a lesson from this awful history, it may be in the early warning signs; the use of law in a police state as the "thin edge of the wedge" to initiate the normative changes to follow.

The "end years" of the Nazi regime are chronicled in Antony Beevor's brilliant book.[412] They were depicted by an implosion of extreme violence now directed within the group. The SS (following Hitler's orders to fight to the death) pursued and killed Germans, even the Wehrmacht (German Army) who saw the hopelessness of the situation as the Red Army closed in on Berlin from the east and the Allies from the west. Suicides were commonplace, especially by German women who heard of the coming rape and brutality of the Russian Red Army. The SS began terrorizing Germans to fight on[413] through threats of castration and by killing would-be defectors. (The Russians had done the same, even sending soldiers wounded and captured by the Germans to a Gulag after the war. Stalin's order, as was Hitler's, was to die fighting.) The German army was so overcommitted that 15-year-old boys were sent to fight the Red Army with no training and poor weaponry. Roadside executions of Hitler Youth were commonplace; they were hanged from trees on the flimsiest of proof that they had not fought hard enough.[414] Some of these boys had simply become exhausted and were then murdered by the SS instead of the Russians. The slaughter of political prisoners escalated and included decapitation.[415] A "scorched earth policy" was put in place; anything of value was destroyed. The violence fed on itself, destruction of everything human marked the last days, signifying a collective group suicide for the true believers.

MILITARY MASSACRES

Q: What is the law?
A: Not to spill blood.
Are we not men?

—*The Island of Lost Souls* (film, 1933, from the novel by H.G. Wells)

The genocides in Rwanda and Nazi Germany were implemented, in part, by a series of slaughters or massacres carried out by the military or a group under governmental control. These massacres might be thought of as planned massacres similar to premeditated murder in a civilian context. The massacres we review here are more ambiguous. Previous planning is not so evident as a certain mind-set of disdain for the victims as a group. These more "spontaneous" massacres are similar to "unplanned" homicide or manslaughter or second degree murder in a civilian context. Military massacre has been documented over the ages from Genghis Khan to the U.S. Cavalry.[i] In the former case, massacre was used

---

[i]In the spring of 1864, while the Civil War raged in the eastern United States, Cavalry Commander Chivington launched a campaign of violence in Colorado against the Cheyenne and their allies, his troops attacking any and all Indians and razing their villages. The Cheyenne, joined by neighboring Arapahos, Sioux, Comanche, and Kiowa in both Colorado and Kansas, went on the defensive warpath. After a summer of scattered small raids and clashes, white and Indian representatives met at Camp Weld outside of Denver on September 28. No treaties were signed, but the Indians believed that by reporting and camping near army posts, they would be declaring peace and accepting sanctuary.

Black Kettle was a peace-seeking chief of a band of some 600 Southern Cheyennes and Arapahos that followed the buffalo along the Arkansas River of Colorado and Kansas. They reported to Fort Lyon and then camped on Sand Creek about 40 miles north.

Shortly afterward, Chivington led a force of about 800 men into Fort Lyon, and gave the garrison notice of his plans for an attack on the Indian encampment. Although he was informed that Black Kettle had already surrendered, Chivington pressed on with what he considered the perfect opportunity to

strategically as a weapon of terror. As with the Crusaders described in Chapter 1, other fortified towns would hear of prior massacres and surrender.[1] In this chapter, we concentrate on some notable twentieth century massacres for which there is independent documentation.

THE RAPE OF NANKING

Chang graphically described the rape and slaughter of captured Chinese soldiers[ii] and civilians that occurred during the Sino-Japanese War in 1937.[2] By

---

further the cause for Indian extinction. On the morning of November 29, he led his troops, many of them drinking heavily, to Sand Creek and positioned them, along with their four howitzers, around the Indian village.

Black Kettle, ever-trusting, raised both an American and a white flag of peace over his tepee. In response, Chivington raised his arm for the attack. Chivington wanted a victory, not prisoners, and so men, women, and children were hunted down and shot.

With cannons and rifles pounding them, the Indians scattered in panic. Then the crazed soldiers charged and killed anything that moved. A few warriors managed to fight back to allow some of the tribe to escape across the stream, including Black Kettle.

The colonel was as thorough as he was heartless. An interpreter living in the village testified, "They were scalped, their brains knocked out, the men used their knives, ripped open women, clubbed little children, knocked them in the head with their rifle butts, beat their brains out, mutilated their bodies in every sense of the word." By the end of the one-sided battle. as many as 200 Indians, more than half women and children, had been killed and mutilated (scalped).

While the Sand Creek Massacre outraged easterners, it seemed to please many people in Colorado Territory. Chivington later appeared on a Denver stage where he regaled delighted audiences with his war stories and displayed 100 Indian scalps, including the pubic hairs of women (see www.pbs.org and Dee Brown[56]).

Waller raises the point that several levels of socialization may contribute to such collective violence.[57] As he puts it, "what about the men who perpetrated the slaughter at Sand Creek? Was it their membership in the Third Colorado Volunteer Cavalry regiment that best accounts for their active and willing participation in the atrocities? Or was it their membership in an even larger collective, the American culture, steeped in an extraordinary ideological hatred against Indians, which made them unusually fit to perpetrate extraordinary evil? He concludes, "Admitting that culture or ideology may simply be the pretext by which we rationalize a more general wish to dominate or destroy is much more discomforting."[58]

An investigation was conducted by a Joint Committee on the Conduct of the War who found:

As to Colonel Chivington, your committee can hardly find fitting terms to describe his conduct. Wearing the uniform of the United States, which should be the emblem of justice and humanity; holding the important position of commander of a military district, and therefore having the honor of the government to that extent in his keeping, he deliberately planned and executed a foul and dastardly massacre which would have disgraced the verist [sic] savage among those who were the victims of his cruelty. Having full knowledge of their friendly character, having himself been instrumental to some extent in placing them in their position of fancied security, he took advantage of their inapprehension and defenceless [sic] condition to gratify the worst passions that ever cursed the heart of man. (Wikipedia)

However, Chivington was not punished, nor were any of his troops.

[ii]Technically, both soldiers and civilians in Nanking were prisoners of war—the Chinese army had surrendered. The killing of POW's, although forbidden by the Geneva Convention, is not unusual. Ferguson describes the killing of German POW's in WWI by the British,[59] and Boswell describes their killing by

historical standards, Chang views the Rape of Nanking as the largest short-term mass extermination in history (the Romans killed 150,000 during the sack of Carthage, but numbers of victims in Rwanda surpassed even Nanking, with 800,000 being killed in eight months). While estimates vary, it seems 250,000 dead is the accepted estimate, but the slaughter is infamous for the cruelty with which the victims were dispatched; the majority of the victims were killed and/ or raped in a six week period. Chinese men were used for bayonet practice, and women were gang-raped, were sodomized, and had their vaginas crammed with foreign objects. Men and women were disemboweled. Both men and women were torn apart by dogs. Races were practiced where bound prisoners were lined up and decapitated. Babies were thrown into the air and impaled on bayonets, cut in half or quartered (this practice is also reported by Danner[3] as occurring during the civil war in El Salvador: see below). I remember my reaction to first hearing of this practice, I was so shocked, revolted, and numb that I could not function for some time.[iii] Although the Japanese government has officially denied that this event occurred (despite a war crimes trial in Tokyo and Nanking in which Japanese officers were found guilty and hanged),[iv] Europeans living in Nanking at that time (who were spared) have largely confirmed the carnage (also see Woods).[4] Ironically, one of the Europeans who wrote of the carnage was a member of the Nazi Party, John Rabe, who wrote somewhat naively to Hitler, cautioning him against political alignment with the Japanese.[5] It is clear from

---

Canadians (after they had surrendered), by dropping hand grenades into the German prisoners' great-coats.[60] Ferguson argues that too much animosity had developed during combat for a sudden cessation of hostilities to lead to favorable treatment. In WWII, Chang argues that a higher percentage of POW's died in Japanese (33 percent) than in Nazi (4 percent) prison camps.[61] Eventually, the combat motive for humane treatment is that it encourages surrender when the surrendering army is not forced to fight to the death.

[iii]Iris Chang was found dead in her car on November 9, 2004, on a rural road south of Los Gatos, California. Investigators concluded that Chang had shot herself through the mouth with a revolver. At the time of her death she had been taking medication for mania and sleep deprivation. In addition, she was working on another book, *Bataan Death March*. There is some speculation that the subject matter took a toll on the author. There was suggestion of increasing paranoid schizophrenia in her suicide notes (see Wikipedia.org under her name).

[iv]There was some breakdown in the chain of command at Nanking, when the commander (General Matsui) became ill.[62] Military massacres (My Lai, El Mozote) appear to occur despite background social order. My Lai occurred when the United States was a democracy (March 1968) that tolerated dissent. In response to a description of the My Lai situation (your commanding officer orders you to shoot unarmed civilians), Kelman and Hamilton found that survey samples (n = 400) of U.S. citizens said that most people believed 62 percent of others would obey the order but that they personally would only do so 34 percent of the time.[63] There was some variation by education, gender, and geographic location (less educated people were more obedient). There were groups of people who believed the army should have shot civilians and that they themselves would do so. These people tended to see Calley as not responsible. This group was more likely to agree with trying foreign officers than American officers for war crimes. They were high on authoritarianism, obedient to in-group norms. Another group believed that no one should shoot under illegal orders. They saw Calley as responsible. They were less likely to have a double standard about war crimes as a function of whether their group or a foreign nation committed them.[64]

Rabe's diaries that the Japanese Embassy was fully informed of the events at Nanking as they were occurring. Japanese denial of these events has been complete, testifying, I suppose, to the shame and disbelief that any group has about the horrific capabilities of its own.[v] The issue of denial of verifiable atrocities would constitute a book itself and would include the phenomenon of Holocaust deniers.[6]

The event was precipitated by the surrender of the Chinese army at Nanking in December 1937. According to Chang, an order was issued to "kill all captives."[7] Chang presents some evidence that the order was forged by a Japanese intelligence officer as a means of solving the logistical nightmare of feeding a large group of captured and despised enemy and eliminating the possibility of retaliation. About 500,000 civilians and 90,000 troops were trapped in Nanking and surrendered to 50,000 Japanese troops. The slaughter began with the killing of the Chinese troops, for whom the Japanese had great contempt. That contempt was enhanced by their surrender, which Japanese soldiers were trained not to do. An article of the Japanese warrior code of Bushido was never to dishonor one's lord by avoiding death. The Japanese warrior culture valued suicide over surrender and highly valued Kamikaze (suicidal mission). The Chinese soldiers who surrendered were shot en masse, in groups of 50 each. Their bodies were cremated or dumped into the Yangtze River.

The Japanese then started a house-to-house search of Nanking, shooting any civilians they encountered. Evidence for that series of events comes from diaries kept by some Japanese soldiers and by Japanese journalists, who were appalled by what was transpiring.[8] At this point, mass rape began. Every woman available was raped regardless of age. There was a military policy forbidding rape, but, according to Chang, it could not overcome centuries old Japanese military practice (although raping enemy females is clearly not exclusive to the Japanese, since it happened in Rwanda, El Salvador, Bosnia, Russia, and Germany as well). Chang claims that the Japanese military culture taught that raping virgins made one more powerful in battle (similar to beliefs in the Congo and elsewhere about cannibalism). One of the Japanese soldiers (Shiro Azuma) later wrote to Chang saying, "Perhaps when we were raping her, we looked at her as a woman but when we killed her, we just thought of her as something like a pig."[9] The postrape killing included mutilation, insertion of foreign objects into the vagina, disemboweling, and vivisection. Men were sodomized or forced to perform sexual acts with members of their own families.[10] The degradation of entire families was a common practice of sexual torture. Some family members chose death rather than participate, a choice made easier by the belief that one would be

[v]This belief in the essential "goodness" of the in-group transforms the perception of in-group actions while simultaneously projecting the worst atrocities onto the out-group. The Spanish typically view the horrific ritual abuse of bulls and horses that occurs in their national sport as a sign of the machismo in the bullfighter.

raped then savagely killed immediately afterwards by the sexually frenzied soldiers. As was reported in Rwanda, children were killed in front of their parents. Chapter Four in Chang's book represents some of the most grisly descriptions of human action anywhere recorded.

The rape and carnage lasted for six weeks. By contrast, during that time the Japanese observed an International Non-Killing Zone where Americans and Europeans lived. Some Chinese found refuge there where no non-Chinese were killed or hurt. John Rabe, a German businessman and member of the Nazi party, saved numerous Chinese and cabled Hitler to rethink his connection with Japan,[11] and occasionally put himself at risk to save Chinese.[12] The Japanese demonstrated that they were capable of self-control in not killing non-Chinese, even during the six week killing spree. Hence, some form of social control, in terms of defining who was a target and who was not, based on the race of the person, was at work even at the height of the massacre. In fact, this aspect of the slaughter, that some territorial boundary was respected in the midst of the carnage, is perplexing. Against any Chinese outside the safety zone, anything was permitted. Against Europeans or Chinese in the safety zone, the normal rules applied. There was a line of demarcation in the minds of the killers.

Even though the Japanese had been trained to kill civilians,[13] the newly arrived soldiers who witnessed the torture were shocked. After some time, that aversion had changed. This conversion of aversion to acceptance and even rewarding arousal is also evident in Browning's descriptions of German *Ordnungpolizie* (Police Battalion 101) killing Jews[14] and is explored in detail in Chapter 9. Chang interviewed Japanese veterans who reported experiencing a lack of remorse even when torturing helpless civilians.[15] However, in some cases remorse occurred with a delayed onset. Nagatomi Hakudo, later a doctor in Japan, built a shrine of remorse in his waiting room where patients could watch videotapes of his war crime trial (war crimes trials were held in Tokyo and Nanking) and confession. He said,

> Few know that soldiers impaled babies on bayonets and tossed them still alive into pots of boiling water. They gang raped women from the ages of twelve to eighty and killed them when they no longer satisfied their sexual requirements. I beheaded people, starved them to death, burned them, and buried them alive, over two hundred in all. **It is terrible that I could turn into an animal and do these things. There are really no words to explain what I was doing. I was truly a devil.**[16] (boldface mine)

Chang reported that Japanese soldiers interviewed after the war reported that it was easy for them to kill because they had been taught that, next to the emperor, all individual life was valueless. To die for the emperor was the greatest glory, and to be caught alive by the enemy was the greatest shame. As one former soldier wrote to Chang, "If my life was not important, an enemies' life became inevitably less important."[17] Hence social features of a combatant's socialization that lessen the importance of individual life will make slaughter easier to implement. War and conflict inevitably carry such messages: that the "cause" is greater than the individual. Any belief system that includes a notion of life (or awareness) after death will similarly devalue the present, the individual, and the "enemy." Suicide bombers who believe in reward after death also share this view.[18]

The U.S. government had cracked the Japanese cipher in 1936[19] and knew what was transpiring in Nanking, but kept it from the U.S. public. It was years before Pearl Harbor (in 1941), and the U.S. government believed the public outcry would force U.S. involvement in a war they did not yet want.

Chang views some explanations for the Japanese brutality as specific to Japan: the hierarchical nature of Japanese society coupled with the brutalization of the Japanese soldier as part of training that included exercises to numb men[20] "against the human instinct against killing people who are not attacking."[21] Japanese culture originated as tribal without an embracing concept of humanity. Moral obligations in Japanese society, as in other collective cultural systems,[22] were not universal but local and particularized, so they could easily be broken on foreign soil when confronting out-group members.[23]

Desensitization was part of Japanese military training. Soldiers were taught how to decapitate and bayonet living prisoners. Initially recruits were repulsed by such practices,[24] eventually they became inured, and atrocities became banal. That regimen goes some way toward explaining the beheadings and the "killing contests." It does not explain the tortures or rapes that were not part of training in the Japanese or other military training camps.

Also, according to historian Theodore Cook,[25] there is no historical precedent in Japanese history for the Rape of Nanking. Such atrocities had not occurred in Japanese civil wars. It may be that ethnocentrism in Japan was extreme, fuelled by the vision of the Greater East Asia Co-prosperity Sphere with Japan as its leader,[26] and that the Chinese were viewed as resisting that social order and hence as subhuman. Diary reports of Japanese soldiers reflect the belief that Chinese were a subhuman species. However, being subhuman does not "explain" the furious sadism the Japanese soldiers exhibited. For example, there is no evidence that the Japanese are especially cruel toward animals. Chang's analysis goes some way toward explaining the sadistic violence evidenced by the Japanese army. However, the question is raised: Chang focused exclusively on the Japanese. What if, in studying other massacres, she found other soldiers from differing cultures to be just as capable of sadistic violence? Would this suggest a universal propensity in humans that can be raised or lowered by social forces?

It could be argued that knowledge of human attributes (such as human capacity to feel pain) provides another area of exploitation for sadism; for example, the killing of children in front of their parents requires a knowledge of what would be most painful for a human to witness. It requires an awareness of human family attachment and parental protectiveness. It then turns these universal norms upside down and acts against them to maximize psychological as well as physical pain. Hence, "dehumanization" as an explanation of barbarous acts is called into question by the actions of the soldiers in both Nanking and Rwanda. If anything, they acted on "too human" traits—knowledge of the psychological pain that would be felt by a target selected because he/she was human and a member of an enemy group. What may be the hardest truth to face is that, as humans, we exhibit more sadistic violence than any "subhuman" group or animal and that members of our own race/culture/nation (that is, people like us) are capable of this violence. We may have to rethink our use of terms like "inhuman violence" or "humane treatment."

MY LAI

According to Herbert Kelman and Lee Hamilton[27] and based on descriptions by Seymour Hersh,[28] later corroborated at the trial of Lt. William Calley,[29] U.S. Army C Company's Second Platoon of the 11th Light Infantry Brigade, Americal Division, attacked a village in Viet Nam, killing between 128 and 500 unarmed civilians, raping the women, and bayoneting children.[30] A substantial amount of this killing was organized and some occurred spontaneously during "mop up" operations. The massacre was officially reported as a military victory over the Viet Cong.

Robert Lifton's[31] descriptions of My Lai, based on eyewitness reports, suggested that the killings were accompanied by a generalized rage and by expressions of anger and revenge towards the victims. Kelman and Hamilton suggest that rage occurs in the course of the killing as a way of explaining and rationalizing the actions. After the slaughter, the soldiers shared lunch with surviving Vietnamese children whose families and neighbors they had killed hours before.[32] The authors do not explain why these children would go anywhere near the Americans.

The My Lai operation was planned as a "search and destroy" mission with an objective to root out a Viet Cong battalion. The men in C Company were frustrated by an inability to find an elusive enemy and felt that, finally, they would get into combat;[33] the combination of losing men to booby-trapped mines and the inability to find the enemy had created a climate of animosity and a hunger for revenge. Hence, some evidence for an elevated baseline level of rage amongst all soldiers existed. This preexisting state is different from that described for soldiers in Nanking or El Mozote.

The men in C company were 18–22 years old and had volunteered for the draft (hence, similar to the profile of U.S. soldiers in Iraq).[34] The company commander, Captain Ernest Medina, had given the men orders to expect resistance, to burn the village, and to kill the livestock. It was not clear whether an order was given to slaughter the inhabitants. Medina's second in command, Lt. William Calley, claimed he had heard such an order. Medina denied it.

Hersh described the platoon entering the village "with guns blazing."[35] All there were women, children, and old men. The platoon began to ransack the village and kill everyone, shooting into huts without knowing who was inside. Atrocities occurred spontaneously: rapes, tortures, killings (see also Brownmiller).[36] One of the soldiers, Vernado Simpson, recalled killing about 25 people. "I cut their throats, cut off their hands, cut out their tongue, their hair, scalped them."[37]

About a third of the entire unit was later charged with war crimes. About 10 to 20 percent of those present committed no atrocities. Some disobeyed Calley's orders to machine gun civilians. One, a helicopter pilot named Hugh Thompson, witnessed the atrocities from the air and realized he was witnessing a massacre.[38] He landed his helicopter between a group of fleeing Vietnamese women, children, and old men and a pursuing group of soldiers. He told his crewmen to train their M-60's on the troops and to fire if they saw civilians being shot. According to Kadri, this action was "unprecedented in US military history."[39] Thompson helicoptered survivors to safety. The encounter included an enraged standoff between Thompson and Calley (mimicked in the film *Platoon*) where Thompson insisted on rescuing civilians and Calley insisted on killing them. Eventually Calley gave in. Thompson immediately reported the massacre, but there was an immediate cover-up with an official report of 128 enemy being captured from a "Viet Cong stronghold."[40]

According to testimony given later at the trial of Lt. William Calley, the inhabitants were rounded up and executed. Calley, the only soldier tried in court, had ordered the executions and was found guilty. He had also killed several civilians himself, although so had many other soldiers. Some men refused to carry out Calley's orders to execute civilians. This refusal was significant in court, signifying that the orders were not reasonable.[41] The Army command knew something had gone wrong and began an instant cover-up by reporting the operation as a victory over the Viet Cong. An individual soldier with knowledge of the incident, Ronald Ridenhour, began a letter writing campaign that started the subsequent investigation.[42] Kelman and Hamilton's survey, done in 1971, indicated that about two-thirds of Americans felt it was wrong to try Calley, some because they believed his superiors should have been tried.[43] There were two men higher up than Calley at My Lai; one was killed in action, and the other (Medina) was not tried.

Calley's court-martial was stacked in his favor with a seasoned defense counsel appointed against a rookie prosecutor (Captain Aubrey Daniel). One of the defendants, Paul Medlo, accepted under cross-examination that many of those he shot were children but insisted that they still posed a threat. "Even the babies, he claimed, might have attacked him...They might have been booby trapped, he explained, He had feared that at any point their mothers could have lobbed them, like human hand grenades from the ditches in which they were being killed."[44] Was there any basis in reality to this belief? Calley's cross-examination found him referring to the "Battle of My Lai." When asked repeatedly under cross-examination whether he or his company had come under fire, he eventually admitted they had not. He also admitted he had not seen any Vietnamese who were not either dead or in the process of being killed. Most of Calley's testimony was a series of contradictions and evasions. When asked why he told Hugh Thompson he would evacuate women and children from a bomb shelter by using a hand grenade, Calley looked blank and answered, "I don't have any idea, Sir."[45] While there is clearly an extreme element of danger in war, it also seems the case that exposure to danger generates a form of paranoid psychosis in some. Unfortunately, given the difficulty in finding troops, even with the unpopular draft in place for the Viet Nam war, the U.S. Army, like others, does not screen out applicants because of this risk.

Calley had some interpersonal problems: he had failed at school, was only 5 feet 3 inches tall, and was universally hated by his men, who made plans to kill him by "fragging" or using a fragmentation grenade. He was described as "hostile" and "nervous" by his men. However, he had no criminal record before or after the war. Calley spent three years under house arrest. His civilian profile suggests someone who would have problems in a position of power and would have a need to compensate for his failures and lack of physical stature. Lieutenant Calley was given just such an opportunity.

It is tempting to view My Lai as an aberration. Kadri puts the lie to this: brutality and mutilation was so common in Viet Nam that the general in charge, Westmoreland, issued a blanket order in October 1967, instructing all commanders to prevent their men from severing human fingers and arms. A second massacre, at My Khe, occurring at the same time as My Lai, was also investigated, but all suspected claimed memory loss or the "right to silence."[46] As Kadri puts it, "several more cases were discontinued, in the supposed interests of justice, over subsequent months."[47] The debate essentially was to try as few men as possible to show how exceptional atrocities were and to preserve the notion of the essential nobility of war.

EL MOZOTE

In the 1980s, a civil war was fought in El Salvador between guerillas (the People's Revolutionary Army) and the government of Alfredo Cristiani.[48] As with the Viet Cong, the Salvadoran guerillas proved elusive. Support for the guerillas was fairly high in the general area of Morazan in southeastern El Salvador, around a tiny town called El Mozote but not within the town itself where the people were essentially born-again Christians. There people were staunchly anti-Communist while the guerilla army was a left wing political group. Up until that time, a "dirty war" had been taking place with skirmishes and death squads who killed, mutilated, and raped their victims. Those death squads left signature knife cuts on victims, which signified their connection with the right wing Martinez Brigade. The El Salvadoran Army decided to launch an offensive in Morazan under the direction of a Colonel Domingo Monterrosa Barrios, and they warned prominent citizens of El Mozote to stock up on provisions and stay inside the town. As the Army chased guerillas through the hills of Morazan, some guerillas warned the citizens of El Mozote to flee but, believing they had nothing to fear, they decided to stay. The Army, however, had begun a procedure of "zone killing" whereby they would make an example to terrorize the guerillas by slaughtering all residents of a geographic area. The general order was to kill all the men who were suspected of being guerillas. The paranoia became so great that officers even began to suspect one another of being guerillas.[49] The hard-line Army officers always referred to the guerillas as a virus, an infection, or a cancer. This justified killing all members of a suspected guerilla's family.

When the Atlacatl Battalion of the Salvadoran Army reached El Mozote in December 1991, they marched all the inhabitants (women, children, old men) into the center of town, screaming abuse at them. They stripped them of jewelry and then ordered them back to their houses, planning initially to interrogate them about logistical connections to the guerillas. Then they ordered the men outside and into a church where they shot them all. A few who tried to escape were shot then beheaded. Eventually they stopped shooting and decapitated all remaining men. They ordered the women and children into an adjacent building and, once the men were dead, began raping and killing the women. At last they returned to the crying children and began to shoot, bayonet, and slash them with machetes.

In a rationalization reminiscent of that given by Talaat during the Armenian genocide, one captain ended soldiers balking at killing the children by arguing that,

If we don't kill them now, they'll just grow up to be guerillas. We have to take care of the job now (italics added).[50]

He then threw a child into the air and impaled him on a bayonet, then most of the children were killed either by bayoneting or hanging. A few children and women were overlooked and left for dead; in some cases they escaped into the jungle and avoided search parties. The women (particularly one named Rufina Amaya) eventually told what had happened.

The story was relayed to the U.S. press and reported after reporters from the *New York Times* and *Washington Post* visited El Salvador. The government denied any atrocities had occurred. In 1992–1993, a UN sponsored investigation, led by the Forensic Anthropology team from the University of Buenos Aires, unearthed skeletons of women and children on the El Mozote site. It was the largest mass slaughter in modern Central American history. Colonel Monterrosa at first denied the killing when asked by U.S. Army Intelligence,[51] but, subsequently, he claimed the Salvadoran Army was under attack in the village of El Mozote. Of course, the subsequent investigation by the United Nations proved this story to be a lie. Exhumation of corpses revealed 143 remains of which 132 were children (and one fetus). On another occasion, Monterrosa admitted a *limpieza* (cleaning out) had occurred[52] (but he did not call the massacre by its Spanish name, a Matanza). A subsequent investigation listed names of 794 dead. The ensuing peace accord, signed in 1992 contained an agreement that the El Salvadoran Army be purged of "known human rights violators."[53] A subsequent Truth Commission investigation that used forensic anthropological techniques (including searching for bone fragments in the soil) established that at least 500 people were killed by at least 24 different guns (not all planned exhumations were completed).[54] Final estimates put the total killed at about 733–926 people in one day.[55]

It is enormously difficult to overcome the glorification of war. Typically this takes the form of admitting that some atrocities occur (without describing them, or admitting that the victims were, in some cases, babies). It is as difficult to overcome the belief that one's own group would do such things, while simultaneously overattributing their frequency to the enemy. Pope Urban did this in 1088. George W. Bush described "weapons of mass destruction" as a rationale for invading Iraq. While these were never found, a CNN Poll as late as August 2006, found that 51 percent of Americans still believed they existed.

LYNCHINGS

Southern trees bear a strange fruit
Blood on the leaves and blood at the root
Black bodies swingin' in the Southern breeze
Strange fruit hangin' from the poplar trees

Pastoral scene of the gallant South
The bulging eyes and the twisted mouth
Scent of magnolia, sweet and fresh
Then the sudden smell of burning flesh

Here is the fruit for the crows to pluck
For the rain to gather, for the wind to suck
For the sun to rot, for the tree to drop
Here is a strange and bitter crop

—Billie Holliday, "Strange Fruit," 1939

At first glance, one may wonder what the subject of lynchings is doing in a book about genocide and military massacre. There are two reasons: lynchings represent group violence at its extreme, and they represent a form of social control through terror that is often consistent with government goals, although not "officially" sanctioned by the government. Lynchings typically occur, not during a war, but in civilian conditions. However, as we shall see below, they carry the ferocity of military violence. As Clarke showed, when official government policy becomes enacted by state executions, lynchings diminish in frequency.[1] Lynchings became less frequent in the U.S. South during the early twentieth century (after peaking in the 16 years after the Civil War was lost), because state sanctioned executioners replaced lynch mobs in carrying out the will of the white majority. As such, lynchings represent a social control condition for our explanation of massacres. They are, in effect, a massacre of one person (or a few people) by a mob of civilians—people who are not in the anxiety ridden anomie of the war context. The questions then are as follows: How were lynchings implemented? Did the mob violence resemble that of military massacres?

Approximately 3,724 people were lynched in the United States from 1889 to 1930.[2] Whether evidence was present or not, the accused were lynched for crimes such as murder, sexual assault, nonsexual assault, theft, and robbery. However, there are many recorded cases of individuals being lynched for crimes much less severe, including insulting a white person, frightening school children, seeking employment in a restaurant, expressing sympathy with the lynched victim, and using offensive language.[3] Many lynching victims were captured after extended organized manhunts by armed men, who then proceeded to torture, mutilate, drag, or burn the accused, and finally left them hanging dead from a tree to be viewed and prodded by thousands of onlookers. This aspect of lynching, the torture that preceded the hanging, is omitted from popular notions of the action.

Although there were varying levels of crimes committed as well as different degrees of torture inflicted, there remains one commonality amongst all lynchings: the mobs acted illegally, ignoring the rights of an individual to the formal system of criminal justice, and instead executed a fatal punishment that they felt the suspect deserved. Mobs ranged in size from five members to 15,000. They were composed of the community's citizens—men, women, and children. Virtually all lynchings shared important common elements. Mobs, on the pretext of punishing an alleged lawbreaker or violator of local norms, abruptly executed their victims with little regard for proof of guilt. The fact that virtually none of the perpetrators were ever punished by the local courts suggests the degree to which the mobs' violence was accepted.[4] The question remains: What drove these mobs to commit such heinous crimes?

SAM HOSE

In 1898, an African American, Sam Hose, began working for a white man, Alfred Cranford. On April 12, 1899, Hose asked his employer to allow him to return to his home to visit his ill mother, as well as asked him for money. Cranford refused to advance him any money, and the two men quarreled. The following afternoon, while Hose chopped wood at Cranford's home, his employer resumed the previous day's argument. Cranford grew increasingly angry, drew his pistol, and threatened to kill Hose. Hose hurled his axe in self-defense, which hit Cranford in the head, killing him instantly. Hose then fled the area.[5]

The next day, newspapers printed extra editions that blazoned the story of Hose's crimes across the country, with enormous embellishments, including fictitious accounts that he had also sexually assaulted Mrs. Cranford and attempted to kill her baby. *The Atlanta Constitution* printed the following: "When Hose is caught he will either be lynched and his body riddled with bullets or he will be burned at the stake."[6] Further, in the same issue the *Constitution* suggests torture in these words: "There have been whisperings of burning at the stake and of torturing the fellow low, and so great is the excitement, and so high the indignation, that this is among the possibilities."[7]

On April 16, the newspaper continued to build on the events that would occur when Hose was caught. There was no mention of due process, but rather encouragement for burning. The headlines state: "Excitement still continues intense, and it is openly declared that if Sam Hose is brought in alive he will be burned," and in the dispatch it is said:

> The residents have shown no disposition to abandon the search in the immediate neighborhood of Palmetto; their ardor has in no degree cooled, and if Sam Hose is brought here by his captors he will be publicly burned at the stake as an example to members of his race who are said to have been causing the residents of this vicinity trouble for some time.[8]

The Constitution then stated on April 19 that the search for Sam Hose had not been abandoned, and the editor declared through the paper that there would be a reward of five hundred dollars for the capture of the fugitive. Wells-Barnett argues that this offer of a reward, along with the constant suggestions that Hose be burned alive when caught, shows that the idea to burn Hose at the stake was formed by the leading citizens of Georgia.

Wells-Barnett reported that on the night of Saturday, April 23, 1899, Sam Hose was caught and it was decided to take him to another town in Georgia to burn him. The governor had ordered that Hose be taken to Atlanta, the state capital, but the arresting officers did not obey. They refused to take the prisoner to Atlanta, but arranged to take him to a town called Newman, where they knew a mob was waiting to burn him. There was no train going to Newman that Sunday morning, so the captors needed to secure a special train to take Hose to the place of burning.

The news of Hose's capture was known all over Georgia. It was known in the early morning in Atlanta that the prisoner was not going to be brought there, but rather would be taken to Newman for the burning. A special train was then ordered as an excursion train to take people to the burning. The governor of Georgia did nothing to prevent the lynching.

The following is a report on the events that took place that April afternoon after the community left church:

> Some 2,000 men and women witnessed it [the lynching] on Sunday afternoon, April 23, 1899, near Newman, Georgia. After stripping Hose of his clothes and chaining him to a tree, the self appointed executioners stacked kerosene-soaked wood high around him. Before saturating Hose with oil and applying the torch, they cut off his ears, fingers, and genitals, and skinned his face. While some in the crowd plunged knives into the victim's flesh, others watched "with unfeigning satisfaction" (as one reported noted) the contortions of Sam Hose's body as the flames rose, distorting his features, causing his eyes to bulge out of their sockets, and rupturing his veins. Before Hose's body had even cooled, his heart and liver were removed and cut into several pieces and his bones were crushed into small particles. The crowd fought over the souvenirs.[9]

Wells-Barnett adds to this account, stating that when all the bones and flesh had been taken by the early comers, others scraped in the ashes. Even the stake that Hose was tied to was quickly chopped down and carried away as the largest souvenir of the burning. The annihilation of the lynch victim was accompanied by what forensic psychologists call the gathering of trophies,[10] which is typically associated in forensic analysis with serial sexual murderers. For example, Gilles de Rais, the most notorious of sexual murderers, kept severed heads of victims.[11] In the current case, the lynch mob comprised normal citizens leaving church.

A federal detective was sent to Georgia and reported that he found no difficulty in securing interviews from the white citizens. They found no reason to conceal their participation in the lynching, but rather discussed the details with the freedom that one would talk about "an afternoon's advertisement in which he has pleasantly participated in."[12]

COTTON AGRICULTURE IN RELATION TO NUMBER OF LYNCHINGS

The majority of lynchings occurred as a Southern phenomenon, and many researchers have noted that lynchings in the South were even further concentrated in certain sites while virtually unknown in others.[13] The majority of lynchings of African American victims occurred in the prime cotton growing areas, which raises the possibility of a connection between cotton agriculture and racial violence.

Beck and Tolnay examined the relationship between cotton price and number of lynch victims from 1882 to 1930.[14] Between the early 1890s and mid 1910s, there was a rise in the market price of cotton that paralleled a reduction in African American lynch victims. As the price of cotton went up, the number of victims decreased. It may be that as competition between marginal black and white laborers increased, so did lynching.[15] The economic hardship caused by a poor profit from the cotton crop leads to an effort by whites to replace black workers with unemployed white laborers. Mob violence was a form of intimidation used to facilitate this labor substitution.[16]

Whether the cause was competition or economic frustration, violence towards blacks increased as economic conditions worsened. Low cotton prices threatened whites' economic security, so they blamed the subordinate black population, thus justifying their violence against them.

It is interesting to note that an analysis of the lynchings occurring during any given period clearly reveals the poor economy of the communities where the lynchings occurred. For example, when the 21 different counties where the 1931 lynchings occurred are compared with other counties in the same states, they are found to be far below the economic average.[17] The data collected by the Southern Commission on the Study of Lynching (as cited in Cantril)[18] revealed that:

> In approximately nine-tenths of these counties the per capita tax valuation was below the general state average; in almost nineteen-twentieths the bank deposits per capita were less than the state average; in three-fourths the per capita income from farm and factory was below the state average, in many cases less than one-half; in nine-tenths fewer and smaller income tax returns were made per thousand population than throughout the state; in over two-thirds, the proportion of farms operated by tenants was in excess of the state rate; and in nearly three fourths of the counties, automobiles were less common than in the state.[19]

The role of economic competition is also indirectly seen in the fact that lynchings were more frequent in areas that had been relatively recently settled where a strong rivalry for jobs existed and the expectations on the status of racial groups was not yet clearly defined.[20] Hence, lynchings demonstrate the role of background economic factors in producing extreme violence when that violence was committed with impunity and when a clear scapegoat existed.

POPULATION AND MOB VIOLENCE

It was more probable that one would be a victim of a lynch mob if he lived in the sparsely settled rural counties of the South. There is an inverse correlation between the rate of lynchings and the population per county, which is those who lived in the counties with the fewest inhabitants were in the greatest danger of being lynched versus those who lived in the most populous counties being the safest.[21] In rural communities of less than a 10,000 population, the lynching rate over a 30 year period was 3.2 per 100,000 of the population. In urban areas of 300,000 or more, it was .05 (per 100,000). This greater rate of lynching in the sparsely settled areas could be explained by the fact that the Southern rural communities were known to be the least policed of any communities in the United States.[22]

Also, African Americans who lived in counties where the proportion of African American population was less than one-fourth of the population were in the greatest danger of becoming victims of mob violence. If they constituted more than half the population, that risk dropped significantly. Clearly, one explanation for this finding is that the higher the African American majority, the fewer the whites, and hence the fewer the occasions for conflict and the fewer the opportunities for whites to take part in mobs.[23]

POLITICS AND CONTROL

As previously mentioned, there was inadequate police protection in the rural areas, possibly allowing for increased mob violence. Clarke expands on this point, stating that violence became more public after the removal of the federal troops and restoration of states' rights in 1877.[24] No longer was it necessary to disguise crimes or commit them at night. Instead, lynching could occur as a public display as a means of enforcing White's social control and power.

As well, the ratification of the Fourteenth Amendment to the U.S. Constitution in 1868 extended to freed blacks the full rights of citizenship, including due process of law. Thus, the right for Southern blacks to vote gave them the power to affect the construction of the Southern politics. They were able to be elected into office at all levels of government and to serve on juries that sat in judgment of whites.[25] They were then capable of expressing their opinions and able to make changes to their society.

> With Black Americans' vote, the traditional dominant Democratic Party was losing its power to the expanding Republican Party, which caused a hysterical concern among many who were threatened by the prospect of "Negro domination."[26] Whites attempted to prevent the increasing freedom and rights of Black individuals by creating codes that dictated the separation of blacks and whites in rail cars, jails, hospitals and schools.[27] The codes were overturned by federal civil rights legislations and thus it has been argued that whites turned to violence to control and restrain Black freedom.

However, the extent to which politics contributed to mob violence is debated. Clarke argued that, although the election year of 1892 was the worst since 1861 with 161 lynchings, there is, in fact, no electoral pattern of lynchings, and rates of lynch victims differed from state to state.[28] Thus, political influence on lynching could be due to the racial hysteria that coincided with it, rather than the actual voting rights granted to African Americans.

CLAUDE NEAL

Claude Neal (also African American) was lynched in Greenwood, Florida, on October 26, 1934. Neal lived across the road from a woman named Lola

Cannidy, who on October 18, 1934, went to a nearby water pump and did not return. Her body was found after an all-night search, and Neal was arrested a couple of hours later when the local sheriff found a piece of cloth that allegedly fit Neal's torn shirt. Other fragments of evidence that served to incriminate Neal were that the two had been seen talking together, and there was the bloodied piece of torn shirt, a bloody hammer (ownership never identified), cuts on Neal's hands (his employer testified that Neal explained this to him as a consequence of working on a fence), and a ring from the watch stem found near the body (believed incriminating because the ring from Neal's watch was missing when he was taken into custody).[29]

Before the completion of hearings by the coroner's jury, a large number of whites concluded that Neal had killed Cannidy. Thus, Neal was moved from one jail to another in northwest Florida, just steps ahead of the mob. The mob went to the city jail and demanded Neal be turned over to them. When they were refused, they went to the sheriff's house demanding to know where Neal had been taken. When the mob failed to learn any information from the sheriff, they next went to another nearby jail and called for officials to give up Neal's live-in relatives, two women named Smith. The two Smith women had nothing to do with the murder of Cannidy, but they were threatened by the mob who wanted to lynch them only because of their close association with Neal. Authorities incarcerated these potential victims for their own protection.

On October 22, the sheriff claimed that Neal had made a complete confession. Details of the conditions under which Neal made his confession were never made public. At this time, Neal was housed in the Brewton (Florida) jail. A motorcade consisting of a scout car with three other vehicles, which contained four or five men, descended on Brewton in the middle of the night. They flashed guns on the lone jailer and threatened to "blow up" the jail if Neal was not released to them. According to the jailer, they took the keys from him and unlocked the cell door. They took Neal, and they made no effort to conceal their faces or their license plates.[30]

The mob returned to Jackson County on the morning of October 26 and made it clear that they were going to lynch Neal that evening. The afternoon edition of the *Dothan Eagle* in Dothan, Alabama, stated in headlines "Florida to burn Negro at Stake: Sex Criminal Seized from Brewton Jail, Will be Mutilated, Set Afire in Extra-Legal Vengeance for Deed."[31] The mob called the sheriff and notified him of the time for the scheduled lynching, as well as to spread the word that the place would be the Cannidy property.

A crowd of several thousand waited in a "good humored and orderly" way near the site where Cannidy had been killed. Neal, meanwhile, had been tortured for many hours by whites who held him captive. An investigator of the lynching after a week had passed, reported the following is the story of "the actual lynching" in the words of his informants:

After taking the nigger to the woods about four miles from Greenwood, they cut off his penis. He was made to eat it. They then cut off his testicles and made him eat them and say he liked it. Then they sliced his sides and stomach with knives and every now and then somebody would cut off a finger or toe. Red-hot irons were used on the nigger to burn him from top to bottom. From time to time during the torture a rope would be tied around Neal's neck and he was pulled up over a limb and held there until he almost choked to death when he would be let down and the torture began all over again.[32]

When Neal was dead, his body was tied to a rope and dragged by a car to the Cannidy property. A witness present at the scene later recalled, "Old man Cannidy came out and shot him [Neal] around the head."[33] The remainder of the crowd then walked by and kicked the lifeless form. His body was then dragged into town and hung nude in the courthouse square. Photographers took pictures of the remains and sold them to those who were disappointed that Neal's body was cut down before they were able to see it. In this case, the trophies were photographs.

The crowd's anger towards blacks was not over after Claude Neal was dead. A mob accused a black man of starting a fight near the courthouse, began to attack the building, and was intent on lynching the man when the police intervened and took him to a safe place. Overwhelmed policemen and the mayor called the state governor and implored him to send the National Guard to assist them. Angry groups of whites meanwhile paraded the streets where they sought out blacks and subjected them to beatings for several hours. The black citizens were forced to leave or hide to avoid confrontation with whites.

The National Guard arrived the next afternoon. One member of the guard remembered, "The troops were unloaded at the edge of town and marched through the town to intimidate the crowd. There was trouble moving the crowd of perhaps 1,000 people." He continued, "They yelled, 'Soldiers Go Home! What business you got here?' and 'We can take care of ourselves.' We posted at ten to twenty foot intervals around the courthouse with machine guns at each corner of the building." He concluded, "Black people were still being beaten up. Many blacks came to the courthouse for protection. We had a rough situation on the first day."[34] On Monday evening, order had been restored, and the military ended its three-day occupation.

White citizens and officials of the area exhibited neither contrition nor remorse over the two-day outburst that required the National Guard to restore order. By implication, their response demonstrated that whites were not deterred from violence against blacks by accusation of conscience. One day after the riot, a reporter observed, "Marianna (Florida) goes on her placid way apparently unaware of the drama that has attracted the attention of a nation."[35] When he asked a waitress what she thought of the excitement of the last two days, she replied, "Well, it has certainly kept us busy with so many strangers here to feed."[36]

Howard states that the response to the Neal lynching by individuals in the criminal justice system in Jackson County was typical of rural Southern counties at this time.[37] The Jackson County grand jury investigating Neal's death commended the sheriff and declared that Cannidy was, in fact, "brutally murdered and raped in the county...by Claude Neal."[38] About Neal's lynching, however, it simply stated, "We have not been able to get much direct or positive evidence with reference to this matter," and it dismissed all information in its possession as "hearsay and rumors."[39] After receiving criticism from across the nation for his failure to send the National Guard to Jackson County to prevent the Neal lynching, the governor defended himself by declaring that "under the circumstances it would have been futile to call out the militia."[40]

These horrific acts committed and witnessed by tens of thousands of individuals can hardly be justified or explained simply by economic or political causes. Although the above factors may have aided in the expression of such violent acts, the actual mind-set of the mob members is eerily similar to that of military massacres or *genocidaires.*

SELECTION OF TARGET GROUP

Preconditions for the selection of a target group or victim involves Ervin Staub's argument (to be outlined at length in Chapter 8) that human destructiveness is a consequence of the frustration of basic human needs and the development of the destructive mode of need fulfillment.[41] The frustration of basic human needs, such as security, control over essentials, and an understanding of the world, initiates a search for a scapegoat who can be blamed for the disturbance of these needs. Of the 3,724 people killed by lynching, the vast majority of victims were African American. Of these African American victims, 94 percent died in the hands of white lynch mobs. Thus, on average, a black man, woman, or child was murdered nearly once a week, every week, between 1882 and 1930 by a hate-driven white mob.[42] Staub's theory can apply to lynchings as there are many instances where a mob was unable to find the alleged suspect, so instead they would lynch any convenient black individual who lived within the community. As Brundage put it, the black community as a whole was accountable, and one black victim for the lynch mob would serve as well as another.[43] This may stem from the fact that white citizens witnessed the status of nearly 4 million Southern African Americans rapidly change from that of personal property to competitors with control and power. Hence, a major threat to an established world view and way of life had occurred. Their social structure had, in effect, been turned on its head. Their beliefs were, of course, wrong, but the instantaneous inversion of these beliefs was potentially shattering. Violence has a function of restoring one's universe, reaffirming one's world view (as Becker put it).[44]

Dehumanization of African Americans was apparent in many of the headlines of newspapers all over the nation. For example, some of the terms used to describe the African American suspects included "black fiend," "ape-like," "Darwin's missing link," and "beast."[45] Whites' superiority and security were threatened, and one way they could try to regain control was to send a message to the African American community that unacceptable behavior (whether it was an actual crime or something as trivial as an insult to a white person) would not be accepted. In some instances, such as with Hose and Neal, the mobs gave increased emphasis by subjecting victims to hideous forms of torture and mutilation.

It was found that a second lynching would not occur in the same community where one had previously occurred, the only exceptions being when a new generation grew up or when a new group of people moved into the community.[46] Thus, the different mob members involved in the brutal lynchings against Neal and Claude were most likely not involved in any other lynching incidents, as the mobs are almost always constructed of the communities' own citizens.[47]

Obviously, the mob members that took part in the horrific tortures and killings of both Neal and Hose were not subjected to any desensitization of the kind Chang suggested had occurred to the Japanese soldier. They were ordinary citizens (like Browning's "Ordinary Men")[48] who took part in a lynching and then returned to their normal day's activities afterwards. There was no "recruiting" of mob members as with, for example, the Greek military police, who would convert ordinary men into torturers using a five-stage process (and would lose one-third who just could not do it).[49] Hence, in some ways, lynch mobs represent a pure example of "normal" people behaving viciously.

Thousands of people voluntarily took part in both the Hose and Neal lynchings without any desensitization or training. One mob member stated during the manhunt for Hose: "If Hose is on earth I'll never rest easy until he's caught and burned alive. And that's the way all of us feel."[50] He was right; approximately 2000 people traveled to witness Hose's torture and killing. No one, not even the mayor, attempted to prevent the lynching. Instead, newspapers printed articles days before the event stating that Hose would be tortured and burned. The leading mob members did not wear a disguise, and they were never charged. Thus, not only were normal citizens capable of committing crimes as heinous as those committed by trained and abused Japanese and Greek militia, but thousands of people, including women and children, also took part and even fought over the dead victims' body parts and ashes. In these ways, the extreme violence of the Southern U.S. lynch mobs was unique (as far as we know) and can only be attributed to the combination of rage over losing the Civil War and a way of life and the blaming of this situation on the African American. Coupled with the history of viewing the African Americans as subhuman and seeing them as the symbol of the loss, the rage displayed was extreme, even by the standards we now examine.

In military massacres, there is an immediate transition to a killing rage state, which occurs after an order to kill (implicitly or explicitly) is given. Indeed, the lynch mobs did, in fact, have implicit orders to kill. As we mentioned above, during the manhunt for Hose the *Atlanta Constitution* printed multiple headlines stating that if Hose was found alive he would be tortured and burnt. This also occurred with Neal, as the *Dothan Eagle* paper printed that he would be mutilated and killed when he was caught. In both cases, it was known all over their respective states what would happen, and no one attempted to prevent either lynching from occurring. Hence, at the outset, the act of lynching appears to follow the same steps as the Nanking or the El Mozote massacres.

Many soldiers who took part in massacres were frustrated and angry at the time that they began to kill, especially at My Lai. Their mind-set when killing was more than just following orders to kill—it was a combination of orders to kill and the act of killing itself, which produced increased levels of preparatory arousal and rage. On the other hand, the killings of Neal and Hose could not have been generated by preparatory arousal. In the case of Hose, the mob went to church services in the morning and then proceeded to go to the place where the lynching was to occur to commit the brutal killing. There were clear wishes to annihilate the victims, but not all present could participate. The number of people involved in the killing of a single person made it impossible for everyone to fire the fatal shot, jerk the rope that would break the person's neck, or, in the case of Hose, start the fire that burned him to death. Yet, because so many people had come to take part in a lynching, they wanted to have some role in the actual event. The torture, therefore, would often be deliberately prolonged so that everyone interested could have a hand in punishing and annihilating the victim.[51] This communal annihilation explains the post-mortem violence as well, such as cutting out Hose's organs for trophies. The extended brutality allowed for mass participation rather than the actions of a few individuals, like in military massacres.

In the words of one member of a Georgia mob:

> I reckon folks from the north think we're hard on niggers, but they just don't know what would happen to the white people if the niggers ran wild like they would if we didn't show them who's boss....If that nigger out there in the woods gets jumped before the sheriff finds him, it will all be over and done with by sundown, and everybody will be satisfied.[52]

Mob members did not seem to suffer from any guilt, but rather they seemed to celebrate the fact that they had reprimanded a deserving criminal. Only in a society where norms direct violence rather than restrain it could such reactions, or lack thereof, occur. We examine this "long term transition" that alters societal norms in Chapter 8.

Thousands of individuals were killed without judge or jury, many for crimes that they did not commit. For at least four decades, "normal" citizens settled their differences in a brutal and heinous manner—by torturing and lynching victims who were sometimes accused of serious offenses, such as murder, but most were charged with insignificant crimes, including insulting a white person and using offensive language. How were hundreds of thousands of people capable of participating in these appalling events? Economic considerations have been proposed by some researchers. However, inflating and deflating cotton prices, population, and politics cannot fully explain the cause of countless individuals committing such horrific atrocities. Neither can the widely accepted idea that lynch mobs knew they would not be punished and believed that they would be community protectors, not destroyers. Instead, they are all small pieces of a larger puzzle.

There are many lenses through which to view the phenomenon of lynching, with many different researchers suggesting different theories. Raper tended to view mob violence as the product of the deprived and backward culture shared by many poorer whites, and also to the unwillingness of more respectable citizens to intervene.[53] Others have described the rise of radical racism in the South, where the Southern attitudes towards African Americans were fundamentally transformed. Accordingly, this psychological transformation was to blame for the mob violence that spread throughout the country.[54] Thus, the explanation of lynching and, more specifically, the question of how mob members were capable of such revolting acts, has no simple answer. Ultimately, these mob members were men, women, and children. They were neighbors, teachers, farmers, and sheriffs. They were only killers for one tragic day.

PRISON RIOTS

Oh! cold March winds your cruel laments
Are hard on prisoners' hearts.

—Bobby Sands, IRA Volunteer, died of hunger strike in prison

Prison riots represent a special form of extreme group violence. The participants are, by self-selection into prison, violent. Target groups are presented by the conditions of incarceration: guards, other ethnic gangs in the prison, snitches (those who have, in the past, passed information to prison authorities). We describe here some of the more famous prison riots in U.S. prison history. Prison riots have come in waves, demonstrating some form of contagion born by inmate transfer. The first wave began in 1929 in New York State,[1] leading the state to build the ultimate escape-proof and riot-proof prison: Attica.

ATTICA

The world's most expensive prison opened in 1931 in Attica, a town in upstate New York, 275 miles northwest of New York City. In September 1971, Attica was the scene of the world's most famous prison riot, in part because of the relevance of the riot for emerging trends in U.S. society (especially the emergence of the Black Panther Party and the Black Muslims) and its proximity to New York City. Several accounts of this riot have been written, as well as a lengthy 500 page report by the state committee set up to investigate the riot, called the McKay Report,[2] drafted by lawyers and academics, and based on interviews with 1600 inmates, 400 guards, and 270 state police.

Attica was built around four long cell blocks (A to D), each of which had access to a central recreation yard. The cell blocks and yards were segregated from each other by tunnels (solid and ill lit aboveground passageways with catwalks on top for patrolling guards). The prisoners did intermingle, however, in the dining hall.

Guards at Attica had been well trained in the 1930s, but by the 1950s funding for training was cut and the guards, who were largely rural and white, were not trained at all. In contrast to the demographic of the guards, the prisoners had become increasingly urban and nonwhite. By September 1971, nearly half the prisoners were from New York City, 54 percent were black, and 9 percent were Hispanic. This change was rapid, with the prison going from being 80 percent white in 1969 to 63 percent black and Hispanic in 1971. Radicalization of black and Hispanic prisoners was greatest in New York and California, where black power politics took hold and both the Black Panther Party and Black Muslims generated converts in the prison population. Guards sought to avoid contact with prisoners; senior guards took night shifts to avoid them. As a result, the least experienced guards had the most contact with prisoners during the daytime.

Prison conditions were described in the McKay Report as abysmal: cramped cells, inedible food, and poor medical care. However, the report pointed out that these conditions were not specific to Attica. Legal self-help by prisoners was beginning at that time (1971) and was viewed as a challenge to the authority of the system. At Attica, legal self-help, challenges by prisoners of their convictions and the conditions of their imprisonment, was a near obsession. Any prisoner who publicly showed allegiance to black or Hispanic power groups was immediately viewed as problematic: his reading material and mail were censored, and his only means of retrieving them was to go to court. Hence, race, ethnicity, rapid change, and an increase in legal challenges by prisoners constituted a "perfect storm": a confluence of forces clashing with the authorities.

To further the conflictual features of the situation, a battle was also occurring within the prison correctional system itself between liberal reform that sought to improve prisoners' living conditions and traditionalist forces backed by the guards and old-line prison officials. One of the issues, the prison system's "right" to punish and limit the rights of inmates, was declared unconstitutional by a Federal District Court in 1970 because it violated the inmates' right to due process. A liberal prison administration was stymied in efforts to reform by passive resistance from the guards. Ordered to allow the inmates to receive periodicals, they began to snip out individual articles they believed the inmates should not read. In many ways, the guards sabotaged reform measures. In June 1971, prisoners wrote to the commissioner of prisons with a list of reform demands: legal representation before the Parole Board, improved medical care, upkeep of facilities, and an end to segregation because of political beliefs. The McKay Commission characterized these demands as a "strikingly reasonable and civil approach."[3]

Soon after this approach had produced no visible results, inmates began to develop unity and intra-inmate factions began discussions to end their disagreements. These groups included the Black Muslims, the Black Panthers, and the Young Lords (who represented Hispanic inmates).

Some preliminary skirmishes foreshadowed the chaos to come. On September 8 and 9, confrontations between guards and inmates became physical. In one, an inmate had struck an officer and then been backed up by a crowd of fellow inmates. The officers were forced to retreat, and the offending inmate was not punished. Later the decision not to punish the offending inmate was reversed by the acting superintendent. This led to greater agitation amongst the inmates, leading to the hurling of garbage and insults at the guards. All actions in the prison were the subject of rumor and misperception. The punishment of the inmate, which involved his being put in solitary confinement, was rumored to have been accompanied by beatings. Even the event on which it was based, the confrontation in the prison yard, was viewed differently by inmates and guard, as later reported to interviewers for the McKay Commission. The upshot of this event and similar others that occurred in this same time period was to give the inmates an increased sense of efficacy in conflict with the forces of the state. The rebelliousness of the political ideology was being played out in minor testing of the limits.

What triggered the riot was an escalating series of events that began with an apparently minor problem: a can of soup was allegedly thrown at an officer by a Latino inmate, William Ortiz, striking the officer in the head and drawing blood. Ortiz was to be sent to solitary confinement as punishment, but the inmates stymied attempts to leave him in his cell by opening the cell during breakfast. A subsequent attempt to get Ortiz into solitary (by letting all inmates except him out for yard exercises) was botched, bringing to the scene a guard lieutenant whom the prisoners believed had lied about the prior inmate punishment.

Inmates attempting to enact the separation of Ortiz and other inmates got into a melee with guards, attacking some with baseball bats. The guards escaped, but the inmates were now in control of a section of the prison. Because of faults in the communication system in the prison, a general alarm was slow in coming. In addition, a locking rod was faulty. When the inmates shook it, it collapsed and inmates spilled into the prison exercise yard, striking a guard with a baseball bat. The guard died two days later. The inmates then opened up gates that theoretically separated the inmates into four quadrants; all gates were faulty and easily opened. The rebellious force had now grown in numbers. Not all inmates joined; however, numerous groups either took cover or left quietly with guards. In some instances, there was violent inmate resistance to the riot; a 72-year-old black inmate, armed with a lethal iron bar, kept rioters away from the prison gasoline supply. Within the inmate community, a status hierarchy existed based on jobs, and the riot was started by those with the least desirable jobs or no job at all. At this point, off-duty guards began firing at the rioting inmates with automatic weapons (which violated regulations) and passed the weapons among them so fingerprints could not be detected.

After the first chaotic outbreak, 1,300 inmates were left holding one quadrant of the exercise yard (D yard) and 45 hostages, guards, and civilians. The initial atmosphere was euphoric, and there had been little inter-inmate violence thus far. A debate developed over what to do with the hostages. The Black Muslims seemed protective of the hostages and favored leaving them in a corner for their own protection. Others wanted them in a more exposed position as insurance against an assault by authorities. A compromise was made to put them in the center of the yard but ringed by Muslim guards. An "open mike" session followed where inmates took turns expressing views on the riot. The main theme was a call for solidarity and declarations that the riot was not a "race riot" but a protest against a litany of common grievances for all inmates. Far from being anarchic, the inmate group immediately proclaimed some rules: no drugs, no fighting, no sexual activity. A "security guard" was developed to take over the job of breaking up fights and internal policing. There was an effort to ensure that all racial groups were represented in the security guard. Injured guards were handed over to the authorities. A political order developed that was essentially democratic. Contact with the state developed, and food was the first demand; others included amnesty, safe transportation out of the United States, and reconstruction of Attica by inmates. They promised safe passage to anyone who would come to see the conditions at Attica. A leadership was elected and ran the group in a tolerant fashion, encouraging and protecting dissenters. However, on the outside, amongst 1,100 armed men (state troopers, sheriffs, and deputies from surrounding counties) rumors spread that hostages were being tortured, sodomized, and killed. This group had no clear command structure and in-group discussion was grossly racist.[4] The mood voiced was one of unrelieved hatred for the rioting inmates. At the top of the organizational structure was New York State Governor Nelson Rockefeller, who saw the Attica uprising as "an ominous world trend," opposed negotiating with the inmates, and viewed the situation as an affront to the capitalist/democratic world order.[5] Needless to say, the governor's hysteria did nothing to calm the small army gathering outside the prison.

This conflicting set of forces nevertheless began with some attempts at direct negotiation. The commissioner himself appeared in D Yard for these negotiations, which, depending on which side's version you later read, focused on prison conditions or the demands for amnesty and safe transportation. The latter were unacceptable to the prison administration, who saw them, if they were met, as an inducement for riots in other prisons. During the attempts at negotiation, group polarization occurred on both sides, where initial positions became more extreme and polarized in opposite directions. Negotiations broke down, and the inmates demanded observers present for any further talks. Observers were persons named either by the inmates or by the state. These later negotiations produced some agreement on prison condition issues and even on the issue of amnesty for inmates. However, word arrived that an officer who had been attacked in the initial riot and handed over to the state for treatment had died. Killing a prison guard was a capital offense in New York State; hence without the amnesty agreement, some inmates who surrendered might go to the electric chair. At this point, without agreement, the talks broke down. The deal breaker seemed to be the incompatibility of the inmates' view that the violence had been caused by prison conditions and the state view that it was the responsibility of the inmates. The commissioner at this point gave the inmates an ultimatum to accept the 28 point concession to which he had agreed and to release hostages and surrender. Unfortunately, he did not make it clear that an assault with overwhelming force was to be the consequence of refusal. Subsequent interviews revealed that the inmates did not believe the state would do this. Some believed the hostages were insurance against such an action. As a consequence, the ultimatum was not taken seriously.

The entire incident from hostage taking to the subsequent assault by police lasted only four days. By the fourth day (the day before the police assault), the inmates were beginning to show signs of psychological disturbance. A doctor sent to care for them reported "psychic or hysterical reactions," including seizures and fits, and inmate fighting increased with an increase in slash and stab wounds. Three inmates who were themselves deemed dangerous or who were believed to be naming names in interviews with the press, were incarcerated (literally, a prison within a prison) and were found, after the subsequent police assault, dead of numerous stab wounds—deemed "overkill" by sociologist Marvin Wolfgang,[6] literally more than was needed to kill and indicative of a rage-based killing. It is unclear whether these killings may have driven the inmates to hold out for amnesty out of self-interest and also unclear whether any specific individuals could have ever been identified as the assailants. The final day also saw a confrontation over the fate of the hostages with one group (20 black inmates) announcing they had come to get the hostages and the Black Muslims refusing to hand them over. Within the stresses of impending doom very different reactions were expressed by inmates.

Radical statements given at Attica were being broadcast worldwide by the press coverage given to the event. In their analysis of the eventual assault, social scientists Useem and Kimball concluded that the reasons for the assault were essentially political: Governor Rockefeller decided that the press coverage given to revolutionary statements by the inmates would give support to other revolutionary movements.[7] Responsibility for the assault was given to the New York State Police who were not trained in military maneuvers. The effect was that the troopers acted essentially as free agents, and little thought was given to the impact this may have on the hostages. The troopers were instructed to expect fierce resistance and to react with deadly force. They were instructed not to engage in hand-to-hand combat because they might lose a weapon. The upshot was that the only strategy available to them was deadly force. It had been determined that corrections officers should not be involved in the assault because of the likelihood of overreaction. However, 11 corrections officers obtained weapons and joined the police. At 9:46 AM, teargas was dropped, and within seconds rifle squads opened fire on inmates. The inmates had knives and eight blindfolded hostages were presented on the catwalks—all inmates were killed. However, the inmates holding hostages were not the only ones killed. There was a 50 second barrage of fire aimed at any and all inmates. Police were firing shotguns loaded with "00" buckshot—each pellet capable of killing. Several of the hostages were later found to be dead—killed by buckshot or rifle fire. Police essentially shot at anything not in a police uniform; there were 38 dead and 90 wounded.

Once the prison was secured, the violence did not stop. Instead, fueled by rumor of inmate brutality toward hostages, the police beat inmates mercilessly, even the wounded. That night, autopsies revealed that the ten dead hostages had died from gunshot wounds, not stabbings (the inmates were unarmed). According to Useem and Kimball, the belief still persists in Attica that the autopsy was performed by a left wing doctor and the truth was that the hostages were stabbed.[8] As we have seen in the Japanese governments' denial of the Nanking massacre or the denial of the Armenian slaughter by the Turkish government, denial of atrocities is commonplace.

Eventually, two inmates were charged with the murders of the three inmates who had been killed before the assault. Three inmate leaders were charged with 34 counts of kidnapping, and 62 inmates were indicted on 1,289 counts of criminal activity. As for the police activity, evidence was destroyed, and the investigation was stifled to such an extent that a special prosecutor went public in 1975. As a result, a general amnesty was declared. Some mundane details of prison living conditions were improved, and in subsequent prison hostage takings, both sides have declared they "did not want another Attica."

SANTA FE PENITENTIARY

There are two riots that are legendary amongst prisoners: Attica and New Mexico. The New Mexico riot occurred on February 2 and 3, 1980. The New Mexico riot was unlike Attica: no radical political groups, no militant inmate orators, no anti-imperialist demands. Where the inmates at Attica had, with the exception of the murder of three unruly inmates, been nonviolent, the New Mexico (NM) riot is considered the most violent in U.S. history. The New Mexico prison conditions had deteriorated for a decade. At the same time, the population of the prison increased from 682 in 1972 to 1,569 in 1978. At the time of the riot, 53 percent of the prisoners were Hispanic, 37 percent white, 9 percent black, and 1 percent Native American. However, post-riot interviews indicated that there was no climate of racial harassment amongst these groups. The main problems in the prison were overcrowding and disorganization (this included security, and escapes were commonplace). Previous corruption investigations had led to reform that clamped down on inmate programs just as the population was increasing. The result was to leave inmates idle, bored, and frustrated. The level of incompetence at the prison was attested to by the fact that the riot started at an evening "hootch" (homemade beer) party on February 1. That prisoners could produce and consume illicit alcohol in a large group, in the middle of an open dormitory, indicates the lax security. Half-drunk, the inmates decided to take over the prison that night. Four guards were captured, stripped, and beaten. The riot then spread wing by wing, block by block, enabled by the poor security. The entire prison was under inmate control without state resistance in five hours, including the control center and riot control gear (gas grenades and launchers and acetylene torches). The initial inmate plan seems to have been simple: take hostages, compel negotiations over demands, and bring in news media to tell about conditions in the prison. Incredibly, a group of half-drunk inmates with no leadership took over a state prison without resistance in five hours.

Whereas group membership may have prevented murder in Attica, the lack of membership or leadership led to anomie in NM, allowing an opportunity for personal grudges to be enacted. Snitches were dragged from cells and beaten to death with steel pipes. The dead bodies were mutilated. One "snitch" was hanged, and then the body was dragged back to a higher level in the prison and hacked to bits with a knife. Another victim had his eyes gouged out and a screwdriver driven through his head, his genitals hacked off and stuffed in his mouth. Yet another was slowly killed with an acetylene torch. Some of the dead bodies had the word "rata" (rat) carved on them. Rumor, as usual, fueled events. Inmates heard that a friend had been killed and set out to enact revenge. The violence grew. The killing was initially based on presumptions of someone being a snitch or for a personal beef, then escalated to revenge for the initial killings (true or not). As Useem and Kimball put it, the snitches are viewed as traitors and hence arouse more hatred than the actual enemy. The killing of snitches suggests a purging of traitorous elements, with deliberate cruelty used to dramatize the renunciation of bonds of "fellow-feeling" with the traitor.

The guards were less hated. None were killed, although they were beaten and, in a few cases, raped. In Chapter 10, we discuss the psychological motivation for military rape. Brownmiller chronicled the universality of rape in war and massacre and described it as follows: "rape is the quintessential act by which a male demonstrates to a female that she is conquered."[9] In prison riots, where no women exist, rape still occurs as does everyday sex between inmates who prefer women when outside the prison. Some guards were not harmed and others were helped to escape. This differential treatment seems to have been based on how early or late in the riot the guard was taken hostage (early hostages were released) and their prior reputation for treatment of prisoners. The prison was selectively destroyed: the psychology clinic was the worst hit; it was believed that the clinic director passed on information obtained in therapy sessions. The library, hobby shop, and Catholic chapel were spared. It was later discovered that inmates took large doses of drugs (from the prison pharmacy), injected morphine, and swallowed Valium.

Residual violence potential was present. A group of surrendered Chicano inmates in the prison yard threatened to attack a group of black inmates and had to be backed off at gunpoint by the National Guard.

Negotiations involved hostage release in return for media access. Negotiations went much better than in Attica. Prison officials agreed that there would be no retaliation against the rioters and that riot negotiators would be transferred out of state immediately. In return, the remaining hostages were released. Police entered the prison without incident. As a result of the riot, living conditions at the penitentiary improved. Guards held hostage were traumatized and unable to hold jobs after the riot.

Numerous prison riots have occurred in the United States (and other countries —notably Brazil) in the twentieth century. From a social psychological perspective, prisons are composed of two groups with conflicting goals—the guards to maintain order and prevent escape and the inmates to resist. Social psychologist Philip Zimbardo conducted a famous demonstration of the effect of these roles on behavior by constructing a realistic simulated prison for a "role play" of prison life.[10] Zimbardo created one of the most realistic "simulation" experiments ever designed, even having the local police force "arrest" the prisoners (volunteer subjects whose assignment to the role of prisoner or guard was by a coin flip). Zimbardo found "guards" abusing "prisoners" and prisoners undergoing psychological stress and breakdown after four days in his simulated prison. By the sixth day, he had to terminate the study. The subjects of the study, the guards and prisoners, were all college age men with no prior criminal history and no record of psychological disturbance. Zimbardo attributed the reactions exhibited to the situational pressures established by the oppositional goals between the groups, to power differentials between them, and to rapid immersion in this role-directed behavior. The rapid immersion, in turn, was generated by the 24/7 nature of the experiment and by the power struggle itself. When prisoners failed to defer to orders by guards, the guards forced them to awaken in the middle of the night and do push-ups, as a way of establishing authority. Challenges to authority, in themselves, generated rage in those who believe the authority was theirs. There were some individual differences in the guards' abuse of authority and the prisoners' ability to tolerate the stress. About one-third of the guards exceeded the limits of their role description and were extremely verbally abusive, another one-third seemed to passively go along but not challenge them, and still another third tried in small ways to help out the prisoners by doing them favors. Although not trained to do it, the guards reacted aggressively to any show of solidarity by the prisoners. They actively undermined solidarity by, in one instance, offering the prisoners a small reward (keeping their blankets), if another unruly prisoner was severely punished (kept in solitary).

A brilliant portrayal of this phenomenon occurs in the British film, *The Hill* (not coincidentally about life in a prison). In this film, a hill is used as punishment by forcing any prisoner who breaks the interminable and contradictory set of prison regulations to run over it repeatedly until exhausted. Since the prison is in North Africa, the extreme heat brings on exhaustion rapidly. Sean Connery plays a prisoner who "fights the system" and is treated harshly by abusive guards who seem deeply sadistic. Was their sadism caused by the role they are in or did it precede the role, which then enabled them to act it out? No better examination of the rage behind authority exists on film. Philip Brickman wrote a thoughtful treatise on how reality overtakes people in everyday situations.[11] What makes life feel real, according to Brickman, is two "correspondences." The first is a correspondence between what we feel and whether the social role we play allows us to express through actions the feelings that "correspond" to those emotions. Bank clerks who are feeling depressed cannot express this feeling in their actions as a bank clerk. They have to smile and interact in a pleasant fashion with customers. This lack of "internal correspondence" between inner feelings and external actions precludes feeling real; the day has a sense of unreality about it. The second type of correspondence is between our actions and the reactions of others. If we walk down the street proclaiming ourselves to be Jesus Christ and no one bows or prays, our fundamental belief is shaken. The reactions are not appropriate to the belief and its expression. There is no external correspondence.

In a role play such as the Zimbardo experiment, subjects start with a double negative; nothing is real yet, neither internally nor externally. However, as the situation progresses, events can become real in two ways. The first is that "external correspondence" is generated by the power structure. At the beginning of the prison experiment (astutely video recorded by a hidden camera), guards demand that prisoners do a "count" (give their prison number to be sure all are accounted for). The prisoners begin to play around. The guards assert their authority, barking at the prisoners that if they do not do it right, they will be there all night. The prisoners begin to fall into line and do as the guards demand. Their actions now correspond to the guards' orders. External correspondence is generated, and the guards feel they are true authorities not to be dismissed. The feeling (internal correspondence) follows from the external correspondence. Orders generate obedience, which, in turn, generates feelings of power and authority. Then the cycle repeats itself, spiraling upward to a feeling of real power (as opposed to role determined power).

The second pathway involves the generation of internal correspondence first. Suppose some of the boys selected to be guards had buried motives to act sadistically, to have power over others. These feelings might simply have been buried because there was no realistic way of implementing the feelings in everyday life. The role of guard then provides the role where the feelings can be expressed toward prisoners. Hence, internal correspondence is generated. The guards' role allows them to put sadistic power needs into action. They do so, generating compliance in the prisoners. Now both internal and external correspondence exist. The situation feels real. In the Zimbardo video, it is clear that the more aggressive guards are the ones who generate compliance from the prisoners.

These guards had no prior record of psychological disturbance; however, sadism can be masked.

While the Nazis specifically screened sadists from certain key positions, Joseph Mengele certainly slipped through the screen.[12] Although his background showed no signs of sadism, Mengele worked overtime deciding who would live and die, making his decisions with studied detachment, interrupted by outbreaks of rage.[13] He killed directly, injecting victims with phenol and occasionally shooting them.[14] In one case, he crushed a woman underfoot. He was reported to have thrown babies into crematoria. Was Mengele a hidden sadist in civilian life whose sadism was clearly exposed when the conditions were "right"? And, of course, Mengele's infamous medical experiments, performed on Jews, are the lowlight of medical malpractice. Robert Lifton's examination of Mengel's life indicates clear evidence for sadism, but the evidence did not become clear until he was placed in the power position he held during the war. Mengele, in Brickman's terms, was given internal correspondence by his position and relished it. This may have occurred for some of Zimbardo's guards as well.

Zimbardo was trying to separate individual factors that may give rise to prison violence (e.g., that a violent population resides in the prison) from the situational factors (the power struggle and oppositional goals). He showed that, even with a nonviolent population, abuse develops rapidly from the situational factors alone. Inmates react to the organizational power of guards by organizing themselves, either legally or by forming prison gangs. Sometimes the gangs form along racial or ethnic lines. The historical traditional form of power gathering amongst the powerless is unification—a forming of the herd. Hence, threats to that solidarity will be the subject of the most extreme violence. Snitches in prisons are the first target of riots and are treated more severely than hostage-guards. Years ago, I showed the Zimbardo prison study to a group of real prisoners doing life in a federal penitentiary. I asked them what they thought of the study, whether it was realistic. They thought it was a good portrayal of prison life except for one thing. The prisoners in the study were not organized—they had not formed any solidarity. To the real prisoners, that was essential.

The issue of authority is one theme that runs through social violence. We saw it in the lynch mob mentality; whites in the southern United States had lost their authority over the black population after the loss of the Civil War. They were enraged by this affront to their social order, and the scapegoats were going to be the blacks who were terrorized by lynchings and by the Ku Klux Klan. Just as the snitch most threatens the social power structure of the powerless, the powerful are threatened by any change to the status quo power structure. In the U.S. South, the Confederacy favored whites. Blacks were the symbols of that lost power and the attempt to restate it. In the Zimbardo prison study, college age males in the role of guards spontaneously devised methods to undermine solidarity in the prisoner group. When scapegoat groups that threaten authority do not exist, they must be invented. Hence, the invention occurred of a privileged enemy by Pol Pot through arbitrarily decreeing anyone who wore glasses or had a certain education at level 7 to be privileged.

Prison riots may, at first glance, seem unrelated to genocide or military massacres, but they are important in two respects. First, they show us how authority and its abuse is one theme of social violence. Threats to authority generate vicious rage. Does it do so in everyone? Does it do so in hierarchical militaristic organizations where the emphasis is on authority? Second, riots show us how similar social conditions can produce different reactions: the violence of prisoners in Attica was restrained by comparison to New Mexico. Both prisons had the potential for race-based cliques of prisoners, yet violence by prisoners toward prisoners did not follow racial lines. Finally, despite the viciousness of the New Mexico riot, it was not more vicious than the lynchings by churchgoing Southern whites nor the rape and massacre of civilians by soldiers. The individual characteristics of violence that we may associate with prison populations appear to be swamped by the social characteristics of group violence.

SOCIETAL TRANSITIONS: THE NORMATIVE SHIFTS IN GENOCIDE

> Civilized society is perpetually menaced with disintegration through this primary hostility of men towards each other.
>
> —Sigmund Freud

To appreciate the full impact of changes in social norms on individual thinking and behavior, we turn briefly from cases of genocide and violence to an often cited and disturbing study of the impact of drought on the gradual starvation of an entire people. Anthropologist Colin Turnbull spent years living amongst an African tribe in Uganda called the Ik; the tribe was driven from its natural hunting grounds by government policy and told to hunt in another area (which was impossible because of repeated drought), and was slowly (in less than three generations) starving to extinction.[1] As a consequence, norms of attachment and protection of others had given way to extreme self-interest. Children were abandoned at an early age by their parents and joined gangs of same age peers to forage for food. Fights over food were a daily occurrence, and reactions to someone else's death was of merriment not grief because the death meant more food for oneself. Turnbull's western sensitivities were initially offended by this social display, and he began to share his food, but soon realized it was hopeless. He could not feed the tribe, and how was he to play God and select who would live? Eventually he gave in to the local norms and mores. Turnbull described those attitudinal shifts this way:

> ...the very old and the very young share one great belief in common, a belief in continuity, and a hope that is a hope for the past just as it is a hope for the future.

It is a belief that is a rudely shattered by every violation that is felt when another body dies....that is surely equally rudely shattered for the Ik old when they look at the very young and see the emptiness that has taken the place of the life they knew ...that is why they now look at only the very, very young, for only with them can they retain any belief, any hope. The urge to survive in such circumstances must in itself indicate a belief in some kind of continuity, some kind of future, though whether or not that indicates some kind of hope which would make life more bearable, I do not know. And now that all the old are dead, what is left? The newly old no longer remember...that there was a time when people were kind, looked after their children and children looked after their parents. Every one of the Ik who are old today was thrown out at three...and in consequence has thrown his own children out and knows full well they will not help him in his old age any more than he helped his parents.[2]

Norms of intrafamily helping had been entirely lost in this tribe. Within a much shorter period of time (6 years in Germany, 1.5 years in Rwanda), norms defining acceptable behavior towards and the perception of specified groups would completely change. The function of norms is made clear by this example. Norms help us define the rules of social reality; they define what is acceptable and what is not.

Beevor has a fascinating description of how the norms had changed in a besieged Germany in 1945.[3] When Russian shells went off, killing women standing in line for food, the survivors simply closed the line, stepping over the dead. None of them dared lose their places. There was no attention paid to the dead or dying. In the cellars of apartment blocks (where they hid to avoid the bombing), the fortunate people who had found food ate it, avoiding all eye contact with others. When news came that a nearby barracks had been abandoned, all civility disappeared and a feeding frenzy ensued of looting for food and anything else that could aid survival.

Suedfeld points out that case studies of genocide provide important historical information on particular genocides, whereas comparative studies focus on the common factors present in all genocides.[4] We have focused on the latter approach. In Rwanda, the attack was by one group or tribe (Hutu) on another (Tutsi), based on perceived historical injustices supposedly favoring the target group. Since intermarriage had occurred, it could not have been always obvious what someone's tribal membership actually was. And, as typically is the case in genocides, others are killed through unsubstantiated accusation based on a personal grievance. In the Cambodian slaughter, although other ethnic groups were attacked, the main killing was by Cambodians of Cambodians based on a peculiar communist notion of class membership. In most cases, a target group is selected for reasons having to do with historical animosity. This was true for both the Jews and the Tutsi. In many ways, the Tutsi were more integrated with the Hutu than the Jews were with the Germans. Intermarriage was more common in Rwanda. The parts of Germany where attacks on the Jews were greatest were those where the Jews were relatively segregated (i.e., Bavaria).

One quantitative study has attempted to explore the variation of homicidal activity that exists within a genocide.[5] This work investigated why certain countries under the Third Reich were subjected to a large amount of killing (e.g., Poland and Slovakia), while others experienced comparatively little (e.g., Romania and Bulgaria). Using many sources of information, Helen Fein employed cross-tabulation and regression analysis to show which factors explained the variation in Jewish victimization. From her analysis, Fein concluded that prewar anti-Semitism, German control, state complicity with German activity, and Jewish segregation from the rest of society increased the magnitude of victimization. The number of victims was decreased by early warnings of impending German activity and the degree of mass as well as elite resistance to Jewish persecution.

The genodynamics project at the University of Maryland is attempting to test political theories about genocide in Rwanda based on a rationalist political model of action.[6] For example, there are social-structural factors in genocides. In Rwanda, the Hutu government's propaganda about the forthcoming confrontation with the Rwandan Patriotic Front (RPF) suggested that Hutu would be killed by the RPF when it took power, which increased fear and rage toward the Tutsi. This inciting propaganda was compatible with Hutu socialization about a continuous pattern of Tutsi domination and violence that had extended over generations.[7] Similar to Fein's findings for Germany, there was regional variation within Rwanda, which was directly relevant to the likelihood of ethnic violence. For example, there was a history of strong Hutu political power within the north from which the leadership during the Second Republic emerged to govern the country from 1973 to 1994. Within that area, which was the focal point for numerous Tutsi military incursions, there was also a long history of anti-Tutsi persecution. In contrast, the center of the country was generally associated with a more conciliatory Hutu position. "Hutu Power" organizations were the most extreme anti-Tutsi groups. They were most closely associated with the ruling Hutu party and had, therefore, the most to lose politically if the Tutsi rebel army returned to power. Those organizations drove the genocide.[8] Mamdani described how members of Hutu Power and/or the militias would show up within a cell, bring all nonmoderate Hutus together in one location, inform them who was to be killed, eliminate any resistance within this crowd by killing any dissidents, and then, as a group, eliminate those targeted.[9] After the killing, the original political group would move on to the next location. Hence, their sociopolitical view attempts to locate genocidal acts within a geopolitical structure, focusing on degree of integration and fear of the targeted group.

Davenport and Stam also argue that in a rural, peasant, impoverished economy, survival becomes a prime motive.[10] Such desperation enhances the ability of leaders to generate compliance with genocidal commands. In Rwanda, obedience to those commands was framed in terms of communal labor obligations. The killing was euphemized as "doing the work," and weapons as "the tools."[11] In psychological terms, the subjective perception of Tutsi and the actions against them were transformed by social appeals and linguistic dissociation.

Rationalist political models provide a blueprint of influence showing the geographic spread of animosity and eventual killing. However, they cannot explain many aspects of genocidal aggression, such as why the aggression becomes "over-kill" (more severe than required to attain genocide or subjugate the out-group) or why rape is a universal component of genocide (e.g., Rwanda, Bosnia, El Mozote, My Lai). Such models may attempt to explain why some groups are "targeted" or are even seen as necessary for extermination, but they do not elucidate the causes of brutality. What they do is provide a normative road map of the slaughter, describing why attacks are greatest in certain areas as a function of prior integration, acceptance by the dominant group, etc.

PRECONDITIONS FOR GENOCIDE AND THE SELECTION OF A TARGET GROUP

Staub[12] saw the evolution of "evil" (extreme human destructiveness that is not commensurate with instigating conditions) in societies as beginning with the "frustration of basic human needs and the development of destructive modes of need fulfillment."[13] These basic human needs include security, positive identity, effectiveness and control over essentials, connections to others and autonomy, and an understanding of the world and one's place in it. The frustration of these needs both interferes with the satisfaction of other needs and begins a search for a scapegoat, in the form of a target group that can be blamed for the dissatisfaction. In Germany, World War I left the nation with reparations to be paid, which the Germans viewed as grossly unfair. In the 1920s when Nazism began to form, the economy was in ruins, with the Deutschmark devalued and unemployment soaring. In Rwanda, as in many African nations, a history of colonialism had taken a toll, and precolonial animosities had been suppressed, even exaggerated. As with other African countries, the economy was in shambles. Many nations saw psychopaths, like Idi Amin, step into the power vacuum. In the past 20 years Sierra Leone, the Congo, Uganda, and Somalia, amongst others, have experienced horrific civil wars and numerous massacres. As I write this, a human tragedy unfolds in the Darfur region of Sudan that is reminiscent of what occurred in Rwanda. African Union peacekeepers are about to withdraw, and no UN troops will replace them. The UN passes countless resolutions, but no direct action results. A slaughter has occurred and more will almost certainly follow, and no one is stepping up to help the victims. Jewish groups in New York, all too familiar with the dynamics of genocide, have attempted to raise world concern over the Sudanese tragedy.

What Waller calls "our ancestral shadow" is the essential tribalism that socio-biology argues is part of the human condition.[14] In practice, a target group is identified that is clearly and symbolically made different from the perpetrators, by definition a stigmatized "out-group." With ethnic, political, or religious differences, the target minority is often clearly visible or made so through official identification (e.g., badges, tattoos, identity cards, or the yellow Star of David for the Jews in Germany). Societies whose culture officially emphasizes differences among groups (e.g., Christian versus Jew, rather than merely German; and Jew versus Arab, rather than merely Israeli) facilitate this process. Even relatively transitory or ephemeral characteristics can be identified and recruited to the task merely by promoting xenophobia, a basic human reaction experienced from infancy grounded in sociobiology.[15] As we saw in Cambodia, the target group was designated as "educated people" (defined as anyone above grade 7 in school or those who wore glasses) who had "benefited" from a bourgeois existence. In the Ukraine, it was those peasants who owned "prosperous" farms, who in actuality were no different from the less prosperous in landholdings and livestock, who were initially identified as enemies of the revolution. Eventually, however, everyone was victimized as millions starved. Some writers argue that the Russian oligarchy's ethnocentricity that cast aspersions on Ukrainians played a part in the genocide.[16] The Cambodian situation suggests that when obvious ethnic differences are not available, the creation of an out-group requires more imagination but still occurs.

Janis's notion of "groupthink" comes to mind from this analysis.[17] Janis examined what he defined as "a mode of thinking that people engage in when they are deeply involved in a cohesive in-group, when members' strivings for unanimity override their motivation to realistically appraise alternative courses of action."[18] Although Janis was studying foreign policy decisions, he found that groupthink occurred when there was any highly cohesive group that was insulated from independent judgments plus a perceived threat and an active leader who promotes his own solution. At the societal level, that leader or group generates a support group or "vanguard," a small group of ideologues who seize power.

In Rwanda in 1994, President Juvenal Habyarimana and his close colleagues, who had been in power since 1975, saw a coming loss of political power. In response, they exaggerated the risk posed by Tutsi "freedom fighters" or RPF (Rwandan Patriotic Front). The RPF assembled Tutsi militias who won their first victory inside Rwanda in 1994. Initially, the Hutu elite referred to those on their side as "Rwandans" and to the rest as "ibyitso," meaning, "accomplices of the enemy." The Tutsi, although intermingled with and, in some cases, intermarried with the Hutu, were taller and lighter skinned. Rwandan law required tribal identification, and people generally knew everyone's tribal background. Tribal identification cards had been carried since 1931. They began terror attacks using small boys, kidnapped from their villages and forced to kill a village member so that the boys would be ostracized and could never return. They accompanied this criminal recruitment with nonstop propaganda broadcast over Radio Television Libre des Mille Collines where they demonized the Tutsis as interlopers who had unfairly benefited from Belgian rule. They developed a killer militia called the Interahamwe (literally, those who attack together) who spearheaded the killings.

THE NEW BLUEPRINT FOR SLAUGHTER

Because they killed and massacred with impunity, violence became "normalized." This initial period of norm shifts, which preceded the actual mass slaughter, lasted about three years. During this time, the norm for killing Tutsi began to shift so that other Hutu were dragooned into action. Conformity was developed through extreme social pressure and terror to the Hutu. As they began to join into the violence, the social norm on killing shifted further. Here is the description of a Hutu who killed early in the genocide.

> Some people tried to kill one person in particular. You could tell this obsessed them, to be first at the finding. They searched as if they were sniffing around, then got steamed up when they failed. Maybe because of some old falling out, maybe just for fun. Maybe most often so as to get, that very evening, a well placed field coveted for a long time. Someone who brought proof of an important cutting—a well-known person, or somebody very fast, for example—might be rewarded by a first claim on the victims' land. But usually we hunted without such thoughts.[19]

This quote is from Jean Hatzfeld's remarkable book, *Machete Season: The Killers in Rwanda Speak*.[20] Hatzfeld, a French reporter, interviewed ten imprisoned *genocidaires* about life in Rwanda in the spring of 1994. The impact of shifting social norms on the alteration of consciousness is clear from these quotes. On the one hand, the killing was viewed dispassionately, as an opportunity to get land and with little regard for the victim. On the other hand, some vestige of community attachment remained in place, in that *genocidaires* passed on killing people they knew personally, but did nothing to help them, presumably because they believed nothing could be done. The rules of slaughter, at this point, were an acceptance that everyone must die.

An example of the impact of the early stages of societal transition on individual perception can be gleaned from this startling description of the "rules of slaughter" by other *genocidaires* in Rwanda.[21]

> It was possible not to kill a neighbor or someone who appealed for pity, gratitude, or recognition, but it was not possible to save that person. You could agree together on a dodge, decide on a trick of that sort. But it was of no use to the dead person. For example, a man finding someone with whom he had popped many a Primus (beer)

in friendship might turn aside, but someone else would come along and take care of it.[22]

You could spare a person you owed an old favor to, or who had given you a cowl but there was always someone bringing up the rear who was out to kill. Luck did not exempt a single Tutsi in the marshes. What had to be done was done in all circumstances. You knew it, and in the end, you did not dare go against the truth.[23]

Advancing as a team, we would run into a scramble of fugitives hiding in the papyrus and the muck, so it was not easy to recognize neighbors. If, by misfortune I caught sight of an acquaintance, like a soccer comrade, for example, a pang pinched my heart, and I left him to a nearby colleague. But I had to do this quietly, I could not reveal my good heart...Anyone who hesitated to kill because of feelings of sadness absolutely had to watch his mouth, to say nothing about the reason for his reticence, for fear of being accused of complicity...in any case, these feelings did not last long—they managed to be forgotten.[24]

We killed everything we tracked down in the papyrus. We had no reason to choose, to expect or fear anyone in particular. We were cutters of acquaintances, cutters of neighbors, just plain cutters...Today some name acquaintances they supposedly spared because they know these are no longer living to contradict them. They tell tales to attract favor of suffering families, they invent rescues to ease their return. We joke about those fake stratagems.[25]

We were forbidden to choose among men and women, babies and oldsters—everyone had to be slaughtered in the end...the intimidators kept saying. Anyone who lowers his machete because of someone he knows, he is spoiling the willingness of his colleagues. Anyway, someone who avoided the fatal gesture before a good acquaintance did it out of kindness to himself, not his acquaintance, because he knew it brought no mercy to the other person, who'd be struck down anyway.[26]

The slaughter by machetes was "the cutting," some victims were avoided because of past ties that made the slaughter difficult for the killer. Some victims were prized because of rewards anticipated through their death. We all maintain a hierarchy in civilian circumstances: a sociometric pattern of neighbors or acquaintances whom we like, are indifferent to, or dislike. In Rwanda, this became the sociometric blueprint for slaughter.

In April 1994, after President Habyarimana's plane was shot down (probably by a surface to air missile), the RPF began to drive toward Kigali, the capital. At this point, the genocide of Tutsi escalated to full force. It is still not clear who fired the missile.

STRUCTURE OF THE PERPETRATOR GROUP

Killer groups engaging in groupthink have an illusion of invulnerability and moral righteousness that leads to excessive risk taking,[27] a collective rationalizing of warnings that might temper position, an unquestioned belief in the group's moral superiority, negative stereotypes of out-group making negotiation unfeasible, direct pressure on dissenters from group ideology, self-censorship of deviation from apparent consensus, a shared illusion of unanimity, and the emergence of self-appointed "mind guards" to protect the group from adverse information. Irving Janis proposed groupthink as a small group dynamic, yet the collective shifts in perceptions towards target groups and group goals occurring in Germany or Rwanda are clear examples of groupthink at a national level. The groupthink spreads, becoming a national dogma with an unchallenged "world view" or view that defines reality. When this view is finally challenged, it implodes. When Hitler committed suicide in a bunker, Nazism was finished as a national world view. On a smaller level, the exposure of a cult figure ends the social reality manufactured within the cult. Genocides, viewed this way, constitute a virulent form of social hysteria, one with a hapless target group for extreme aggression. As the group dominates, they define reality within the microcosm of genocide: the victims are evil, they gained unfairly, they are like vermin or a virus, they must be exterminated before they multiply. The Nazi propaganda apparatus produced films showing lice and hordes of rats; Jews were described in these terms and associated with visual images of pestilence. The interested reader is referred to Peter Cohen's brilliant documentary entitled *The Architecture of Doom* for a chilling view of such a constructed reality.[28] In Rwanda, the government radio station broadcast propaganda daily. In Orwell's chilling but accurate novel, *1984*, government-run television screens broadcast the ongoing progress of a war. One does not know whether it is real or fictional. There is no way to know. That was Orwell's point. Information is controlled and reality is reshaped.

Apart from the frustration of basic needs described by Staub,[29] societies clearly differ in the amount of social regulation they generate. One can conceive of a continuum of societies with totalitarian arrangements at one end (e.g., Nazi Germany, Cambodia under the Khmer Rouge (KR), Stalinist Russia, China under Mao Zedong, etc.) and relatively "anomic" or disorganized states at the other (e.g., Rwanda). Democratic states with established legal systems would exist in the middle of such a continuum, if they remained democratic. The Nazis became a minority within a democratic state and then seized power through a series of machinations such as staged assassination attempts and the Reichstag Fire. This fire was, in all likelihood, set by the Nazis (specifically Hermann Goering) and pinned on a hapless communist bricklayer who "confessed" under torture, was found guilty, and was decapitated. It helped the Nazi ascension to power by throwing the Communists (who were a viable party in Germany at that time) into disarray and increasing the vote for the Nazis (see http://www.wikipedia.org/wiki/Reichstag_fire).

Typically, government military or paramilitary militias under direct state control perform the bulk of the killing. (In Germany, Armenia, and Ukraine there were attacks by citizens on the target groups, but the preponderant violence was government orchestrated.) The genocide in these states is "dispassionate," systematic, efficient, and controlled. It is directed toward target groups who were clearly politically selected. The Nazi genocide of the Jews represents an example; although it began with mass shootings, it progressed to the Final Solution using technology: trains and gas chambers, crematoria, and hugely repressive control. In Rwanda, extremist militias (called Interahamwe) initiated the killing spree. Later on, when the genocide reached an apex, other Hutu became killers as well. Surreptitiously taken films of the Rwanda killing show an apparently dispassionate slashing of people, much in the manner one would cut corn or long grass (and just as the killers described it—the cutting).

Similarly, the killing in Cambodia is described as "mechanical." Many victims were struck in the back of the head by a garden hoe or pick, ostensibly to save bullets. Both the Nazis and the KR used euphemized language to describe the process of systematic elimination of a large group of people; "sweep out, discard" were the words used by the KR (cf. the Nazi terms "special action, resettlement"). The Nazi "extermination camps" included Auschwitz, and the famous "interrogation camp" of the KR was Tuol Sleng. Found at Tuol Sleng was a set of instructions for inmates. These included rules such as "during the bastinado (beating to the soles of the feet) or the electrification you must not cry loudly."[30] The killing form of totalitarian regimes is predominately dispassionate (although a minority of killings in Cambodia occurred through torture, and in Ukraine through torture and execution; the "Final Solution" replaced messy shooting with more efficient gas).

According to Human Rights Watch, in Rwanda, the killing began with extreme militias recruited for violence and spread to other Hutu as social pressure increased to join or to be considered with the enemy.[31] These killer gangs (like the SS) were trained by former soldiers to attack the enemy in their community. Many poor young men responded readily to the promise of rewards. Of the nearly 60 percent of Rwandans under the age of 20, tens of thousands had little hope of obtaining the land needed to establish their own households or the jobs necessary to provide for a family. Such young men, including many displaced by the war and living in camps near the capital, provided many of the early recruits to the Interahamwe. They were trained in the months before and in the days immediately after the genocide began. Many militia members were merely children, some as young as nine.[i] They were taken from a village and some were shot—those who did not react were now complicit in the murder. They were drafted and then ordered to return to the village and to kill; hence they were ostracized from their village and bonded to the army.

---

[i]An "advance" in weapons technology has produced automatic weapons light enough to be handled by children.

One official was later imprisoned and executed, and another was murdered with his family. Three burgomasters (mayors) and a number of other officials who sought to stop the killings were also slain, either by mid-April or shortly after. The leaders of the genocide held meetings in the center and south of the country to push hesitant local administrators into collaboration. At the same time, they sent assailants from areas where slaughter was well under way into those central and southern communes where people had refused to kill, and they used the radio to ridicule and threaten administrators and local political leaders who had been preaching calm.

After Habyarimana's plane was shot down in April 1994, a new group under Hutu Colonel Theoneste Bagasora stepped into the power vacuum. The new leaders were consolidating control over military commanders, and they profited enormously from the first demonstration of international timidity. UN troops, in Rwanda under the terms of the peace accords, tried for a few hours to keep the peace, then withdrew to their posts—as ordered by superiors in New York —leaving the local population at the mercy of assailants. Officers opposed to Bagasora realized that a continuing foreign presence was essential to restricting the killing campaign and appealed to representatives of France, Belgium, and the United States not to desert Rwanda. But, suspecting the kind of horrors to come, the foreigners had already packed their bags. An experienced and well-equipped force of French, Belgian, and Italian troops rushed in to evacuate the foreigners, and then departed. U.S. Marines dispatched to the area stopped in neighboring Burundi once it was clear that U.S. citizens would be evacuated without their help. By April 20, two weeks after the plane crash, the organizers of the genocide had substantial, although not yet complete, control of the now highly centralized state. The administration continued to function remarkably well despite the disruptions in communication and transport caused by the war.

Orders to kill flowed from the prime minister to prefects to burgomasters and to local meetings where instructions on killing (how and who) were read to the population. The same language echoed from north to south and from east to west, calling for "self-defense" against "accomplices." Slaughter was known as "the work" and machetes and firearms were described as "tools." Reports on the situation at the local level and minutes of meetings held by people out on the hills were handed back up through the administrative channels (cf. "ethnic cleansing," relocation, etc., used in other genocides). Hence, the normative nature of the killing spread throughout the population to Hutu who were not originally in the Interahamwe.

In the first days of killing in Kigali, assailants sought out and murdered targeted individuals and also went systematically from house to house in certain neighborhoods, killing Tutsi and Hutu opposed to Habyarimana. Administrative officials ordered local people to establish barriers to catch Tutsi trying to flee and to organize search patrols to discover those trying to hide. By the middle of the first week of the genocide, organizers began implementing a different strategy: driving Tutsi out of their homes to government offices, churches, schools, or other public sites, where they would subsequently be massacred in large-scale operations. In one church, girls were told to separate into Tutsi and Hutu factions so the Tutsis could be killed. They refused, so all were killed.

Towards the end of April, authorities declared a campaign of "pacification," which meant not an end to killing, but greater control over killing. Sensitive to criticism from abroad—muted though it was—authorities ended most large-scale massacres. They also sought to rein in assailants who were abusing their license to kill, such as those slaying Hutu with whom they had disputes or those allowing Tutsi to escape in return for money or sexual favors. They ordered militia and other citizens to bring suspects to officials for "investigation" instead of simply killing them where they found them. Authorities used "pacification" as a tactic to lure Tutsi out of hiding to be killed.

By mid-May, the authorities ordered the final phase, that of tracking down the last surviving Tutsi. They sought to exterminate both those who had hidden successfully and those who had been spared thus far—like women and children—or protected by their status in the community—like priests and medical workers. As the RPF advanced through the country, assailants also hurried to eliminate any survivors who might be able to testify about the slaughter. Throughout the genocide, Tutsi women were often raped, tortured, and mutilated before they were murdered.

Both on the radio and through public meetings, authorities worked to make the long-decried threat of RPF infiltration concrete and immediate. Throughout the country they disseminated detailed false information, such as reports that Tutsi had hidden firearms, that they had prepared maps showing fields to be taken from Hutu, or that they had killed local administrative officials. Authorities counted on such news to convince Hutu that their Tutsi neighbors were dangerous agents of the RPF who had to be eliminated. Community leaders and even clergy assured Hutu that they were justified in attacking Tutsi as a measure of "self-defense."

As one of Hatzfeld's interviewees said,

Our Tutsi neighbors, we knew they were guilty of no misdoing, but we thought all Tutsis at fault for our constant troubles. We no longer looked at them one by one, we no longer stopped to recognize them as they had been, not even as colleagues. They had become a threat greater than all we had experienced together, more important than our way of seeing things in the community. That's how we reasoned and that's how we killed at the time.[32]

Authorities offered tangible incentives to participants. They delivered food, drink, and other intoxicants, parts of military uniforms, and small payments in cash to hungry, jobless young men. They encouraged cultivators to pillage farm animals, crops, and such building materials as doors, windows, and roofs. Even more important in this land-hungry society, they promised cultivators the fields left vacant by Tutsi victims. To entrepreneurs and members of the local elite, they granted houses, vehicles, control of a small business, or such rare goods as television sets or computers. In some regions, authorities needed to do little more than give the signal for Hutu to begin attacking Tutsi. In other areas, such as central and southern Rwanda, where Tutsi were numerous and well integrated and where the government party had little standing, many Hutu initially refused to attack Tutsi and joined with them in fighting off assailants. Only when military and civilian authorities resorted to public criticism and harassment, fines, destruction of property, injury, and threat of death did these Hutu give up their open opposition to the genocide. In some places, authorities apparently deliberately drew hesitant Hutu into increasingly more violent behavior, first encouraging them to pillage, then to destroy homes, and then to kill the occupants of the homes. Soldiers and police sometimes threatened to punish Hutu who wanted only to pillage and not to harm Tutsi. The prior integration of the Tutsi and the relative weakness of the government can be likened to fields of force, playing out against each other in different geographic locations.

Just as some communities were more ready to kill than others, so individual Hutu would agree to attack one person and not another or, in an extension of the same logic, would attack one person and save another (as we saw in the above quotes from Jean Hatzfeld's book). Hutu who protected Tutsi ordinarily helped those to whom they were linked by the ties of family, friendship, or obligation for past assistance, but sometimes they also saved the lives of strangers. Many Rwandans say that they killed because authorities told them to kill. Such statements reflect less a national predisposition to obey orders, as is sometimes said, than a recognition that the "moral authority" of the state swayed them to commit crimes that would otherwise have been unthinkable. In this sense, the norms had been transformed along the lines suggested by Staub; a new set of rules prevailed, one that directed citizens to be violent. This incremental alteration of norms was also evident in Nazi Germany—see the list of increases in harassment and murder of Jews in Chapter 4.

When organizers of the genocide gained control of the state, they suppressed dissent but did not extinguish it. In May and June, when the interim government was weakened by military losses and by the first signs of international disapproval, Hutu in one community after another began refusing to undertake further searches or to participate in guarding barriers. As the majority of participants withdrew, they left the execution of the genocide in the hands of smaller, more zealous groups of assailants, who continued to hunt and kill in hopes of profit or because they were committed to exterminating the last Tutsi.

In Staub's model the frustration of basic needs (e.g., material deprivation, political chaos, realistic conflict) and the identification of a scapegoat constitutes the instigating conditions for the destructive process. In Rwanda, long term deprivation, political chaos, and a long-standing belief that the Tutsi were dangerous interlopers coalesced into a perfect storm of violence. The deprivation produces heightened in-group identification, particularly amongst authoritarian people who seek a strong leader, perception of out-group threat, and a destructive ideology. The latter presents an exclusionary world vision and is called, *in extremis,* an *ideology of antagonism.* When subordinate groups demand more, they threaten the basic need satisfaction of the dominant group whose "legitimizing ideology" is threatened and who then react with increasingly harsh acts of repression and aggression. In Rwanda, the push by the RPF and the death of the president served as such precipitating threats. Although not genocide, the lynchings in the Southern United States can also be viewed from this perspective. The loss of the Civil War and the continuing presence of the "free negro" threatened the legitimizing ideology of the South.

Staub argued that two types of out-group stereotyping exist.[33] The lesser is devaluation of the out-group, while the more intense form specifically sees the out-group as having achieved gains through prior injustice. Hitler saw the Jews this way, and the Hutu extremists portrayed the Tutsi in this way.

Once initiated, violence generates an evolution in perpetrators; the personality of individuals, social norms, institutions, and culture all change incrementally in ways that make greater violence easier and more likely.[34] The usual moral principles that prohibit violence and protect people are replaced by "higher" values protecting purity, goodness, and well-being of the in-group, and creating a better society by destroying the victims. A utopian vision is offered that excludes some people and justifies their exclusion in the service of the vision. A progressive restructuring of group norms occurs in line with this ideological shift. Albert Bandura describes the process of *moral disengagement* that allows "reprehensible conduct" to occur and recur.[35]

Through this cognitive process, the acts of violence are viewed differently, in euphemistic terminology—hence, "the work" (Rwanda). These euphemisms protect the actor from the full realization of what he is doing. Normative shifts aid this process. By making an action "normal" we judge it differently, as more morally acceptable. Personal responsibility for the action is diffused by the normative shift. One is less personally responsible for something everyone is doing. The effects of the action are viewed differently as well—without compassionate awareness of the full effects on the victim. Such empathic awareness would render the killer incapable of murderous acts and the rapist incapable of rape. The cognitive shift is generated by the societal normative shifts. As Bandura put it, "the conversion of socialized people into dedicated combatants is achieved not by altering their personality structures, aggressive drives, or moral standards. Rather, it is accomplished by cognitively restructuring the moral value of killing, so that it can be done free from self-censuring restraints."[36] Osofsky et al. monitored this process in prison personnel who were mandated to enact executions.[37] Compared to other prison personnel, the execution teams showed moral disengagement in the ways Bandura described, by rationalizing their actions in moral terms (The Bible teaches "a life for a life and an eye for an eye"; murderers have forfeited their right to be considered full human beings), social terms (nowadays the death penalty is done in a way to minimize suffering; an execution is merciful compared to murder), or economic terms (it is cheaper for society to use the death penalty than to keep a murderer for life).

Behavior towards the victims that would previously have been considered inconceivable now becomes acceptable and "normal." Eventually, killing the victims becomes the "right" thing to do. As Hatzfeld's interviews showed, the killing of Tutsi was taken for granted, even if killing a neighbor was difficult. This process can be slow (in Turkey, Armenians had been persecuted for a long time before the genocide) or relatively fast (in Rwanda, moderate Hutu and Tutsi were positively interconnected only a few months before the carnage, although a long history of tribal animosity existed).

THE CENTRAL BELIEF

In Peter Cohen's film, Goebbels's Nazi propaganda machine depicted genocide as cleansing of an infection or removal of a virus. The central metaphor was powerful enough to alter other thoughts. As Desdemona's father says in *Othello*, "Belief of it [that his daughter was in a relationship with a black man] oppresses me already" (*Othello*, 1.1.154). In other words, some central beliefs oppress or occupy consciousness so that they distort or obliterate all related beliefs. The imagery of Jews as vermin is one such image. The propaganda film showed large masses of rats and wriggling lice. As the evolution progresses, the number of perpetrators spreads and the selected target group expands. In the end, there is what Staub calls a "reversal of morality"; those actions once thought reprehensible (violent slaughter) are now laudable. The killing of a human being has become transformed in consciousness to the cleansing of an infection. Our human capacity for symbolic reasoning, perhaps the essence of our humanity, enables these transformations in consciousness. Sadistic violence occurs only in creatures that have evolved brains such as chimpanzees and humans, but we get ahead of ourselves. As we shall see below, another central belief that can color consciousness is the belief that, if one kills for jihad, one will enter heaven and be rewarded (see Postscript).

SELECTION OF A TARGET GROUP

Michael Ghiglieri views genocide from a sociobiological perspective.[38] This perspective speaks not only to the choice of target groups but also to the origins of tribalism, that when a social group grows too large for men to recognize each other, men then feel impelled to join smaller groups in which they can still belong and recognize the others individually as allies. This, in sociobiological terms, is the origin of ethnocentrism and xenophobia; the out-group originally was those we could not recognize. However, one can join a small group without killing a larger one, and in pluralistic societies in-groups coexist peaceably with out-groups. Furthermore, in Rwanda, the killers recognized their victims; they were not faceless.

Again, from Hatzfeld,

> The leader would repeat, "kill everyone except the Tutsi women properly possessed by Hutu husbands"...which explains why some Tutsi women were spared. But on the contrary, a Tutsi husband of a Hutu woman had to be killed as a top priority... A Tutsi wife, you could try to save her. You offered a cow to the leader and a radio or the like to the organizers.[39]

From a sociobiological perspective, the Tutsi wife was already possessed by the Hutu husband, but the Tutsi husband was capable of generating out-group genes.

The forces that shape the selection of a target group appear to be both political and psychological. In Serbia, religious and ethnic divisions had existed for some time amongst the Serbs, Croats, and Muslims. Those preexisting divisions became exacerbated when conditions led to Yugoslavia's disintegration. In Rwanda, hatred appears to have existed for centuries between the Hutu and Tutsi because of precolonial tribal wars sustained in the memories of the next generation and reinforced by intergroup inequities during Belgian colonization. The Hutu viewed the Tutsi as interlopers who were unfairly favored by the ruling Belgians. Smoldering resentment surfaced as soon as the Belgians left. Typically there is an ethnic or religious distinction that comes to define a target group, yet ethnic and religious divisions are tolerated worldwide, most often when a superordinate definition provides universal membership (e.g., we are all subservient to a colonizing power, or we are all merely Catholics, Moslems, Communists, Yugoslavs, etc.). Yet at certain times, these social labels take on the power to direct hatred.

In the case of Cambodia, while ethnic divisions existed, they were not the essential basis of targeting. Pol Pot and the Khmer Rouge came to define "educated people" (across ethnic lines) as a threat who would side with the West (even though Pol Pot himself had a Ph.D. from the Sorbonne, he took his cue from the French Revolution, Stalin and Mao Zedong who advocated the elimination of the *bourgeoisie*). His definition of "educated" was extremely loose but served his political purpose. Hence, while in some cases, realistic historical conflict provides the germ for the out-group threat (Armenia, Rwanda, Bosnia), in others (like Cambodia) it is completely manufactured on ideological grounds. It is possible that when clearly defined out-groups do not exist, they have to be invented. Out-groups can be viewed as a kind of lightning rod for the collective frustration and rage that builds at a societal level fueled by accumulated frustration and directed by rhetoric.

Inculcation of Fear

Xenophobia is especially potent when a threat is identified. Sherif and his colleagues,[40] amongst others,[41] have illustrated how easy it is to produce the differentiation, denigration, discrimination, and hostility necessary as a first step. Sociologist George Simmel[42] amongst others[43] has shown how in-group self-identity and conformity processes combined with threat of censure from others in the in-group to reinforce and maintain the distinction. To remain members of the in-group, individuals initially move away physically and attitudinally from the identified out-group. Perceived threat (real or concocted) inspires the requisite social polarization, initial avoidance, and eventual hostility. This, of course, was the central motive of Orwell's classic novel, *1984,* where an illusory enemy was fought in battles shown on television in all public spaces on a 24 hour basis. So, too, fear of a Tutsi attack drove Hutu extremists to their call for extermination of the Tutsi, and fear of their so-called generation of disease and social ills drove anti-Semitic violence.

The question is raised as to whether racial/ethnic conflict is either necessary or sufficient for pogroms or genocide. In Cambodia, the KR killed millions of Cambodians who were racially, ethnically, and religiously identical to them. Why do groups sometimes define others as categorically different and seek to end the intolerable situation by eradication of the out-group? For whatever reasons, the process is furthered by defining the out-group so that the entire out-group is perceived as threatening. Typically, this occurs through generalizing the actions of a few out-group members to the entire group. A group of Armenians had sided with the Russians against the Turks; a group of Tutsis had formed a revolutionary party; Jews in pre-WWII Germany were seen as part of an exclusive Zionist conspiracy that controlled an inordinate amount of financial resources and as incompatible with a national goal of "racial purity" set by the Nazis; a small group of the Kurds in Iraq had sided with Iran against Iraq. As the perception of threat spreads to encompass the entire group, all members, even children, come to be viewed as probable future enemies and, hence, as threatening. In the Nanking massacre, the "threat" was initially the sheer number of those captured, which seems to have triggered the mass slaughter.[44]

As Goering put it at the Nuremberg Trials:

> It is always a simple matter to drag people along whether it is a democracy, or a fascist dictatorship, or a parliament, or a communist dictatorship. Voice or no voice, the people can always be brought to the bidding of the leaders. This is easy. All you have to do is tell them they are being attacked, and denounce the pacifists for lack of patriotism and exposing the country to danger. It works the same in every country.[45]

THE VIRUS METAPHOR

It appears that a common perception of *genocidaires* is that their target group is *virus* or *cancer-like*. The notion of the threat spreading is common to these views, justifying extermination of the currently innocent. At the Human Rights Tribunal for abuses in Rwanda, one Hutu woman justified her killing Tutsi children by portraying it as a humanitarian act, saying that she was sparing them the impossibility of living without parents.

It may well be that one quintessential aspect of the human condition is the ability to imagine oneself and one's tribe existing in perpetuity. This requires both a belief in life after death where one will be reunited with one's loved ones and a sense that, on earth, one's community will continue to thrive. The positive aspect of this is the hope for continuity of one's offspring in the future. Generally, it extends to survival of one's values and social philosophy as well. Unfortunately, this "lifestyle solution" (as Becker called it; see Chapter 2) to the existential dilemma of death involves a bolstering of the dominant in-group values at the expense of those who do not share them. Hence, there must be an out-group, or scapegoat group, that will be demonized in order to heighten in-group solidarity. This is done by portraying the out-group as a threat—in Rwanda, the Tutsi were depicted as threatening the Hutu structure; in Germany, the Jews were portrayed as the root of all evil. Media play a role here. In Rwanda, the Mille Collines radio station played anti-Tutsi propaganda nonstop. In Germany, Goebbels, the Minister of Propaganda, had films made depicting the Jews as vermin, like viruses, or as maggots. Hence, they were depicted as a threat that would spread unless eradicated. Peter Cohen's remarkable documentary using Nazi propaganda films shows this footage.[46] Images of rats or lice provided the visual association for audio descriptions of the Jews as undermining German society (in ways not specified). Both genocides included depictions of the target groups as having benefited unjustly in the past. The Hutu portrayed the Tutsi as being favored by the Belgians. The Nazis portrayed the Jews as causing illness and social problems in order to benefit from them. In El Salvador, a military commander convinced soldiers, balking at a command to kill children by intoning, "they will only grow up to be guerillas, we have to take care of the job now."[47]

A Decision Is Made to Eliminate the Outgroup

Fear produces tendencies to fight or flee. If groups feel entitled to their land, or feel the capacity to overpower the target group, a policy of aggression is more likely. The aversive out-group is viewed as controllable.[48] So long as they exist, they remain a threat; hence, the surest method of control is elimination. This is followed by planning on how best to implement this goal. How then, once a group has been targeted, isolated psychologically, and attributed with a threat or injustice, is the killing initiated and sustained? Official sanction and exhortation gives the initiative to grievance, disinhibition of aggression, and personal predilections to implement violence. How this personal predilection plays out generates, in some cases, extreme aggression in persons who had little or no history of aggression prior to the social conflict context. According to Staub, evidence suggests that leaders in genocidal nations (Germany, Rwanda) have attitudes shaped by the culture but in an extreme form. Hitler was, of course, virulently anti-Semitic and saw the Jews as an affront to Aryan "purity," positing a racial ideal (blue eyes, blond hair) that he himself did not resemble.

In his book on mob psychology, Le Bon had also hypothesized that the leader (and by extension, his coterie of followers or vanguard) was chosen in the situation because he was somewhat more extreme than the rest of the group.[49] They possessed the same values as the rest of the group but in the extreme. As they generate more influence, others come to adopt these anti-out-group attitudes as they become popular, in order to belong to an identity affirming group and to generate status within the group. These aspects of conformity are more pronounced with authoritarian followers who prefer a strong leader and the stability of position within an in-group. There is some evidence for authoritarian child rearing practices in both Germany and Rwanda.[50] At the same time, desensitization to the out-group increases, creating a situation where the potential for mass slaughter is raised. They have now ceased to be viewed as human, and actions against them are not viewed as aggression but as cleansing or "the work."[51]

Staub's view is that perpetrators evolve with the commission of evil acts, making the commission of further evil acts more likely. Indeed, Staub makes as a defining quality of evil "the repetition or persistence of greatly harmful acts"[52] and sees the evil he describes as arising out of extreme forms of ordinary psychological processes and not requiring an explanation from psychopathology. This evolution in killing was evidenced in Germany, Nanking, and Rwanda.

Finally, the type of slaughter generated by societal shifts is what we may term "dispassionate slaughter" (look again, at the statements of the Rwandan genocidaires), devoid of the rage and turmoil of the massacres we review in the next chapter. The normative shifts serve to protect perpetrators from a near-universal revulsion to killing other humans. We still see vestiges of that reaction in those who are thrown into the front lines of the slaughter too quickly, such as the *Ordnungpolizei.*

INDIVIDUAL TRANSITIONS TO EXTREME VIOLENCE

Apparently some quirk in human nature allows even the most unspeakable acts of evil to become banal within minutes, provided that they occur far enough away to pose no personal threat.

—Iris Chang, *The Rape of Nanking,* p. 221

In his book, *Ordinary Men,* historian Christopher Browning describes the reactions of Reserve Police Battalion 101 in the German Order Police (*Ordnungpolizei* or Orpo) when first asked to give up their previously mundane duties and to kill Jews in Poland.[1] The men in the Orpo were largely middle aged and had joined the Orpo to avoid conscription into the army. The Orpo was somewhat like the National Guard in the United States. Based on 210 interrogation records obtained after World War I, Browning focused on the "Final Solution" described in Chapter 4. In mid-March 1942, 75–80 percent of all eventual Holocaust victims were still alive. By February 1943, only 25 percent were still alive. The main focus of the slaughter was in Poland, what Browning calls a "veritable blitzkrieg" requiring large numbers of troops.

The failure of the invasion of Russia by the Nazis (which stalled in the siege of Stalingrad), called Operation Barbarossa, threw the Nazis into a killing frenzy. The firing squad method of killing Jews that was used in Russia was deemed inefficient, and the use of gas ovens was instituted for the Polish Jews. These were located at Birkenau, Auschwitz, and Belzec. When the trains carrying Jews to their deaths needed repair, the use of gassing itself became inefficient. A return to the firing squads was ordered, and it was to this end that Police Battalion 101 was drafted to Poland in June 1942. The order was quite specific: the

Battalion commander, Major Wilhelm Trapp, told the men that they were to round up all Jews in Józefów, Poland, load the 300 able-bodied men off to work camp, and shoot the rest. That included 1,500 women, children, and the elderly. The special action required of Battalion 101 was first believed to be guard duty.[2] Once it was made clear to Trapp what was expected, he summoned his men and told them that their job was to murder Jews. He then made an astounding offer; any men who did not feel up to it could hand their rifles and step out.[3] Twelve of his 500 men did so. Witnesses described Trapp as extremely distressed at being given these orders.[4] The job consisted of drumming Jews out of houses and shooting them. The Battalion carried out its duties, although some balked at shooting infants.[5] As one policeman later put it, "I would like to say that almost tacitly everyone refrained from shooting infants and small children."[6] Another rationalized shooting a child this way, "I reasoned with myself that after all without its mother (who had already been shot) the child could not live any longer."[7] When hesitation manifested itself, the commander said the same thing as the captain in El Mozote, that the men should remember this was the enemy, and the enemy was killing German women and children.[8]

The men in the First Company of the 101 Battalion were instructed on how to shoot in order to induce immediate death and then were sent to the marketplace where Jews had been rounded up to begin the shooting. At this point more men tried to opt out, asking for other assignments or saying they could not continue.[9] Some hid in a priests' garden, and others shot past their victims.[10] Most men did not directly opt out but found more passive ways to be unavailable for the actual shooting. The Second Company was not given shooting instructions and resorted to point blank shots in order to compensate for their ineptitude. However, "Through the point blank shot that was thus required, the bullet struck the head of the victim at such a trajectory that often the entire skull or at least the entire rear skullcap was torn off, and blood and splinters, and brains sprayed everywhere and besmirched the shooters."[11]

Some of the shooters could not take it and either slowed down, shot to miss, or left the scene for extended breaks. They were scorned by the other soldiers and called weaklings.[12] Many of the men interviewed reported being able to shoot some Jews but then reaching a point where they could not go on. Since they were already reporting killing, it does not seem to be self-serving to report this reluctance. Some men were upset by individual characteristics of people they shot, indicating that they were still responding to their victims as human. Browning estimates that about 20 percent of the men in the firing squads sought to evade shooting. Those who quit later cited sheer physical revulsion as the cause but did not cite any ethical or political principles. One man remembered with considerable upset that he had killed a Jew who was a decorated veteran of World War I and who had begged for his life.[13] Another policeman reported becoming nauseated and vomiting; he had begun to miss intentionally.[14] The men emerged from the woods where the shooting was taking place, splattered in blood and brains, "morale shaken and nerves finished."[15] When they arrived back at their barracks, they were depressed, embittered, and shaken; they ate little but drank heavily.[16] Neither the drink nor their commanding officers' consolation could "wash away the sense of shame and horror that pervaded the barracks."[17] Browning speculates that the initial refusal rate (12/500) was so small because the order was sudden and the men did not fully understand what they were getting into. One policeman said, "I thought that I could master the situation and that without me the Jews were not going to escape their fate anyway. Truthfully, I must say that at the time we did not reflect on it at all. Only years later did any of us become truly conscious of what had happened then."[18] Furthermore, their basic identification with their comrades and strong urge not to separate themselves from the group worked against refusal. They also did not understand the reactions they would have or the horror of the killing. A similar response was reported by volunteers for a firing squad that shot convicted killer Garry Gilmore in Norman Mailer's report of that event in *The Executioner's Song*. Similarly, Lt. Col. David Grossman reported that studies by U.S. Army Brigadier General S. L. A. Marshall indicated that only 15–20 percent of soldiers in WWII actually fired their guns at the enemy.[19] Those who would not fire would not run and hide; they simply would not fire at the enemy. As Grossman puts it, "There is, within most men, an intense resistance to killing their fellow man. A resistance so strong that, in many circumstances, soldiers on the battlefield will die before they can overcome it."[20] How then do we get from this reluctance to the enraged killings in My Lai or Nanking? Is it that the initial reluctance and revulsion is quickly replaced by anxiety and anger?

Roy Baumeister and Keith Campbell argue that, based on several anecdotal reports, the initial reaction to killing or hurting others seems to be aversive but the distress subsides over time while pleasure in harming others emerges over time.[21] A minority of perpetrators appears to develop pleasure from killing or hurting. One explanation for this development is the opponent-process theory developed by Richard Solomon.[22] This theory, based on animal learning models and research, postulates that psychological processes are homeostatic, so that when an initial response to killing (the A or Alpha process, such as visceral aversion) occurs, it is followed by a restorative (B or Beta process), which is initially pleasant (e.g., recovering from aversion) though weak and inefficient. Over time, according to the learning research of Solomon, the A process diminishes in force and the B process begins to strengthen and predominate. Although the initial theory was developed on animal learning data, the process has been applied to human acquisition of addictions, to the acquired thrill of parachute jumping, and to "traumatic bonding" in battered women.[23] Addiction to the B response explains the attraction to the once-aversive actions. In parachute jumping, the B process is initially relief from terror but then becomes an acquired "high" in itself experienced as a kind of euphoria.[24] Baumeister and Campbell argue that "evil" (sadism), apart from whatever extrinsic motives it satisfies (e.g., threat, dominance) acquires an intrinsic appeal through this dual-process model.[25]

The B process involves a pleasurable feeling (initially escape from aversion, now pleasurable in itself). Baumeister and Campbell cite the presence of laughter among harm-doers as an example. Hence, we are held back from committing harm under ordinary circumstances because of A processes (learned aversions to killing); these reduce with repetition and are replaced by B processes (which strengthen with repetition).

With Police Battalion 101, after the initial revulsion of the massacre at Józefów, they were reassigned to ghetto clearing but not shooting.[26] Instead SS-trained (non-German) Trawnikis recruited from POW camps took over the shooting. This respite did the trick. When it came time to kill again, the policemen did not experience the same revulsion. Instead, they became increasingly efficient and calloused executioners.[27] The initial demand to kill had probably produced an Alpha process of revulsion. With more experience and a temporarily lessened load, it dissipated.

Baumeister and Campbell suggest that the initial violence may serve to terminate boredom, anxiety, or threats, but the violence habit becomes acquired through the opponent process. Baumeister and Campbell as well as Zimbardo examine the potential pleasure of aggression once normative restraints have been reduced. Military massacres prove to be situations where normative constraints are not only reduced but new norms exhorting violence can rapidly develop, in some cases (when an order is given) spontaneously. While individual slayings in Rwanda, El Mozote, My Lai, or Nanking may contain aspects of deindividuated violence, there are elements of controlled violence in these settings as well. For example, violence in Nanking spread from killing by gunshot to rape, torture, mutilation, and "killing games." Yet no one was killed in the "Neutral Zone" created by the international community. The perpetrators had a clearly defined concept of the rules; any Chinese were targets, but Europeans were not. Targets could have anything done to them.

As we described My Lai in Chapter 5, Hersh described the platoon entering the village "with guns blazing."[28] All there were women, children, and old men. The platoon began to ransack the village and kill everyone, shooting into huts without knowing who was inside. Atrocities occurred spontaneously: rapes, tortures, killings (see also Brownmiller).[29] One of the soldiers, Vernado Simpson, recalled killing about 25 people. "I cut their throats, cut off their hands, cut out their tongue, their hair, scalped them."[30] Kelman and Hamilton report that many soldiers were crying as they carried out their orders,[31] although rage seems to have been the most predominant emotion displayed.[32] It is also important to note that the villagers were not resisting, and at least 75 had been rounded up when many were executed, many by Calley himself.[33]

Other soldiers could not engage in the slaughter. A private, James Dursi, testified that when ordered to shoot by another soldier who was screaming and crying, he replied "I can't, I won't."[34] Another soldier, Specialist Ron Grzesik, reported that when ordered by Calley to "finish them off," he refused.[35] Baumeister and Campbell argue that even in such extreme circumstances individual differences in reactions may be based on levels of guilt, high or low sensation seeking, and narcissism.

Both Kadri[36] and Sallah and Weiss[37] depict My Lai as unusual only in the sense that it was reported and resulted in a trial. A U.S. Marine Unit called "Tiger Force" routinely massacred civilians in Viet Nam and wore body parts on a necklace. Initially established as a reconnaissance team (Recon), the 101st Airborne was a 45 man "Special Forces" unit, small, mobile, and trained to kill. After about 18 months, the unit began to lose sight of the conventions of war and embarked upon an apocalyptic trail of blood, death, and mutilation. Director Francis Ford Coppola used them as a model for Colonel Kurtz in his film *Apocalypse Now.* Several members of the unit wore necklaces of ears. As one member later put it, "You think back and say, I can't believe I did that. But now you know what you did was wrong. The killing gets to you. You just can't escape it...it's in the middle of the night when the demons come, that you remember."[38,i]

As Sallah and Weiss put it, "For the Tigers, the severing of ears wasn't only for souvenirs—a practice by other soldiers in the war. Now, they were mutilating bodies to deal with the rage and, in many cases, simply discarding the ears and scalps. Corpses were being repeatedly stabbed in frenzy. Noses and fingers were being cut off. 'Going berserk' is a phrase used to describe soldiers who fly into an incredible rage after long periods of trauma and combat. The soldiers believe that, by carrying out his anger in a bloody, dehumanizing way, 'the gook' can never hurt him or his comrades again. This kind of savagery—a kind of over-kill—goes beyond taking body parts for souvenirs."[39]

As we shall see below, it takes some time to acquire this taste for killing and to generate this rage. What causes these "overkill" practices[40] in massacres/genocides of raping or torturing, or the extreme brutality in killing described above (rape, dismemberment, killing children in front of their parents, etc.)? A

---

[i]One set of sequelae of combat killing is what is known as "peri-traumatic stress disorder" generated by the secretion of neurotransmitters.[61] This involves activation of several brain-behavioral systems including neurotransmitter secretion, emotional regulation (hyperarousal), loss of emotions as signals, and memory malfunction.[62] Prolonged combat exposure alters the structure of emotion-governing brain structures. Gurvitz, Shenton, and Pitman found that Viet Nam veterans with the most intense combat exposure and with the most post-traumatic stress disorder had an average shrinkage of 26 percent in the left and 22 percent in the right hippocampus compared with veterans who saw combat but had no symptoms.[63] The hippocampus can be thought of as the "search and integrate" part of the brain. A soldier who is "on point" (at the front of a Recon unit searching for enemies) has a hypothalamus that is operating at the maximum.

collective sadism emerges in many massacres/genocides that goes beyond mere extermination and has not been explained by previous work on genocide.[41] While opponent-process theory explains the diminution of revulsion at committing atrocities and how one can become enured to the emotional consequences of the actions, it does not explain why such savage actions are used. (Or why we refer to these actions as "savage" since they are used universally, including use by the military from countries we consider cultured or civilized.)

In Chapter 2, we noted a description by Le Bon of men as descending to the primal level in mobs, suggesting a Hobbesian view of the natural state of man as being a state of war.[42]

> By the very fact that he forms part of an organized group, a man descends several rungs down the ladder of civilization. Isolated, he may be a cultivated individual, in a crowd, he is a barbarian—that is, a creature acting by instinct.[43]

These instincts, as Le Bon called them, included a propensity for violence. Violence can, of course, be instrumental or self-defensive, it can take forms that are not sadistic. Sadism seems to involve violence that goes beyond what is required for self-defense or to achieve an end. It describes violence that appears to be enjoyed by the perpetrator. Eric Fromm called sadism "the conversion of impotence into the experience of omnipotence"[44] and defined it in the quote that begins this chapter.

DEINDIVIDUATED VIOLENCE AND BRUTAL MASSACRES

In a massacre, as we described in Chapter 5, one group generally has an extreme power advantage over another group whom they perceive as putative enemies. Social psychologist Philip Zimbardo and his colleagues described this as the pathology of the situation and as capable of eliciting abusive behavior from normally well-behaved people.[45]

Besides this power imbalance, another factor in generating a massacre is a leader or small cadre of leaders who are extremely prejudiced against the target group and capable through the hierarchy to enforce compliance with the execution of the violence. The *decision to eradicate* the target group originates with this hegemony that is able, through coercion, obedience to authority, fear mongering using an appeal to tribal membership, xenophobia, or perceived past inequities (the landowners in China and Ukraine), to generate compliance in others. In El Mozote, soldiers balked at killing children.[46] A major "pushed into the group of children, seized a little boy, threw him into the air and impaled him as he fell. That put an end to that discussion."[47] Both Freud[48] and Redl[49] described initiators of group violence as having no emotional connections to anyone but themselves and, hence, as capable of executing the "unconflicted act" that generated "infectious" copying in followers. After this initial act at El Mozote, other soldiers slaughtered children. Zimbardo describes a similar initial reluctance to engage in taboo behaviors followed by rapid and escalating participation (see below).[50]

Military massacres have a different *modus operandi* than controlled state-directed killing. In the former, rage can develop as a response to a military command to kill through a combination of a dehumanized target, preparatory arousal, and the action of killing itself generating rage. Hence the killing can be rageful and sadistic. From the testimony of perpetrators in Nanking and My Lai, there seemed to be a sense that one could do anything with impunity. In My Lai, and possibly El Mozote, a small minority refrained from killing. In Rwanda, the genocide took the form of a series of massacres perpetrated initially by the militia and then by a large group of Hutus.

In military massacres, there is an instant transition to a killing rage state that occurs after an order is given. The order either is to kill (Nanking) or is ambiguous (My Lai). Lifton's descriptions of My Lai, based on eyewitness reports, suggested that the killing of civilians was accompanied by generalized rage and by expressions of anger and revenge toward the victims.[51] Certainly this was evident at Nanking and El Mozote (but not in Rwanda where the killing seemed more dispassionate and methodical, based more on moral disengagement than on rage). One question is, did rage cause the actions of violence or was it a reaction to the implementation of the order to kill? Historically rooted hostility toward the target can generate dehumanization, but more is required to generate rage killing. In El Mozote and Nanking, there were orders to kill from commanding officers. In My Lai, this is disputed, but what is not disputed is the mind frame of the military at that point in time: frustration and anger that fellow soldiers had been killed in the preceding days by booby traps. This rage is more than mere obedience, but orders to kill and the act of killing itself may generate higher levels of rage. Such extreme levels may drive the overkill actions of massacre.

Zimbardo describes this as "deindividuated aggression," in which prior arousal and anomie combine to liberate a toxic and self-rewarding form of aggression.[52] The anomie can occur through the "fog of war" battle scene anonymity and sense that "anything goes," that no one will be held personally responsible for what transpires. Others are killing too, and no individual action could be traced to the individual. The aggressive acts occur faster and with greater amplitude as they are rewarded through proprioceptive feedback from the musculature (literally internal cues from the body and its movement as we might experience when stretching). Under ordinary conditions of social interaction, one attends to the actions of others and cues the timing of one's response (an answer to a question, or one's turn to speak, for example) to that feedback. This is called differential rates of low responding. This term signifies that we learn to unconsciously pace our responses in normal interaction so they fit into the response paces of others, literally, to interact. In normal consciousness, we focus on external cues from others that allow us to behave and interact properly, in a socialized fashion.

In deindividuated violence, attention is redirected from the ordinary cues of the external world to focus more on one's own bodily responses. Now differential rates of high responding are the source of reward. Zimbardo makes the provocative assumption that, once normal inhibitions are overcome, the acting out of aggression is innately pleasurable; hence the reward structure changes from reward for slow actions (that are based on feedback from the actions of others) to fast actions (rewarded internally). The source of reward is the pleasurable bodily action called proprioception. The result is "gross agitated behavior" that is unresponsive to cues from the victim. The victim can be located in space as a target but no empathic reaction for their plight ensues.

Zimbardo suggests that rage generates rage, that violence self-amplifies so that when no restrictions on violence exist, violence increases in rate and force.[53] Military massacres suggest that violence may also expand in scope. Rage killings appear to occur when the "Rules of War" clearly do not apply—either through orders or tacit consensus—then civilians, women, and children, are killed. By this model, the order to kill generates rage, which then leads to overkill and a range of forms of violence. The form varies with the individual soldier and is improvised under a felt condition of impunity. In Nanking, the initial killing of captured Chinese soldiers was by machine gun and was efficient. The killing of civilians was by sword, prolonged and rageful, and eventually "sport killing" ensued. Although Zimbardo described acute deindividuated states as terminating from exhaustion, the possibility exists that in war circumstances, perpetrators' consciousness is so transformed by their own violence that, once they recover, the "killing norms" have shifted to the extreme. Eventually, the killers take delight in vengeful killing. A new addiction has been formed.

Mawson also developed a theory for what he called "transient criminality."[54] He reviewed evidence that under conditions of significant stress, such as found in natural disasters and combat, there occur the following changes:

> a partial loss of identity (or weakening of ego boundaries), and a sense of being depersonalized; a decline in self-esteem; alterations in memory and perception; a partial loss of other abstract standards including cultural, moral and legal rules; and a general decline in intellectual functioning, for example, loss of concentration, decline in problem-solving ability, etc.[55]

In Mawson's model, combat stress produces chronic increases in sympathetic arousal, which in turn produces stimulation-seeking behavior searching for familiarity, a recapitulation of the attachment activation system used initially by infants searching for a "secure base" (i.e., their mother) when in unfamiliar territory.[56] In combat, since no familiarity is to be found, further increases in sympathetic arousal (SNS) are generated. At this second step arousal, the individuals' "cognitive map" begins to disintegrate; more patterned, abstract, differentiated processes situating the individual in a complex of attachment memories, normative obligations, and familiar people and places disperse. What Baumeister calls the situated identity or individuated self dissolves, and the soldier becomes "deconstructed," that is, having an altered consciousness that is completely focused on the present action, with high SNS and hypothalamic arousal.[57] Instead of seeking the familiar (to soothe the stress), the combatants now turn their stimulus-seeking activities to the intense and the violent (to fulfill the need for stimulation). This generates an increased likelihood of impulsive, potentially injurious actions. Internalized moral standards disintegrate, and stimulus seeking self-generates in an upward spiral.

Dutton and Yamini also discuss "deconstructed thinking,"[58] a concept developed by Baumeister[59] to explain suicides and in which higher senses of social meaning are lost in a devolving focus on concrete action. The concrete action can be destructive and directed either internally (as in suicide) or externally (as in homicide). Based on analysis of the content of suicide notes, Baumeister described a "foreshortened future," narrowed focus onto simple, concrete actions and a loss of higher meaning associations. Dutton and Yamini applied the concept to case studies of matricide, typically an act driven by extreme and unresolvable emotional conflict.[60] In such cases, the killers who commit an ultimate taboo act of killing their mothers had no prior criminal history and appeared to undergo a transitory alteration of consciousness. Both Mawson's and Baumeister's models suggest a psychological transition away from norm regulated behavior and meaningful thought to impulsive, aggressive behavior and focused, concrete thought. The stress of combat, the fear of violence, and orders to kill all combine to increase the likelihood of such transitory actions. Again, individual differences in stimulation seeking and conscience may operate to keep some soldiers from killing (as in My Lai), but for most, the situation overwhelms the individual psychological functions and extreme violence ensues. For massacres, these individual transitions are operative, while for genocide the societal transitions described in Chapter 8 are operative.

From this psychological distinction, the killings in Rwanda were dispassionate slaughters aimed at generating genocide. They were performed more on a basis of moral disengagement, and the killers were not rageful but were nevertheless deadly. They reflected the result of normative transitions to killing as did the lynch mobs in the U.S. South. Rageful massacres appear to result from a "perfect storm" of social circumstances, including an opportunity to strike back at an outgroup that has been frustrating the military for some time, and an order perceived as a "license to kill" leading to deindividuated violence on the part of many perpetrators. They are performed under high emotion (rage but also crying) seemingly indicative of the release of pent-up feelings that accumulated in the preceding time period.

RAPE, SERIAL KILLERS, AND THE FORENSIC PSYCHOLOGY OF WAR

> Fantasy for the lust killer is much more than an escape, it becomes the focal behavior. Even though the killer is able to maintain contact with reality, the world of fantasy becomes as addictive as an escape into drugs.
>
> —Eric Hickey[1]

Where is this escape into fantasy during military rape and murder? Higher cortical functioning does not seem to disappear during massacres despite the high arousal and distorted perceptions reported by perpetrators. Instead, the actions of the military, especially in the massacres in Nanking and My Lai, seem the products of an altered consciousness as described in Chapter 9 rather than a fantasy. They also seem occasionally designed to violate universal taboos—the strongest being the slaying of family members in front of their own family or the commanding of family members to have sex with each other. Staub has termed this a "reversal of morality."[2] If a forensic examination were conducted on these perpetrators, their actions would indicate that they were aware of the humanity of the victims, the status of a family, and the extreme humiliation such actions would cause. It is for this reason that perpetrator reports of the victims as not human must be balanced against a forensic construction of what they had to know in order to behave as they did.

It is common to describe victims as "dehumanized" in these situations, yet no perpetrator group likely had previous sexual practices involving sex with nonhumans. One perpetrator put it somewhat differently. Chang describes the response of a Japanese soldier who answered her inquiry for her book. The soldier, Shiro

Azuma, said of the rape, "Perhaps when we were raping her (a Chinese woman), we looked at her as a woman but when we killed her, we just thought of her as something like a pig."[3] Can radical transformations of perception occur so instantaneously?

Baumeister et al. have found that perpetrator accounts of conflicts cast the conflict as an isolated incident without lasting implications.[4] However, these studies were not done on perpetrators at after-the-fact war crimes tribunals. Perpetrator accounts (such as Azuma's) that describe the enemy as an animal do not explain the perpetrators' behavior any more than their description of being inhabited by devils. It may be the perpetrators' way of trying to make sense of their own brutality, but it does not ultimately make sense. It fails for two reasons: most perpetrators have no history of brutality to animals, and their actions require knowledge of human thinking in order to enact emotional brutality on their victim. Their actions require a "theory of mind," i.e., how the victim thinks.

It is apparent that the actions of brutal rape, torture, and murder that occurred in all military massacres are similar to those committed by sexual sadists who serially kill.[5] The work of forensic profilers describe "the ultimate expression of the murderer's perversion being the (post mortem) mutilation of the victim"[6] and identify elevated rates of prior sexual abuse victimization among eventual perpetrators as a causal factor in murder and mutilation. Susan Brownmiller, in her classic, *Against Our Will: Men, Women and Rape,* compared actions described in the testimony of a U.S. Army soldier about sexually mutilating a Vietnamese woman to those of Albert DeSalvo, the so-called "Boston Strangler."[7] She found no difference. We review here the psychological studies of heinous acts in civilian conditions and compare them to apparently similar acts in military conditions.

RAPE

In the 1980s laboratory studies on "rape proclivity" amongst male college students, social psychologist Neil Malamuth asked students, "If you could get away with it, how likely would you be to rape?"[8] On a five point scale where 5 was "very likely" and 1 was "not at all likely," 35 percent indicated a 2 or higher. Students who indicated some likelihood of rape were more similar to actual rapists than to other students who indicated no likelihood in that they had more callous attitudes toward sex and believed in what Malamuth called "rape myths" (i.e., that women ask to be raped). Students indicating some likelihood were also more likely to exhibit low level nonsexual aggression towards a female confederate of the experimenter.[9] Of course, whether or not these boys would under- or overestimate their capability for actually raping is unknown. They may have had rape fantasies, but, as feminist writers have shown, rape fantasies that occur for 36 percent of women do not mean they really want to be raped.[10] The fantasy is viewed as a safe and guilt-free outlet that combines intense fantasy desire with an absence of guilt. Given that military rapists (such as the ones in Nanking) showed so little insight into their actions, one wonders how college boys' "predictions" of whether they might rape or not would have any validity.

In military situations, the chances of being caught and punished for rape diminish to near zero.[i] In the chaos of battle, all the necessary requirements disappear for an identification by a witness in civilian life. There is no chance for a victim to identify the culprit (if she lives) and no legal mechanism to file a complaint. In other words, the assumption of impunity that Malamuth's college subjects are asked to imagine is realized.

Military rape is especially problematic, it serves no military purpose, soldiers are not trained to rape, and yet, according to Brownmiller, it is commonplace.[11] It is sometimes argued that it serves the function of a terrorist threat, but that argument is undermined by the fact that it is typically covered up by perpetrators reducing its threat value. Documented rape occurred in Rwanda, Serbia, and Nanking, and was reported in El Mozote and My Lai. Beevor reported the universal rape of German women by the invading Red Army (see below). Sallah and Weiss reported rape as common practice by "Tiger Force" (the U.S. 101st Airborne) and described a post-rape murder. The sworn statement of James Barnett, who was in the 101st Airborne, described the doping (on the sedative Darvon), rape, and killing of a young Vietnamese woman, a mother with a baby. The soldier who raped her ordered Barnett to "grease her" (shoot her). Barnett shot her in the chest with an M16.[12]

Brownmiller chronicled the universality of rape in war and massacre.[13] In her words, "Rape is the quintessential act by which a male demonstrates to a female that she is conquered,"[14] and she describes rapes of Scottish women by the conquering British, mob rapes during the *Kristallnacht* attacks on Jews in 1938, rapes (in front of their parents) of Jewish girls during the German invasion of Poland and Russia (similar to Chang's descriptions of Nanking), and mob rapes of Vietnamese women by the U.S. soldiers. The military law of the United States, Japan, and Germany (in the German case it was "race defilement" for contaminating Aryan blood[15]) prohibited rape, yet its occurrence was commonplace. According to Brownmiller, captured German documents presented at the Nuremberg war crimes tribunal in 1946 corroborated the routine use of rape as a weapon of terror. German, Japanese, and Rwandan rapists dismembered and killed their victims afterwards.[16] Feminist notions of rape view men as raping when they can, and the fog and confusion of war certainly provide the anonymity. This view sees rape as sexually motivated with war conditions freeing up the normally constrained impulse.

---

[i]At the time of writing, a U.S. soldier (Sgt. Paul Cortez) was sentenced to 100 years in jail for the rape and murder of a 14-year-old Iraqi girl. However, a plea bargain agreement makes Cortez eligible for parole in 10 years. The rape and murder had been planned in advance and the soldiers covered it up by burning the family's home.

Brownmiller describes a diary page from James McCallum, an American missionary present at Nanking,

> Never have I heard of such brutality. Rape! Rape! Rape! We estimate at least 1000 cases a night, and many by day. In case of resistance, there is a bayonet or a bullet. We could write up hundreds of cases a day.[17]

These missionaries had excluded these rapes from their report of war damage. No raped women were called to testify at the War Crimes Tribunal in Tokyo, although the female director of dormitories at a college in Nanking gave a deposition. Several witnesses gave the same descriptions: girls dragged off by four or five uniformed Japanese soldiers and forced to service 15–40 soldiers at night. Some of these women were killed or mutilated after sex.[18] John Rabe's diary told the same story.[19]

Beevor described the rape of German women by the invading Red Army in 1945.[20] It began with brutal gang rape of women in East Prussia.[21] Survivors who were not too traumatized to talk described being raped by a dozen or more Russian soldiers.[22] These rapes were euphemized by the Russian Army as "immoral events," and soldiers were not punished.[23] Of interest to the sociobiological perspective (see Ghiglieri below) that armies use rape to inseminate conquered women is Beevor's observation that Red Army soldiers raped Ukrainian, Russian, and Belorussian women as well as German women.[24] The former three groups did not constitute "conquered peoples." As Beevor points out, "The widespread raping of women taken forcibly from the Soviet Union completely undermines any attempts at justifying Red Army behavior on the grounds of revenge for German brutality in the Soviet Union."[25] Beevor described four stages of rape by the Red Army.[26] The first was brutal or "aggravated" gang rape of all women by the first wave of Soviet soldiers. This occurred in East Prussia, the first German territory to be invaded, and was completely indiscriminate; any and all women encountered were raped. The second stage, which occurred in Berlin, was "selection" of women by "second-line" troops[27] who shone flashlights in the captured women's faces and chose their victims. The second phase did not involve gratuitous violence if the victim did not resist.

As Beevor puts it, "In war, undisciplined soldiers without fear of retribution can rapidly revert to a primitive male sexuality. The difference between the incoherent violence in East Prussia and the notion of carnal booty in Berlin underlines the fact that there can be no all-embracing definition of the crime."[28] The Red Army was drunk on both alcohol and power given the turn of events at Stalingrad where the situation had initially looked hopeless for them.[29] The third and fourth stages emphasize this point. The third stage, which also occurred later in Berlin, was the buying of sex for cigarettes or food, still a form of sexual coercion but without the violence.[30] The fourth stage involved cohabitation with "occupation wives" or "campaign wives" who were forced to choose a monogamous relationship with the invader in order to avoid multiple rapists.[31] Some of these latter relationships proved desirable to the Russians who chose to defect in order to stay with their occupation wife.[32] From these depictions, it appears that military rape is not a unified phenomenon. The first stage rapes were brutal expressions of victory and entitlement but were not focused on the vanquished women exclusively (non-German women were raped too). All forms of rape capitalized on a power advantage but differed in brutality and selectivity.

Simon considered the issue of military rape, focusing on the interplay of sexual and aggressive motives.[33] From studies of civilian rapists, he differentiated rapists whose primary motive was aggression and those whose primary motive was sexual. The latter, Simon argued, rarely used more force than was required to complete the rape (i.e., restraint), whereas the aggression-motivated rapist had a *modus operandi* that included "defilement, humiliation, injury and occasionally death."[34] In attempting to answer the question "Is every man a rapist at heart?" Simon gives a very psychiatric answer. Most rapists are not psychotic, he argues, and, apart from their tendency to rape, lead normal lives. Therefore, they are not different from the rest. Simon claims that a study of 94 men's erotic fantasies revealed that 33 percent included rape fantasies. He notes, though, that women have rape fantasies as well and that it is some distance from fantasy to action. Normal aggression, he points out, is often a part of sex play.[35] Of course, sexual and aggressive motives are often intertwined in serial rapists who kill.[36] Gilles de Rais (see below) typified the sexual sadist whose sexual arousal was increased by the pain and suffering of his victims. Serial killers often kill to gratify a sexual impulse in civilian conditions.[37] Murder after rape can occur as a way of preventing identification by the victim, or as a continuation of aggressive actions against the victim, which include aggressive rape.[38] Ressler and his colleagues describe a civilian rapist who stabbed his victim 50–100 times after raping her.[39] Such overkill is consistent with enormous rage and is far beyond violence required to dispatch a potential witness. Rape in military conditions also seems more consistent with this heightened aggression profile, consistent with the feminist notion of rape as an impulsive and expressive aggressive act, one not necessarily directed at any specific political group.[40]

Ghiglieri[41] posited a sociobiological motive for rape, of displacing genetic transmission of the enemy group by inseminating enemy women but fails to note that in military conditions, raped women are often killed after the rape.[42] This killing and the nonspecific nature of the selection of rape victims are contraindicative of genetic displacement through rape, and, if soldiers were motivated to spread their genes to the conquered group, they should protect women they had raped in order to maximize their own contribution to the gene pool. It seems that sociobiology must do more than select actions with apparent function and then claim genetic advantage for these actions while ignoring proximal actions with no genetic advantage. This tendency to "cherry pick" actions (which have apparent sociobiological function) in isolation from their action sequence is self-serving with regards to theory protection but does not accurately depict the entire action sequence. Sociobiology, for example, emphasizes genetic transmission as a motive while ignoring the simple fact that orgasm is pleasurable. If orgasm is pleasurable and can be obtained with an enemy woman with impunity, why is not military rape simply opportunistic sexual selfishness? Both feminists[43] and sociobiologists[44] miss this obvious point. In a thoughtful piece on rape motivation, Palmer reviews arguments that rape is solely power motivated and comes to the same conclusion, that these arguments are flawed.[45] In part, the argument turns on issues of rape, by definition, sex without consent, necessitating a power motive. However, this being said, motivation of sexual gratification is not dismissed. Palmer cited research where convicted rapists, interviewed after the fact, and hence having little to gain by giving self-serving answers, reported sexual motivation "solely or in part," in 84 percent of the cases.[46] In Beevor's description of rape by the Red Army, the victims were not exclusively German but Ukrainian, Russian, and Byelorussian as well; hence, the "pleasure-entitlement" notion seems better supported by historical evidence than does the sociobiological.[47]

Still, outside the pathology of serial killers such as Jeffrey Dahmer, Ed Gein, and Edmund Kemper, the mutilation and dismemberment of woman victims (such as occurred in Nanking and Croatia,[48] among other places) are hard to explain if the victim is viewed as human.[49] Yet the rape itself cannot be understood in terms of the victim being nonhuman. Her humanity is what invites either the sexual license or threat-dominance motives to play out. Both rape and bestiality are relatively (but equally) uncommon in civilian circumstances.[ii] Based on Krafft-Ebing's classic taxonomy of the "sexual deviations," the *Psychopathia Sexualis,* Hartwich argues that certain forms of animal sex were more accepted in other cultures and other times.[50] He cites a "well-known anecdote" that Frederick the Great, informed that a cavalryman had had sex with his mare, was reported to have replied, "The man is a swine and ought to be in the infantry."[51] However, in the military rapes reviewed here, no known perpetrator

---

[ii]Based on several research studies, estimates of sexual contact with animals is around 2–10 percent of the adult population, although it varies with region (and Kinsey's estimates were higher). Many countries have strict rules: Peru, for example, prohibits single males from owning alpacas. The U.S. Bureau of Justice Statistics puts rape incidence at 5–7 percent of adult females.[73] Only a small percentage of rapists use force beyond restraint. Even smaller percentages of zoophiles use force beyond restraint. As with pedophiles, many zoophiles justify their "relationship" as a love relationship. As Wikipedia puts it, "Defenders of zoosexuality argue that a human/animal relationship can go far beyond sexuality, and that animals are capable of forming a genuinely loving relationship that can last for years and which is not functionally different from any other love/sex relationship." Hence, killing someone "as a pig" does not really ring true; it is an invented "justification," along the lines of the "devil made me do it." Note that both Japanese and Rwandan soldiers also described themselves as possessed by devils during their onslaught.

or culture had prior acceptance of animal sex. Also, the raping of family members in front of their family suggests that a knowledge of a human social taboo against family sex is part of the consciousness of the military rapist. Its function is sadistic —to generate a human emotion of humiliation in the victim and her family. Rape in military situations seems to fulfill an ultimate expression of sexualized power and its presumed pathological extension—sadism.

In this context, social psychological studies of rape that used a measure called a "rape proclivity index" (the likelihood, given by a subject in a laboratory, that he would rape in the circumstances described) can be seen as naive.[52] These studies were predicated on the wrongful assumption that a college student actually knew what he would do and would reveal that tendency, both of which are demonstrably false. Imagine Malamuth asking recruits at boot camp how likely they would be to rape and break military law, and you will have some idea of how artificial and misguided this approach was. In military rapes, some amalgam of sexual opportunity and desire to humiliate and annihilate the victim seem to be at play. These darker motives are inaccessible to the college students studied by Malamuth. As further evidence, recall that Japanese soldiers arriving late at Nanking were appalled by what their fellow soldiers were doing.[53]

SEXUAL MURDER

The most famous sexual murderers are Caligula (Gaius Caesar) who routinely raped and murdered dinner guests and enjoyed watching executions[54] and the French fifteenth century nobleman Gilles de Rais who was convicted and executed for the torture, rape, and murder of hundreds of boys.[55] Both were sexual sadists; they derived sexual excitement from the pain of their victims. The extensive witness testimony convinced the judges that there were adequate grounds for establishing the guilt of de Rais. After he admitted to the charges on October 21, the court canceled a plan to torture him into confessing. The transcript, which included testimony from the parents of many of the missing children as well as graphic descriptions of the murders provided by de Rais's accomplices, was said to be so lurid that the judges ordered the worst portions to be stricken from the record.

According to surviving accounts, de Rais lured children, but mainly young boys who were blond haired and blue eyed (as he had been as a child), to his residences, and raped, tortured, and mutilated them, often masturbating over the dying victim or sodomizing them as they died. He and his accomplices would then set up the severed heads of the children in order to judge which was the most fair. The precise number of de Rais's infanticides is not known, as most of the bodies were burned or buried. The number of murders is generally placed between 80 and 200; a few have conjectured numbers upwards of 600. The victims ranged in age from 6 to 18 and included both sexes; although de Rais preferred boys, he would make do with young girls if circumstances required. One of de Rais's accomplices testified in court that de Rais seemed to take more pleasure in watching dismemberment than in sex per se.[56] After tearfully expressing remorse for his crimes, de Rais obtained absolution from the Church's punishment and was allowed confession, but the secular penalty remained in place. De Rais was hanged in France in 1440. Schlesinger[57] describes a number of famous "compulsive killers" such as de Rais, "Jack the Ripper," and Peter Stubbe, all of whom apparently derived sexual pleasure from mutilation (and, in the latter case, cannibalization) of their victims. Ed Gein, the Wisconsin compulsive killer who made lampshades from his victims' skin and decorated his house with body parts, was the basis for "Hannibal Lector," the Anthony Hopkins character, in the film, *Silence of the Lambs*. Most of these compulsive killers took "trophies," generally body parts from their victims. It is generally believed that taking trophies serves a power motive for the killer, generating a collection of reminders of his absolute power over his victims. If this is true, what then do we make of the taking of trophies by the lynch mobs in Georgia and Florida? Were these also reminders that the racial superiority ideals on which they had been raised were still validated by the souvenirs of the deaths of those who transgressed against them? In truth, the concept of power is often used in a circular fashion in explaining civilian violence. Sadistic killers are assumed to have greater power needs that they satisfy sexually, even up to the point of murder.[58] However, serial killers like Gary Ridgway (the Green River killer in Seattle) show no obsession with power outside of their penchants for killing, typically living mundane, unremarkable lives. There is no independent evidence for their powerlessness outside of their extreme violence, hence the circularity. Thousands of similarly powerless men are not violent. In some unusual way, a sense of power may have been fused to sexual fantasy and may provide some of the Beta process reinforcement for violence.

The trophy taking by the citizens in lynch mobs indicates another way that power may play out in mob killings. The power dynamic in these cases is sociohistorically determined. Losing the Civil War, with the ensuing threat to a lifestyle, it may be presumed, caused a sense of powerlessness in Southerners. Simultaneously, it presented a pathway to regain a sense of power, by defining who was the symbol of the war issue: African Americans, especially those who may presume to rise above their ranks in the subjective social order. Hence, the cause of the powerlessness also created the target group and focused the aim, so to speak. The target group was implicated (in the minds of the perpetrators) in the need deprivation that Staub described. The trophies indicate yet another of the many social behaviors described as power-enhancing by McClelland in his classic study of power motivation.[59] Collectors, McClelland described, enhanced their personal sense of power by the size of their collection. Each addition expanded the sense of self-worth. If one is collecting stamps, this is innocuous; if one is collecting body parts, it is pathological.

Through the use of "crime scene analysis" the FBI's Behavioral Science Unit has established different categories of sexual killers, typically differentiated into "organized" and "disorganized." The former is psychopathic and emotionless, a type of sexual sadist who kills for sexual arousal. Many serial killers fit this profile (such as Gary Ridgway).[60] Ridgway claimed responsibility for 48 documented corpses, with an estimated 12 more never found. He killed for 20 years without getting caught, a North American record for murderous longevity. Ridgway's confession, which he agreed to in court by pleading guilty to murder 48 times, took him five months to disgorge. The prosecution's 133-page narrative account of that confession offers a chillingly detailed and surprisingly literary look into his homicidal methods. As the narrative unfolds, what first becomes clear is that Ridgway took a more disciplined, careerist approach to serial murder. He sweated through every detail of finding, killing, and disposing of human beings. Though his IQ tested in the low eighties (normal is 100) and he barely made it through high school, he could recall each detail with a level of precision that staggered investigators.

Before his confessing began, Ridgway had been remarkable for his ability to keep his mouth shut. Investigators say that from the time he started strangling prostitutes in 1982 until he cut the deal in 2003 that spared him the death penalty, he never told anyone about his killings. After his arrest, his flabbergasted third wife, who had been with him for 17 years, told one of his lawyers: "He treated me like a newlywed." He kept no incriminating trophies of his kills. Police never found any evidence in his modest suburban house, although he said he strangled dozens of women there.

If a prostitute scratched or ripped his clothes, he would clip her fingernails before disposing of the body. He liked killing prostitutes, he said, because they were easy to pick up, they were slow to be reported missing, and, if they had any money on them, they ended up paying him for their own murder. Occasionally he would have sex with decaying corpses because necrophilia was less risky than killing another woman. If he pulled a muscle while dragging a body out into the woods, he said, he would claim a work-related injury and collect worker's compensation. Everyone who knew Ridgway well expressed amazement. One brother, who grew up sleeping in the same bedroom and who had gone on family outings with him up until the time of his arrest, told police that Ridgway had never behaved abnormally. Longtime co-workers and former girlfriends echoed this assessment. He was not a loner, he controlled his anger, he had no significant (known) juvenile criminal history, and he was either married or had a steady girlfriend all of his adult life. Ridgway's gift was to bury evil so deeply in the trappings of an ordinary life that it did not exist—except on the nights when he was out polishing his career skills. "His containment is amazing, especially given his pride in what he did," said Reid Meloy, a forensic psychologist and associate clinical professor of psychiatry at the University of California in San Diego.[61] "To have strong feelings of pride in one's career as a serial murderer and then not communicate that to anyone for 21 years is a measure of remarkable discipline." Meloy said Ridgway seemed to focus obsessively on self-preservation. "His sexualized homicidal aggression is very narrowly channeled and does not carry over into any other antisocial behavior" said Meloy. Fortunately, killers like Gary Ridgway are extremely rare. Most serial killers are not so careful nor appear so normal. Hickey describes the etiology of civilian serial murder as composed of early trauma, a tendency to dissociate, low self-esteem, and increasingly violent fantasies during "rehearsal," all leading to violent behavior.[62] Although, as Hickey points out, these predisposing factors are hidden from public view and "the vast majority of serial killers not only are judged sane by legal standards but are indistinguishable from non-offenders as they move within our communities."[63] Based on forensic evidence, organized or nonpsychotic serial killers appear normal until they are discovered. The typical response to the discovery is the typical news clip of neighbors saying what a "nice boy" he was and how amazed they are. The psychiatric diagnosis given to such perpetrators is sexual sadist, sadistic personality disorder, or antisocial personality disorder. One explanation, then, for the prevalence of military rape and murder is that these tendencies are split off in civilian conditions and, while experienced in fantasy, are held in check by almost everyone. In military conditions, the need to check the impulses is removed.

Disorganized serial killers are not so normal and are typically considered psychotic. They tend to position their victims' dead bodies and to insert foreign objects into the vaginas. Both these practices were also reported at Rwanda and Nanking. However, the killers in military cases were following orders to dispose of the "enemy" and took that order as license to wreak havoc on the enemy. No specific order was given to employ the practices they used. Also, the military sexual killers in these two locations had prior sex with living women, just before they killed them, more consistent with the profile of an "organized" killer.

As described above, murderers who mutilate the victim's body were found to be more likely to have been sexually abused[64] and are considered psychotic[65] (in the sense that they live within a sadistic fantasy world that captures their reality). Of course, we know nothing of the backgrounds of *genocidaires* in Rwanda or Nanking. However, the high level of participation in the killing and its public nature suggests several explanations: (1) that situational rather than predispositional (long term traits) factors explain the actions, (2) that early trauma is prevalent in military inductees and is acted on when conditions present themselves, or (3) that "hidden" sexual sadists are drafted into the military. The high incidence of military rape, however, argues against the last explanation. Sexual killers often

11

INDIVIDUAL DIFFERENCES IN VIOLENT AGGRESSION

It is always a simple matter to drag people along whether it is a democracy, or a fascist dictatorship, or a parliament, or a communist dictatorship. Voice or no voice, the people can always be brought to the bidding of the leaders. This is easy. All you have to do is tell them they are being attacked, and denounce the pacifists for lack of patriotism and exposing the country to danger. It works the same in every country.
—Hermann Goering, Commander in Chief of the Luftwaffe,
at the Nuremberg Trials

What kind of person can become a killer in combat? So far, the answer seems to be "everyone." From the killers/rapists in Nanking to the *genocidaires* in Rwanda to the U.S. Army, all combat killers were normal civilians without criminal records, before or after combat. The title and premise of Browning's classic study of "reserve police battalion 101," which we discussed in Chapter 9, was *Ordinary Men*.[1] Both Browning and Baumeister and Campbell pointed out that, in this group, there was evidence for extreme aversive reactions to the acts of killing and traumatic memories.[2]

In studying different types of heinous acts, Conroy came to the same conclusion. Calling his book *Unspeakable Acts, Ordinary People*,[3] Conroy reviewed torture of suspected IRA (Irish Republican Army) members by the British, of suspected criminals by the Chicago police and heretics by the Catholic Church (official policy since 1252), and of the murder and torture of civilians by the Israeli military. He concluded that the torturers were not pathological. Haritos-Fatouros examined torturers in Greece and also concluded that there was no evidence of sadistic or abusive behavior in their lives before they entered the army harbor beliefs about their target population that are similar to the intense form of out-group stereotyping described by Staub, often viewing woman as "whores" or targeting only prostitutes.[66] It appears that some sexual urges of their own are viewed as abhorrent, repressed, and then projected onto the victims.

While most "lust killers" who mutilate their victims are viewed as psychotic,[67] the same actions committed during mass social violence appear to be committed by men who have no prior signs of psychosis and who function well as soldiers. Prior to their sadistic outbursts, most held a rank in an army requiring discipline and surveillance of one's private life (e.g., Japan, United States, El Salvador) or lived, as far as we know, unremarkable lives (Rwanda). Many returned to normal social functioning after the orgy of violence (e.g., Nagatomi Hakudo, the Japanese doctor, and Lt. William Calley) or even after their "day's work."[68] Although some serial sexual killers appear "normal" (e.g., John Wayne Gacy, Ted Bundy, Gary Ridgway, *inter alia*), they live lives that do not bear the same scrutiny as members of the military. The question remains whether the situation provokes such horrific excesses or merely allows their potentiation.

The forensic model applied to "lust killers," an especially terrifying form of individual serial murderer, is one of acting out an arousing and repetitive fantasy. Hickey argues that the urge to kill is fueled by

> . . .well developed fantasies that allow the offender to vicariously gain control over others. Fantasy for the lust killer is much more than an escape, it becomes the focal behavior. Even though the killer is able to maintain contact with reality, the world of fantasy becomes as addictive as an escape into drugs.[69]

Hickey also describes "spree killers" who resemble military killers in that the killing is confined to a short span of time. However, Hickey reports that the forensic *modus operandi* of spree killers does not include sexual attacks,[70] whereas rape is commonplace in military massacres. The problem with all forensic explanations is that soldiers who commit massacres behave normally up to the point of the massacre. There is no evidence that, as with lust killers or spree killers, they have been harboring and are motivated by individual fantasies. Of course, as we described with Gary Ridgway, this is also undiscovered in civilians as well. Military rape presents some challenges to civilian forensic analyses that view crime as an outgrowth of an individual trait. At present, we cannot differentiate two explanations for rape and other brutalities against civilians. The first is that military conditions release a potential for brutality that is part of the human condition as described by Becker[71] or the "ancestral shadow" as described by Waller.[72] The second is that there are "hidden dispositions" in some persons that are activated by the arousal and impunity of the war situation. The latter explanation allows us to recognize that some soldiers decline to commit rape and murder.

and that there was nothing in their personal histories to differentiate them from an age-matched control sample of Greek males.[4] In an interview with infamous Greek torturer Michaelis Petrou in a Danish film called *Your Neighbor's Son,* Petrou admits he would have performed any type of torture he was asked to perform, including the torture of children in front of their father. In that interview, Petrou says he never thought he could do anything but obey.[5] War historians debate whether torture can shorten war and save lives.[6] With proper training, it seems, anyone can be taught to torture and to view it as a job that has to be done.

The U.S. Army's commission of inquiry concluded that the soldiers at My Lai were "generally representative of American youth assigned to combat units throughout the Army."[7] Social psychologist Phil Zimbardo, whose work was cited in Chapter 9, served as an expert witness for the defense of Sgt. Chip Frederick, accused of abusing prisoners at Abu Ghraib prison in Iraq. Zimbardo reviewed Frederick's performance file prior to his posting at Abu Ghraib (based on his being a prison guard in the United States), and found Frederick had received nine medals and awards.[8] Frederick was dishonorably discharged and sentenced to eight years of hard labor. Zimbardo maintains it was a show trial and argues that the entire system encouraged Frederick's behavior. The killers and torturers in war are "only following orders" (as Eichmann put it). They reenact the famous experiment by social psychologist Stanley Milgram where average citizens gave increasingly painful shocks (or so they believed) to a fellow participant in an experiment.[9] For those who hesitated, the statement "the research requires that you continue" was sufficient to get them to obey and administer shocks at the next more severe level. In one version of the experiment, when the shock recipient screamed in pain, 63 percent of subjects still shocked him to the limit. In another version, subjects had to hold the recipients hand down on a shock plate. In this version, 30 percent shocked to the limit.

Milgram, too, in his explanation for the degree of obedience he elicited, emphasized the power of the situation rather than personal aspects of the subjects in determining obedience. In My Lai, the "only following orders" defense was used but failed because 10–20 percent of those present committed no crimes at all.[10]

Since we tend to think in terms of psychological traits to explain extreme behaviors in civilian conditions, these trait explanations also get applied to war violence. However, those with sadistic or psychopathic personalities seem no more frequent in war conditions than in civilian life. The sadists, such as the infamous "Nazi doctor," Josef Mengele, were exceptions ("Dr. Auschwitz").[11] Mengele worked overtime at his job of deciding who would live or die. With his riding crop in hand, he examined each prisoner for a few seconds before stating "Links" (left) or "Rechts" (right). He also committed murder personally, including administering lethal injections, shootings, and beatings.[12] His studied detachment in selecting victims for the gas chamber was "interrupted by out-breaks of rage and violence, especially when encountering resistance to his sense of Auschwitz rules."[13] In some cases where mothers resisted being separated from their children, Mengele shot them both. Mengele's personal file recommended him for promotion and listed his numerous personal qualities and character.[14]

Eichmann was more typical of the efficient Nazi killing apparatus. Eichmann who "only followed orders" was never directly involved in killing but signed death papers for millions of Jews and was instrumental in the Wannsee Conference planning of the "Final Solution." Eichmann was also assessed by Jewish psychiatrists prior to his trial in Jerusalem, eager to discover what pathology could lead someone to sign off on the deaths of multitudes. He was found to be sane, leading to Hannah Arendt's comments on the "banality of evil."[15] Kelman found that Americans who were willing to find Calley "not guilty" were not equally predisposed toward Eichmann.[16] Our judgments about violence are extremely elastic depending on whether the in-group or out-group commits the action. The reader interested in how our feelings about authority and responsibility color judgments in such circumstances is referred to Herb Kelman's thorough study.[17] Those who thought Calley was responsible believed "even a soldier in combat has no right to kill defenseless civilians."[18] Those who thought he was not responsible believed "it is unfair to send a man to fight in Viet Nam and then put him on trial for doing his duty."[19] This latter group believed they would have shot civilians too and that most people would under those circumstances. Only 21 percent of them (compared to 34 percent of the group that thought Calley was responsible) believed that Japanese General Yamashita should have been convicted for war crimes.

No prewar evidence for sadism could be adduced from Mengele's life either (he was an "unremarkable" medical student interested in physical anthropology and genetics),[20] although it appeared in his behavior at Auschwitz. In his case, a submerged trait, repressed in civilian conditions, seems to have surfaced when given the opportunity. As Brickman put it, internal correspondence between Mengele's actions and a deep trait of sadism was created first, leading to external correspondence between his actions and the demands he placed on others.[21] Arendt claims that the Nazis "were not sadists or killers by nature; on the contrary, a systematic effort was made to weed out those who derived physical pleasure from what they did."[22] It is possible that they missed Mengele because he was adept at concealing "physical pleasure."[23]

Waller's example of Franz Ziereis also supports the notion of infinite malleability from normalcy.[24] Ziereis commanded Mauthausen, the most extreme of the Nazi killing camps. Stunned by the mundane appearance of Ziereis in a picture in the Holocaust Museum,[25] Waller repeats the reactions of court attendees at Eichmann's trial. Some passed out when he appeared in court as so nondescript. (Auschwitz prisoners also described Mengele as tall, blond, and Aryan. He was, in fact, of average height and dark haired.) Ziereis shot prisoners at random, personally beat some to death, gave some to his son to shoot, and was planning to blow up the rest when the Allies arrived at Mauthausen on May 5, 1945. Again Ziereis's background was unexceptional. As Waller put it, "those who knew him spoke of him as a model husband and father."[26]

ARE THERE NO INDIVIDUAL DIFFERENCES?

There seem to be two theories of what happens in extreme military violence conditions. One is that the social forces simply swamp individual differences and everyone acts the same way. The other is that, even in extreme situations, individual differences may persist. In My Lai, for example, some men refused the order to kill civilians, and one man (Hugh Thompson) aggressively resisted the orders and confronted Calley.[27] The film, *Schindler's List,* describes the actions of Oskar Schindler, who found ways around the predominant Nazi policies and acted to save the Jews he was able to hire. Some of the *Ordnungpolizei* declined to kill Jews,[28] despite the propaganda to which they had been exposed and the military pressure. Furthermore, those who did kill experienced severe reactions to the initial killings, including nightmares and emotional distress. Lifton estimated that 20 percent of German soldiers ordered to kill civilians suffered psychiatric problems such as anxiety, depression, and sleep disorder.[29] Greek torturers also experienced depression, nightmares, and irritability.[30]

Waller's escape from this conundrum is to suggest that "emphasizing that ordinary people commit extraordinary evil does not preclude the possibility that certain types of individuals may be more likely than others to engage in destructive obedience."[31] Waller develops a multifactor model to explain this process composed of four levels of contributing factors. These are the following: (1) our ancestral shadow: ethnocentrism, xenophobia, and a desire for social dominance, and (2) identities of the perpetrators: their cultural belief systems, moral disengagement, and rational self-interest. Both of these are "actor" (perpetrator) level factors. They then combine with (3) a culture of cruelty: professional socialization, binding factors of the group, and the merger of role and person, and (4) us-them thinking, dehumanization, and blaming of the victims. Waller argues that these four levels of factors acting in concert produce a new self for the perpetrator and that extraordinary evil becomes a part of that self. Waller's theory is a nice conceptualization of these various factors. Since level 1 factors exist for everyone, only level 2 factors could produce differences in reactions to the extreme situations occurring as a result of levels 3 and 4. The questions remain: Have we adequately explained why extraordinary violence existed for some perpetrators when routine killing would have sufficed? Can extreme violence be accounted for by the forces acting on perpetrators in the situation or do individual differences still exist?

Baumeister and Campbell argue that a shift to B process action (described in Chapter 9) does not hold for all soldiers because differential levels of guilt moderate the response.[32] If guilt did not operate, they argue, opponent process theory would predict that everyone would turn into a sadist. Hence, moral differences would still operate even in extreme circumstances. Toch found that 6 percent of his sample of violent men (in civilian circumstances) found pleasure in harming others.[33] Groth concluded that 5 percent of rapists derived pleasure from their victims' suffering.[34] Judging by descriptions of the massacres above and the universality of military rape, that number may be elevated by the context of war, possibly by lowering the restrictions placed by guilt under normal circumstances. Baumeister and Campbell see evidence for this contention in the number of hunters who enjoy the activity (far above 6 percent) because, compared to killing humans, the guilt is less. Given the "moral disengagement" and reconstruction of the violent event described in Chapter 8, the chances that guilt will be invoked lessen. Third, threatened egotism is a third form individual variable leading to violence. In the context of the Japanese Army or the Hutu, there was ample historical bases for lowered self-esteem. In the Japanese Army, it was part of basic training; with the Hutu, it was a historical belief of their inferior status vis-à-vis the Tutsi. It seems fair to conclude that, in situations of extreme violence, the majority of soldiers can be induced to commit atrocities and that a small minority will enjoy doing so. Another small minority declines or experiences extreme psychological distress from the perpetration (see also MacNair).[35] Of the soldiers who comply and kill, long term stress disorders are common,[36] typically PTSD (post-traumatic stress disorder), composed of unwanted recollections or "flashbacks," hyperarousal, nightmares, depression, or "psychic numbing." The latter symptom is often experienced during the killing and, hence, is called "peritraumatic."[37] Solomon et al. studies these combat stress reactions in Israeli soldiers, using clinical records of soldiers in the Lebanon War and finding that 48 percent experienced acute anxiety, 26 percent fear of death, 21 percent crying, and 18 percent psychic numbing. Psychic numbing is an automatic defense that serves to blunt threat and anxiety. Solomon compared these reactions with other published reports of combat reactions in other soldiers in other wars and found similarity. They concluded that the reactions were universal. Fear reactions are so intense during combat that paralysis of limbs and loss of sphincter control is common. Long term interpersonal and somatic complaints occur. Psychopaths, however, are unusually resilient and are not distracted by irrelevant anxiety stimuli.[38] While it seems that psychopaths may make effective soldiers, there are loyalty issues that make drafting psychopaths problematic.

Mawson's notions of the origins of arousal in combat situations, the cognitive shifts, and the high-intensity, escalating aggression that is a hallmark of deindividuated behavior begin to add explanatory texture to the forms of brutality displayed in massacres.[39] High intensity killing of long duration suggests a type of trance state accompanied by extreme arousal. There is a strong likelihood that actions carried out in short term transitional states are done under altered states of consciousness. Zimbardo describes an "expanded present"[40] and Baumeister a "foreshortened future"[41] and focus on discrete concrete acts as hallmarks of this cognitive state. Mawson also cites evidence (as did Solomon et al.) that dissociation (compartmentalization of experience) and "psychic numbing" are commonplace in PTSD[42] and that perpetration of violence can induce trauma in some individuals.[43] Less is known about peritraumatic states, but the neurological and physiological hyperactivity that contributes to PTSD originates in peritraumatic stress. Baumeister and Campbell provide evidence that 20–30 percent of battle soldiers suffer from PTSD caused by their own violent actions.[44] Hence, while some differences exist in the readiness of soldiers to act violently, still other differences exist in the emotional reaction they have to the killing.

A theory to account for the individual differences that appear to occur even during massacres must somehow point to the relative restraint shown by some soldiers (the "Hugh Thompson" profile), the routine "killing as ordered" by others, and the overkill (rape, torture, mutilation) performed by still others. This latter form of killing is inefficient and makes no sense militarily (unless it is used as a threat to others). In the Zimbardo et al. Stanford prison study, one-third of the guards became abusive, one-third followed the directives of the study, and one-third tried to do small favors for the prisoners.[45] Bandura[46] and Waller would argue that differences in "moral disengagement" in perpetrators may account for these differences, but this needs to be independently assessed so as to not be a circular argument. Also, moral disengagement better describes the robotic killing in Rwanda than the rageful extremes of other massacres.

There may also be differences in the extent to which Beta process enjoyment of killing occurs. Ferguson mentions one soldier describing a blood lust where the "ecstasy of battle, by which even the physical ecstasy of love...is less poignant."[47] A certain type of soldier, he notes, "comes to grips, kills and grunts with pleasure in killing."[48]

In one war memoir, a soldier described killing as follows: "(He) was at once the most abject and most exalted of God's creatures. The effort and rage in him made him pant and sob, there was some strange intoxication of joy in it, and again his mind seemed focused into one hard bright point of action. The extremities of pain and pleasure had met and coincided too."[49]

While these processes may occur in situations of violent anomie where orders to kill are understood (although not always issued), not all combatants engage in overkill. Waller argues that it is differences in "moral disengagement" and "identities." Mawson argues for individual differences in ego strength and stimulus seeking (arousability, identity maintenance).[50] Baumeister and Campbell argue for differential levels of guilt operating on B process shifts. None of these accounts per se explains the form of violence used by individual perpetrators.

To date, interviews with perpetrators have yielded little in the way of insight. Perpetrators in Nanking, My Lai, and Rwanda have been interviewed.[51] None could say anything more than that they did not understand their actions and seem to have been possessed by devils. Torturers in My Lai and Greece have been interviewed.[52] All seem to report a dramatically altered state in which violence was simply unquestioned, as with the normative acts we routinely practice. In My Lai, soldiers either rationalized killing as having been ordered or initially denied involvement in rape, etc., and then eventually described the Vietnamese women as "it wasn't like they were human...they were a gook or a commie and it was OK."[53]

It seems that, where possible, more thorough psychological assessments that go beyond self-reports of massacre perpetrators should be done. Suedfeld reported that "psychometric instruments and content analyses" were used to examine the Nuremberg defendants,[54] but Conroy reported that they were just Rorschach tests.[55] None of the assessments were able to pinpoint anything unique in the Nazi's personalities, family histories, or personal histories that would explain their actions in the Holocaust. It may well be that psychological assessment instruments designed for "normal" circumstances simply cannot make meaningful distinctions between those who act horrifically in war and those who do not.

In reviewing personality factors in becoming a torturer in Greece, Argentina, and Germany, Staub found the same traits as with *genocidaires:* authoritarianism, strong in-group conformity, and out-group devaluation.[56] However, in the final analysis, Staub warns about inferring personality traits from the in-role behavior, citing the immense pressures to behave according to the role demands. The explanation of extreme violence seems to be that of social pressures initiating some deeper violent process. Nevertheless, even in extreme circumstances where a majority of soldiers rape and kill, others do not—it is simply that we do not yet have the means of assessment to differentiate. It may well be that this distinction will be revealed, not by self-report assessments, but by brain scans of systems of neural connections.

FINAL THOUGHTS

As long as one believes that the evil man wears horns, one will not discover an evil man.

—Eric Fromm, *The Anatomy of Human Destructiveness,* p. 574

In Chapter 2, we reviewed Le Bon's description of the group mind, a state of consciousness that men in crowds descend to, which is characterized by impulsivity, thirst for obedience, and savagery.[1] Waller called this the "ancestral shadow," which he described as tendencies of human nature: ethnocentrism, xenophobia, and a desire for social dominance.[2] The latter emerges into aggression and violence. Waller's examination of these features is essentially sociobiological. He reviews studies that argue genetic fitness is served by favoring one's own and dominating outsiders. Waller argues that the origins of "us-them" thinking reside in early attachment, that the development of infant-caregiver bonds, essential for human survival, develop a strong sense of "us." In the first year of life, when these bonds are developing, an observable human universal is anxiety to strangers, what is called in adults xenophobia. As the attachment bonds develop, the stranger anxiety increases. By the age of six, children exhibit a strong preference for their own nationality—even before they fully understand what a nation is.[3] Hence, ethnocentrism and xenophobia may be human universals based on the attachment process itself, literally a dark side of attachment. As Waller puts it, "in forming bonds we deepen fissures,"[4] the definition of the in-group requires what is outside that group: the out-group. As Tajfel puts it, "We are what we are because they are not what we are."[5] We have seen that vicious propaganda usually precedes genocide, and this propaganda exaggerates the in-out group differences and portrays the out-group as having unjustly benefited from a historical event. In this view, Waller makes a profound point. We now know, since the groundbreaking work of Bowlby, that attachment is the most powerful human motive, grounded in our early survival.[6] The dark side of this powerful motive is the tendency to form out-groups to whom we can behave badly.

The conditions of this misbehavior have been thoroughly reviewed in this book: the toxicity of war and conflict, the manufactured gossip demonizing the out-group, the progression of actions toward a new norm of violence towards them, the individual changes toward rageful violence as acceptable. These conditions map a pathway to the existence of that state of consciousness called the group mind. Now some new evidence suggests that the group mind may exist, not just as a descriptive concept, but neurobiologically.

In reviewing both paleontological and anthropological evidence, Nell argues for a sociobiological development of cruelty.[7] More specifically, he argues that cruelty is a behavioral by-product of predation (seeking and killing prey), it is driven by reinforcers that derive from this historical adaptation, it provides benefits for genetic fitness (passing on one's genes) in forager, pastoral, and urban societies, and its enjoyment is a "culturally elaborated" manifestation of the initial predatory adaptation. Nell's argument, then, has implications for affective neuroscience and social psychology and, ultimately, for the understanding of cruelty in military massacres. His view leads us very close to and points toward a neural locus for the group mind.

CRUELTY

Nell defines cruelty as the intention to inflict and the actual infliction of pain on another living creature and sees it as an exclusively hominid behavior, originating with *Homo erectus,* dating back 1.5 million years. Punishment is cruel if its purpose is not to vanquish or disable the victim but to inflict pain, if the victim has no control over the intensity or duration of the pain, and if the victim is restrained and helpless. An act is cruel if the perpetrator or witnessing audience experiences arousal triggered by the victims' pain. Strong emotions are generated by the commission or witnessing of cruelty.

Hunting is defined as killing for nutrition and is also reinforced by the "pain-blood-death" complex. The non-nutritional use of hunting also derives from these reinforcers. Paleontological evidence shows that hominids were eating meat by 2.5 million years ago and that archaic *Homo sapiens* obtained almost all their dietary protein from animal sources. Hominids were hunters and hunted and used fire since 1.4 million years ago to both cook meat and repel larger predators (yes, the conclusion is that *Homo sapiens* ate raw meat for almost 1 million years). These twin roles of predator and hunted prey drove brain intelligence. As Nell puts it, "Folded within this brain development were the emotional drivers of the predatory adaptation, responding powerfully then as now to any opportunity to pursue, butcher and consume prey animals, whether as hunters making the kill or as scavenger."[8] Anthropological studies of hunting societies (such as the !Kung in Africa) find that humans hunt much as felines—with stealth and focus—and experience great arousal during the kill and for some time after.[9] Hunting is uneconomic for both animals and humans—the meat yield is sparse—wolves kill moose on only 5 percent of all hunts, and the !Kung generate only 100 calories of food per hour of hunt. Human hunters could do better if they focused on small game and plants. Nell argues the thought that big game hunting has another objective: it confirms male sexual desirability through the shedding of blood and the taking of life. In his view, predation, hunting, and the human fascination with pain-blood and death are homologies stemming from one common source, which he calls "the archetypal emotional-motivational processes that all mammals share,"[10] and argues that these processes are transmitted by biogenic amines produced in dendritic projections from neurons present in the nervous system of all mammals.

PREDATION AND PAIN-BLOOD-DEATH COMPLEX

Predation initially developed from competition for scarce resources in mammalian carnivores and carried over to the great apes and hominids. The reinforcers that are involved in its transmission are a set of linked conditioned stimuli called the pain-blood-death (PBD) complex—the prey's terror, its struggles to escape as it is brought down, the shedding of blood, the prey's vocalizations as it is wounded and eaten (often while still alive). A range of anticipatory reinforcers are triggered by this complex, including dopaminergic release and positive affect. The PBD complex served primitive man as a signal for impending satiation and sexual access and of the animals' death and, hence, his own survival (since primitive man was both the hunted and the hunter). Hence, it would serve, along with cues of secure attachment, as an ultimate signal of survival, the strongest of human motives.

With hyenas and lions, observations of killing indicate that victim death can take from ten minutes to an hour after the initial attack. Some victims are eaten alive, and most victims appear to go into a state of shock, initially fighting and struggling then ceasing to struggle. Most emit distress calls or screams when they are wounded and give off scents particular to death, including the scents of blood and semidigested stomach contents. Perpetrators also experience proprioceptive reinforcers from their own expression of violence and from the victims bucking and writhing and their own visceral reinforcers (i.e., through gastric distention). The experience is extremely arousing, with wild runs and victims' cries. Chimpanzees tear apart colobus monkeys:

> the chimpanzees visceral reaction to a hunt and kill is intense excitement. The forest comes alive with the barks and hoots and cries of apes, and aroused newcomers race

in from several directions. The monkey may be eaten alive, shrieking as it is torn apart. Dominant males try to seize the prey, leading to fights and charges and screams of rage. For one or two hours or more, the thrilled apes tear apart and devour the monkey. This is blood lust in its rawest form.[11]

Chimpanzees do not restrict their violence to nutritional hunting; 52 percent of Gombe chimpanzees die from attacks by other chimpanzees.

Electrical stimulation of the mammalian brain reveals three distinct "aggressive circuits" (neural networks): predation aggression, intermale and sex related aggression, and rage aggression. Predatory aggression is mediated by the "seeking system" (foraging, exploration, curiosity, expectancy, stalking). The neural network involved is the ascending dopamine pathways from the midbrain nuclei through the extended lateral hypothalamic corridor. This evokes the most highly energized exploratory and search behaviors,[12] although the specific behavior varies with the species (e.g., foraging vs. stalking). This dopaminergic response indicates that predation, per se, is highly rewarding—pleasurable despite the high level of energy demands on the predator (aversive exertion to the point of exhaustion involved in chasing and killing). The final stages of predation—aggression, the kill—associates pain cues (from the victims' cries and scents) with this pleasurable brain activation and with pleasurable proprioceptive feedback. This is the origin of the PBD complex. Nell argues that this complex has been shaped by millions of years of evolution. As Nell puts it, "one may thus hypothesize that a necessary condition for the success of the predatory and hunting adaptations is the conjunction of pain—the stress of exertion and the pain of injury—with a high level of pleasurable reward intermixed with sexual arousal, and that this is also true of fighting in its various forms—single combat...and war, though fighting is not by definition cruel, pain is inseparable from combat."[13] The regeneration of arousal and pain (the PBD complex) is rewarding. Aggression, pain, and sexuality are interconnected; "many neurons in the amygdala that are aroused by aggressive encounters are also aroused by sexual activity...the underlying motivation may be the seeking of safety."[14] Nell reviews the anthropological debate over the evolution of predation from ape to man, including the debate over whether australopithecus (a predecessor of *Homo sapiens*) was a violent carnivore. Neanderthals had high frequency of traumatic injuries—serious wounds, sprains, and breaks—which may indicate premortem twisting of limbs by a human killer.[i]

When consummation begins (eating, sex), brain opioids are released and arousal in the seeking system diminishes. The opioids may signal that the body is returning to homeostasis. The "rage system" circuit runs from the amygdala

---

[i]Anthropologists and paleontologists had not, by the time of Nell's writing, developed a technique to discern premorbid twisting of limbs from other traumatic assaults.

through the hypothalamus. Electrical stimulation in these areas potentiates aggression as does high levels of testosterone or low serotonin. Testosterone is highest in the mating season. The rage system and the seeking system are mutually inhibitory; when one turns on, the other turns off. Predatory attack is endogenously generated, and the cycle begins before the target is present. Rage attack, on the other hand, is triggered by the target's presence.

Cruelty, with its affective reinforcement, requires sufficient cognitive development for intentionality and a sufficient social basis to be carried out and elaborated. Once these foundations have been laid, cruelty comes to serve a variety of social functions such as punishment, amusement, and social control. Each of these modalities affirms the power of the perpetrator over the victim, recapitulating the original predation complex, and being further reinforced by survival and sexual access.

In the military massacres we reviewed, Nanking, El Mozote, My Lai, Sand Creek, the army was looking for the enemy (predation). In Nanking, there was minor resistance from the Chinese army, but it was not a battle where the Japanese were seriously threatened. In all cases, extreme cruelty ensued. The same with Tiger Force; they were predators, stalking the North Vietnamese and killing everybody in their path, maiming and taking body parts as trophies. Rage is obviously possible in war and massacre as we have seen, but Nell's sociobiological analysis, based on paleontological research, suggests that "search and destroy" missions generate the utmost cruelty.

In Nell's analysis, with the development of "civilization" and the early state, disciplinary cruelty became a modern extension of predatory cruelty and was put in place by states to serve several purposes. These included the control of enemies through terror, to punish captured slaves (and drive them to greater productivity) and to reaffirm the status of kings as regulatory authority. For these reasons, public entertainment such as the Roman Forum came into being as the new form of cruelty. Such cruelty was based on the principle that the harsher and more painful the punishment, the greater was the perceived status of the perpetrator in relation to the victim, and the more terrible the punishment, the more permanent its effects on the social system. The crowd in the Roman Forum is typically described as highly aroused and agitated. Occasionally, they became actively involved in the killing: when the monk Telemachus leaped from the stands in 404 CE and demanded that the killing be stopped, the crowd tore him apart.[15] The erotic force of blood and death had such an impact on raging sexuality that the prostitutes routinely gathered at the exits from the Coliseum where they did a brisk trade.

Nell argued that these social control functions have existed historically and presently include "public entertainments that are unwillingly stopped short of frank killing...technologies of cruelty as instruments of war...(and) coercive forces of the state and its opponents to use confessional and disciplinary cruelty for political ends...deliberate infliction of pain, as with any other manifestation of interpersonal power, enhances the status of the perpetrator...the striking stability of the social uses of cruelty for punishment, amusement and social control suggests that the underlying motivational structures have a species-wide evolutionary origin."[16]

Nell sees the contemporary warrior as the progeny of the hunter/predator and our fascination with pain-blood-death as also having this origin in our early prehistory. Nell proposes the study to confirm his theory, a study that, at the time of writing, has not yet been done. It would involve exposing research subjects to scenes of pursuit, mutilation and killing of human victims, and their pain vocalizations, as well as doing functional MRIs[ii] to see if cerebral pathways could be found that were homologous to those that evoke predatory gratification in felines, canid, and primate predators. A fascinating idea and one that most university ethics committees would never pass—the idea of showing "search and snuff" films to research subjects—is not going to happen anytime soon. Apart from that issue, there are others; namely, would parts of the orbitofrontal cortex that govern impulse control also light up in conjunction with the cerebral pathways associated with predation? If so, it might demonstrate an oppositional neural response to cruelty. Brain research seems at times to focus on only selected parts of the brain, omitting other relevant brain structures. Some current research with humans indicates considerable individual differences in neural regulation of the ability to regulate negative emotions[17] and appear to involve inhibitory connections from the prefrontal cortex to the amygdala, well known to involve anger processing[18] or deactivation of the ventromedial frontal cortex (during imagination of aggression by the subject)[19] or reduced activity in frontal areas (in affective but not predatory murderers).[20] If, as Nell defines it, cruelty requires an intention to inflict pain, how can we study it using animals who do not have the cognitive ability to form such intentions? Yet, if we study humans, we find that, even with the development of sophisticated brain scans, we still do not know enough to localize "cruelty" in one brain area or to explain individual differences. Different studies find activation in different areas. Raine et al. characterize the results of their study as indicating a "brake failure" (reduced prefrontal function) in concert with generation of high effect (amygdaloid function increases) similar to stepping on the accelerator.[21] Yet this occurred only in "rage killing" where the perpetrator was found not guilty by reason of insanity. Nell would have predicted atypical brain activity for predatory murderers, but

---

[ii]FMRIs measure microscopic fluctuations in blood volume in the body, including the central nervous system and brain. Hence, it can provide a new look at brain function that was previously unknown. FMRI measures "light up" neural networks that function simultaneously when certain stimuli are viewed or thoughts imagined.

in the Raine et al. study predatory murderers did not differ from nonviolent controls.

Miller cites studies that show frontal lobe injury rarely produces postinjury violence in previously nonaggressive persons.[22] Miller views serial predatory killers in civilian contexts as "antisocial variations on phylogenetic predation"[23] with brain mechanisms on the same continuum as those related to normal forms of hunting. On the other hand, Money views sexual sadism as a brain disease that affects the limbic centers and pathways in the brain responsible for sexual arousal, mating behavior, and reproduction, including the amygdale, hippocampus, and hypothalamus.[24] Money's view is more compatible with that of Nell as to the existence of a potential neurological structure housing the "group mind." Davidson et al. posit a neural circuit for impulsive aggression consisting of the orbital frontal cortex, amygdala, anterior cingulate cortex, and "other connected regions."[25] They see impulsive violence as a consequence of faulty emotion regulation due to dysfunctions in the prefrontal cortex. However, this may apply to consistently impulsive civilian perpetrators but not to military aggression by people who are not aggressive in civilian conditions. Certainly the neurological contributors to aggression are known,[26] and some even are state dependent,[27] including both anticipated loss of attachment, impulsivity, and predation. To date, however, more consistency and specificity in the brain scan research is required before a neurological group mind is proclaimed. By this, we mean that replications of neural network findings by independent studies are required and that only these specific neural networks and not other brain areas are found to be involved. Stein echoes this position in a paper on the "neurobiology of evil."[28]

Differentiating what he calls "banal evil" (e.g., Eichmann) from sadistic evil, Stein argues for a preliminary approach to psychobiological bases. Banal evil, he argues may involve a dissociation of corticostriatal processing from limbic input (literally, reason without emotion) while sadistic evil involves a dissociation of limbic processing from frontal controls (literally, passion without reason). These "dissociations" beg the question of how they could arise in a sociopolitical context. Stein warns against reductionism, the attempt to explain all evil as a psychobiological process. He sees the proposed psychobiological dissociations as an end product set in a sociopolitical context. However, the explanatory role of neurobiology is limited in this context; it can guess at individual differences in neural functioning during extreme sociopolitical conditions but not much else. The best case scenario for future fMRI research may be this: that "predatory sequence stimuli" shown to subjects might reveal a brain-behavioral network that reacts to predation. If this is so, it might weaken the argument that rage and violence is primarily fear-based. Until that time, however, we are stuck with two competing hypotheses for extreme violence; as either the "disguise of panic" (Becker) or as an extension of acquired predation (Nell).

WAR CRIMES TRIALS

As much as one might desire some form of retributive justice in the horrendous events we have described, war crimes trials have had mixed results.[29] Although the Japanese commanding officer for the Philipines was found guilty of war crimes and hanged, such severe punishment is rare. Of 1,000 Nazis tried for war crimes between 1959 and 1969, less than 100 received life in prison. In the years that followed, 6,000 were convicted but only 157 received life imprisonment.[30] The trials of Nazi judges were highly controversial.[31] They had handed out 26,000 death sentences for "crimes" such as making an anti-Nazi joke, but not one judge was ever convicted.[32] The trials of the *genocidaires* in Rwanda have been stalled, delayed, and largely unproductive, bogged down with debate over whether trials should be conducted before an international tribunal or before Rwandan courts (USIP.org). No severe punishments and no death sentences have been meted out. Saddam Hussein, on trial in Baghdad for his massacre of the Kurds, "sat in the dock in his trademark double breasted suit, sometimes looking uninterested, ignoring proceedings and reading the Koran."[33] His disinterest occurred while a woman was describing her family being buried alive. Eventually, Saddam was sentenced to hang, as were two of his "henchmen," and several other party officials received 15 years to life. Kurds and Shia Muslims in Iraq celebrated. One father "danced with his son's bones in the street."[34] The son had been killed by Saddam's forces. "In the north, a Sunni man strapped an explosive belt around his waist and vowed to take justice." Some political journalists speculated that the only thing that would unite Iraq was another dictator like Saddam.[35] Although Saddam was "put to justice" and hanged, at the time of writing, Iraq was in chaos with more killings than before it was invaded by the United States and Britain.

At the International Military Trial of the Far East in Tokyo in 1946, over 200,000 people attended and the evidence overwhelmed the defense. Estimates of the number killed ranged from 3,000 (by the Japanese) to over 300,000.[36] When all was said and done, seven Japanese officers were convicted and hanged.[37] The commander of the Japanese Central China Expeditionary Force, Matsui Iwane, took the major share of the blame. He was sick, however, and not present in Nanking at the time of the atrocities.

At the trial, evidence was presented that Nanking was just one of a "tiny fraction of atrocities committed by the Japanese during the war,"[38] just as Sallah and Weiss argue that My Lai was just one of numerous slaughters of the Vietnamese.[39] Hence, because of the "fog of war," the so-called "*chiffe noir*" (unreported statistic) of war crimes is huge. El Mozote was reported only because two survivors hid and crawled out to tell the story.

Besides the detection problem, there is the problem of laying blame. How far up the hierarchy of command does one go in a situation where soldiers are duty bound to obey? This was the issue at the trials of both Adolph Eichmann[40] and William Calley.[41] We saw these latter issues in the debate between Goldhagen's analysis of the Holocaust as being carried out by "willing executioners"[42] versus Browning[43] and Eley's[44] view that the response was mixed with currents of ambivalence and resistance. Eichmann famously declared that he was "only following orders" and that, had he not enacted them, someone else would have. This rationalization is exactly what the *genocidaires* in Rwanda described after their court hearing. Iris Chang[45] suggests that Commander Matsui Iwane was a scapegoat and that Japanese policy of brutality extended far beyond Nanking.[46]

The most famous of all war crimes trials, the Nuremberg trial of Nazi war criminals, was originally proposed by a person who was guilty of genocidal acts himself: Joseph Stalin.[47] Stalin wanted a "show trial" where the verdict was known in advance but the public display was important. Such trials had been used in the Soviet Union against political foes in the 1930s. Churchill proposed in November 1943 to take the 50–100 Nazi leaders out at dawn and shoot them and to reserve trials for subordinates.[48] Churchill's view was that the political decision to shoot the leaders was the only way to approach the severity of their crimes and had an expeditious quality that drawn out legal wrangling lacked. The United States was in agreement and War Secretary Henry Stimson was checking the basis in international law for U.S. soldiers participating in such firing squads without facing legal repercussions themselves.[49] Churchill had the list of 100 top Nazis drawn up, and it was to be presented to Stalin for his approval. Stalin had argued for the show trial so the decision would have had the appearance of legal outcome and not vengeance. In his memoirs, Churchill wrote, "On major war criminals Uncle Joe took an unexpectedly respectable line... there must be no executions without trial otherwise the world would say we were afraid to try them."[50] U.S. Justice Robert H. Jackson pressed the U.S. case for a real trial, based on new developments in international law. The Soviets argued that a real trial was not necessary because the Nazis had already been convicted by governments. Eventually, the U.S. position held the day and Jackson became one of the chief prosecutors.[51]

The Nuremberg trial charged the Nazis with "crimes of peace"; that bellicosity itself was an international crime, with war crimes—mistreating POWs and civilians, and "crimes against humanity" (systematic murder, extermination, and deportation). The word "genocide" was not used at the trial. Jackson was interested only in the first category of crimes and assigned the British and U.S. prosecutors to them, leaving the French and Soviets to prosecute the other two categories. Of the 12 Nazis prosecuted, 11 were found guilty and sentenced to death. Twelve other trials ensued and 200 top Nazi officials were convicted. The Americans began hanging Nazis on October 15, 1948, in batches of up to 15, every Friday for the next four months.

However, as Kadri reports, the trial became a case against Germany. Prosecutors paid lip service to individual guilt and repeatedly slammed the entire German people (almost the opposite of the Far East Trial in Tokyo).[52] The trial was seen across Germany as a political swindle that exaggerated atrocities. It took some time for Germany to come to terms with the Holocaust. Japan still denies the Rape of Nanking and refuses to pay reparations. Even in Nuremberg the prosecution was difficult, despite the reams of evidence against the defendants. The prosecution of Hermann Goering was a case in point. Goering was arrogant and contemptuous of the proceedings, in much the same way as Saddam Hussein. Goering was also very bright and during the proceedings wavered between anger and amusement. Jackson himself cross-examined Goering. Goering was up to the task, parsing questions about the early days in Germany with the arrogance of a world class historian. Jackson began to cut off Goering's answers and was corrected by the judge (Francis Biddle of the United States). The cross-examination hit a nadir when Jackson thrust a piece of paper at Goering and demanded that he accept that Germany was preparing to invade the Rhineland in 1935. Unfortunately for Jackson, the paper had been mistranslated and Goering took great pleasure in pointing out that it spoke only of dredging arrangement if military movements were to take place. Jackson rebuked Goering for his "arrogant and contemptuous attitude" and was himself rebuked by the judge adjourning for the day.[53]

Scottish prosecutor, Sir David Maxwell-Fyfe, took over the next day (March 20, 1945) with a set of questions that focused on war crimes, specifically, the shooting of 50 British RAF prisoners of war (converted into Americans in the film, *The Great Escape*). The line of questioning rattled Goering whose Teutonic chivalry embraced a code whereby enemy combatants were expected to try and escape. Goering went on the defensive and wound up concluding that the incident "was the most serious incident of the whole war."[54] Then Maxwell-Fyfe asked him about the deaths of 6 million Jews. Goering claimed he knew nothing of this and stated, "Not even Hitler knew the extent of what was going on," to which Maxwell-Fyfe asked, "Do you feel that you still have to be loyal to Hitler?" Goering responded, "I believe in keeping one's oath not in good times only, but also in bad times when it is much more difficult." At this point Maxwell-Fyfe read aloud a statement from Hitler in April 1943 that Jews "had to be treated like tuberculosis bacilli, with which a healthy body may become infected...Nations which do not rid themselves of Jews perish."[55] Maxwell-Fyfe asked Goering if he still believed Hitler knew nothing of extermination plans. Goering confirmed that Hitler did. In November, film footage of the walking cadavers of Belsen and Buchenwald was shown in court.

Public memory was kinder to Jackson. He was portrayed as a successful prosecutor by Spencer Tracy in the film, *Judgment at Nuremberg*. The closing speech by the prosecution at Nuremberg was given by British Attorney General Sir

Hartley Shawcross at the end of July 1946. Shawcross's spellbinding two day summation was peppered with instances of human suffering and ended with what Kadri calls "the real meaning of genocide."[56] This was the unforgettable description of a Ukrainian engineer named Herman Graebe who had watched Jewish families being herded out of trucks by whip-wielding SS militiamen. He recalled one family in particular, naked and saying goodbye for the last time:

> An old woman with snow white hair was holding a one year old child in her arms and singing to it and tickling it. The child was cooing with delight. The couple were looking on with tears in their eyes. The father was holding the hand of a boy about ten years old and speaking to him softly, the boy was fighting his tears. The father pointed to the sky, stroked his head, and seemed to explain something to him...I well remember a girl, slim and with black hair, who, as she passed close to me, pointed to herself and said "twenty three". I walked around the mound and found myself confronted by a tremendous grave...Some were lifting their arms and turning their heads to show that *they were still alive. The pit was two-thirds full. I estimated that it already contained about one thousand people.*[57]

The ultimate problem with a military tribunal is that no punishment can fit the crime.

POSTSCRIPT: THE FINAL SUMMATION

Our approach in this book has been to use an examination of generalized social-psychological processes that are common to all genocides or to massacres. Where relevant, we have pointed out shortcomings in our understanding of extreme violence. Hence, we have sought to outline psychological processes engaged in during the events (or, in the case of genocide, just prior to the event) and especially those that contribute to transformation of the perpetrator. We have paid scant attention to historical precedents. Initially, we have attempted to relate the behavior of *genocidaires* to forensic explanation. Historical and socioeconomic explanations seem better at accounting for the conditions initiating genocide or pogrom, but, once the violence begins, individual actions require individual explanation. We have struggled with the issue of whether toxic situations can produce extreme violence in all, and, if so, whether they do so by disinhibiting a sadistic aspect of the human condition[1] (e.g., Goldhagen's argument for actions of many Germans during the Holocaust) or whether certain individuals enact disproportionate violence while others passively enable. It seems that even in "toxic situations" where the level of individual atrocity is raised, individual differences continue to exist. Zimbardo et al.[2] and Baumeister and Campbell[3] both provide evidence on this point, and in My Lai, as we recounted, some soldiers shot civilians, others refused, and some tried to stop the massacre and rescue Vietnamese.[4] That being said, it appears that the majority of members of any group, regardless of nationality, religion, or any other demographic indicator, are capable of the most horrific violence against fellow humans when a "perfect storm" of social conditions exists.

Taking into account Staub's work and viewing the extreme violence described here, it seems that one conclusion regarding mass slaughter is to say that, symbolically, an out-group becomes a threat to an in-group's view of their place in the world. It is also safe to conclude that the division of in-group and out-group is entirely subjective. DNA results showed no differences in victims of tribal violence in Bosnia, but to each group the definition of Serb, Muslim, or Croat was of utmost importance at a life and death level. Also, political alliances are ephemeral and with them go the differentiation into in- and out-groups. Few Americans would regard the Khmer Rouge or Saddam Hussein as allies, but they both were at one time. This "primal division" may originate, as Conroy suggested, in the initial attachment bond, and it may constitute a form of "group egotism" similar to that described by Baumeister and Campbell. The in-group view may be inflated or exalted but once held with conviction and socially supported in the ways Staub describes, it generates the conclusion that any and all actions against the out-group are justifiable acts of perceived revenge. Without "subjective revenge" as a motive, it is difficult to explain the sadism and savagery displayed. Of course, subjective revenge can include the perception that an out-group is standing in the way of a groups' exalted view that they are entitled to world dominance.

It is apparent, too, that the explanation of the specific forms of violence directed toward the out-group—rape, mutilation, torture, etc.—is not forthcoming from current psychological knowledge. All are forms of extreme sadism, but how sadism is developed in specific ways is still not clear. We do know that perpetrators are stressed, fearful, and desensitized, and view their victims as threats or as subhuman, yet they utilize forms of sadism that require human mores and reactions in order to have effect. We know that B process dominance with time diminishes revulsion to one's own brutality. Forensic psychology views such actions as the consequences of pathological developmental issues. Social psychological explanations (e.g., Zimbardo[5]) have suggested that "state" aggression can be produced by pathological situations. Zimbardo suggested that power imbalances, lack of oversight, and competing purposes amongst groups were a toxic mix and produced abusive behavior from normal college age men under such circumstances. It seems, however, that psychology has not attempted to account for the extremity of massacre or the implications of massacre for notions of the human condition. Part of this shortcoming may be due to the limited methods of experimental psychology.

SUICIDE BOMBERS

As I write this, suicide bombing has become commonplace. Generally perpetrated by Muslims (although used worldwide by groups such as the Tamil Tigers in Sri Lanka and Japanese kamikaze who crashed their planes into U.S. ships),[6] the suicide bomber generates two questions for many: Why would someone kill innocent civilians? Why would they give up their own life? The answer to the first question seems to be that they see the action as publicizing a political cause; hence, the innocent civilians are expendable. The second question has an answer, I believe, in the mix of political and religious motives for suicide bombers. The Japanese kamikaze believed he was serving his emperor who was next to God. His place in the hereafter would thus be assured. This belief in "attachment in perpetuity," as we saw back in Chapter 1, was also generated in Christian Crusaders, who believed they were fighting a holy war and, hence, that their war was just and they would be rewarded with heaven. Islamic suicide bombers also believe they will be ensured a place in heaven for fighting the jihad—the holy war. This place in heaven will be accompanied, in many cases by a supply of virgins (72 is the usual number given)[i] and reconnection with family and loved ones. This belief in a heaven where one will connect with the family is as widespread as the range from Christian gospel music to Islam. Gospel lyrics are filled with references to meeting one's dear departed on the "other shore" (i.e., across the River Jordan separating us from heaven). As such, this belief constitutes the most powerful wish in the human imagination: that of perpetual attachment. Resting on the twin pillars of attachment security and a sense of an infinite future after death, the belief erases our fears of both separation and death simultaneously. It is for this reason, with some sociopolitical direction, that people are willing to blow themselves up for the cause.[ii] Note that having a political objective is not inconsistent with this religious reward so long as pursuing the political objective has become "sanctified" as were the Crusades by the pope or in the case of jihad.

---

[i]The 72 virgin view is explained in thestraightdope.com this way: Nothing in the Koran specifically states that the faithful are allotted 72 virgins apiece. For this elaboration we turn to the *hadith,* traditional sayings traced with varying degrees of credibility to Muhammad. Hadith number 2,562 in the collection known as the *Sunan al-Tirmidhi* says, "The least [reward] for the people of Heaven is 80,000 servants and 72 wives, over which stands a dome of pearls, aquamarine and ruby." The 72 virgin view is disputed in a Web article in commondreams.org by Abhinav Aima written in 2004 who argues that the rage is political not religious.
[ii]But see this excerpt from an interview with Dr. Robert Pape[13] (University of Chicago): Over the past two years, I have collected the first complete database of every suicide-terrorist attack around the world from 1980 to early 2004. This research is conducted not only in English but also in native-language sources —Arabic, Hebrew, Russian, and Tamil, and others—so that we can gather information not only from newspapers but also from products from the terrorist community. The terrorists are often quite proud of what they do in their local communities, and they produce albums and all kinds of other information that can be very helpful to understand suicide-terrorist attacks. This wealth of information creates a new picture about what is motivating suicide terrorism. Islamic fundamentalism is not as closely associated with suicide terrorism as many people think. The world leader in suicide terrorism is a group that you may not be familiar with: the Tamil Tigers in Sri Lanka. This is a Marxist group, a completely secular group that draws from the Hindu families of the Tamil regions of the country. They invented the famous suicide vest for their suicide assassination of Rajiv Ghandi in May 1991. The Palestinians got the idea of the suicide vest from the Tamil Tigers. The central fact is that overwhelmingly suicide-terrorist attacks are not driven by religion as much as they are by a clear strategic objective: to compel modern democracies to withdraw military forces from the territory that the terrorists view as their homeland. From Lebanon to Sri Lanka to Chechnya to Kashmir to the West Bank, every major suicide-terrorist campaign—over 95 percent of all the incidents—has had as its central objective to compel a democratic state to withdraw. Dr. Pape is the author of a book called *Dying to Win.*

The question is, Is there any limit to the potential destruction in the present and on earth when one believes in the infinite future in heaven? Feldman, for example, argues the chilling thought that the combination of jihad and nuclear war is inevitable.[7] Furthermore, since jihad precludes any possibility of deterrence, the launching of a nuclear warhead, despite the inevitable retaliation and Muslim deaths, is a distinct possibility. This is because those Muslims killed in the retaliation would also be guaranteed their place in heaven since they died as "collaterals" in jihad. Feldman reviews the elastic and expanding definition of acceptable targets for jihad; first Israeli woman and children, then Americans, then Shi'ites, and then Sunnis of unstinting orthodoxy. Feldman argues that a nuclear Islamic state would be willing to use nuclear weapons for jihad and that those killed in retaliation would all be seen as martyrs. What is more, as with some Christian sects, Islam has an apocalyptic vision of the end of the world and a religious renaissance. Our destructive technology has grown immensely but our tribalism remains. How far have we evolved from Pope Urban's urging for a crusade?

Psychology needs a form of "forensic ethology" that reconstructs the patterns and motives for behavior from "natural observation" tribunal transcripts of massacres or survivor reports that exist and can be followed up with studies of massacre perpetrators under "normal" (i.e., postwar) conditions. Corroborative information could be sought regarding violent tendencies in civilian settings. Conroy already used some of these techniques in his book, citing testimony about abuse of civilians given by Don Dzagulones, the Americal Division interrogator at My Lai, given to the Viet Nam Veterans Against the War hearings in 1971,[8] as well as books written by torture victims. Some of these techniques are used in psychohistorical approaches.[9] However, in a forensic analysis, more weight is put on what information and state of mind would have been required for specific actions to occur (see, for example, Dietz et al.[10]). Darley has suggested "probes into the conceptual world of individuals who are enlisted into real-world harm-doing socialization processes."[11] Only such a methodology may answer the ultimate question of whether normal men who show no prior propensity for violent crime can act like sexual sadists during a pogrom. It may be that a propensity for such actions is supported by neural structures that have developed from our times as hunters/predators. It may be that this is the structure of the group mind alluded to by Le Bon. If we are to thrive on the planet, however, we need a political will to collectively stop the violence and an understanding of its basis. Instead of denying atrocities, we must accept that they have been common in war. In the film *Apocalypse Now*, Colonel Kurtz, the "rogue" officer who has severed heads sitting around his compound, marvels at the resolve of the Vietnamese. He recounts how the Americans have inoculated the children in a Vietnamese village and the Viet Cong came through the next day and severed all the arms that had been inoculated (see epilogue). Those who believe that the war in Iraq, described by U.S. Defense Secretary Donald Rumsfeld as the first war of the twenty-first century, is different from the horror we have seen in this book, should read Evan Wright's *Generation Kill.*[12] According to Wright, these soldiers came "pre-hardened" because of a prior life of video games focused on killing and inner-city gang war. Perhaps, before deciding to enter into a war, we need to factor in this inevitable component of necessary ruthlessness.

EPILOGUE

From Francis Ford Coppolla's film, *Apocalypse Now* (1979):

Kurtz: I've seen horrors...horrors that you've seen. But you have no right to call me a murderer. You have a right to kill me. You have a right to do that...but you have no right to judge me. It's impossible for words to describe what is necessary to those who do not know what horror means. Horror. Horror has a face...and you must make a friend of horror. Horror and moral terror are your friends. If they are not then they are enemies to be feared. They are truly enemies. I remember when I was with Special Forces. Seems a thousand centuries ago. We went into a camp to inoculate the children. We left the camp after we had inoculated the children for Polio, and this old man came running after us and he was crying. He couldn't see. We went back there and they had come and hacked off every inoculated arm. There they were in a pile. A pile of little arms. And I remember...I...I...I cried. I wept like some grandmother. I wanted to tear my teeth out. I didn't know what I wanted to do. And I want to remember it. I never want to forget it. I never want to forget. And then I realized...like I was shot...like I was shot with a diamond...a diamond bullet right through my forehead. And I thought: My God... the genius of that. The genius. The will to do that. Perfect, genuine, complete, crystalline, pure. And then I realized they were stronger than we. Because they could stand that these were not monsters. These were men...trained cadres. These men who fought with their hearts, who had families, who had children, who were filled with love...but they had the strength...the strength...to do that. If I had ten divisions of those men our troubles here would be over very quickly. You have to have men who are moral...and at the same time who are able to utilize their primordial instincts to kill without feeling...without passion...without judgment...without judgment. Because it's judgment that defeats us.

Kurtz: [voiceover] The horror...the horror...

Kurtz: We must kill them. We must incinerate them. Pig after pig. Cow after cow. Village after village. Army after army.

From the film *Apocalypse Now,* screenplay by Francis Coppola
and John Milius
Quoted in Internet Movie Database

NOTES

PREFACE

1. Clarens, C. (1967). *An illustrated history of the horror film.* New York: G. P. Putnams and Sons.

2. Rummel, R. J. (2004). *Death by government.* New Brunswick, NJ: Transaction Publishers.

3. Kadri, S. (2005). *The trial: A history, from Socrates to O. J. Simpson.* New York: Random House.

4. Ibid., 231.

5. Kelman, H. C., & Hamilton, V. L. (1989). *Crimes of obedience.* New Haven: Yale University Press.

6. Sallah, M., & Weiss, M. (2005). *Tiger force: A true story of men and war.* New York: Little, Brown and Company.

7. Phillips, K. (2006). *American theocracy.* New York: Viking.

8. Nell, V. (2006). Cruelty's rewards: The gratifications of perpetrators and spectators. *Behavioral and Brain Sciences, 29,* 211–57.

9. Dallaire, R. (2003). *Shake hands with the devil.* Toronto: Random House of Canada.

10. Danner, M. (1994). *The massacre at El Mozote.* New York: Vintage Books.

11. Power, S. (2002). *A problem from hell: America and the age of genocide.* New York: Harper Collins Perennial.

12. Fromm, E. (1973). *The anatomy of human destructiveness.* New York: Fawcett Crest.

13. Becker, E. (1975). *Escape from evil.* New York: The Free Press.

14. Harmon-Jones, E., Greenberg, J., Solomon, S., and Simon, L. (1996). The effects of mortality salience on intergroup bias between minimal groups. *European Journal of Social Psychology, 26,* 677–81.

15. Tinbergen, N. (1972). *The animal and its world: Forty years of exploratory behavior by an ethologist.* London: Allen and Unwin.

CHAPTER 1

1. Le Bon, G. (1895). *La psychologie des foules.* Paris: F. Olean.

2. Asbridge, T. (2004). *The first crusade: A new history.* Oxford: Oxford University Press.

3. Acocella, J. (2004, December 1). Holy Smoke: What were the Crusades really about? *The New Yorker,* 92–100.

4. Ibid., p. 94.

5. Zanna, M., and Cooper, J. (1974). Dissonance and the pill: An attributional approach to studying the arousal properties of dissonance. *Journal of Personality and Social Psychology, 29,* 703–9.

6. Asbridge. *The first crusade,* 13.

7. Russell, F.H. (1975). *The just war in the Middle Ages.* London: Cambridge University Press.

8. Ibid., p. 17.

9. Ibid., pp. 18–19.

10. Phillips, J. (2003). *The fourth crusade and the sack of Constantinople* (p. 24). London: Jonathan Cape.

11. Ibid., p. 25.

12. Ibid., p. 26.

13. Ibid., p. 27.

14. Ibid., p. 29.

15. Asbridge. *The first crusade,* p. 33.

16. Ibid.

17. Ibid., p. 34.

18. Phillips, K. (2006). *American theocracy.* New York: Viking.

19. Asbridge. *The first crusade,* p. 35.

20. Ibid., p. 36.

21. Ibid.

22. Ibid., p. 39.

23. Ibid., p. 43.

24. Ibid., p. 46–48.

25. Ibid., p. 48.

26. Ibid., p. 48.

27. Acocella. Holy Smoke, p. 94.

28. Asbridge. *The first crusade,* p. 51.

29. Ibid., p. 54.

30. Acocella. Holy Smoke, p. 97.

31. Asbridge. *The first crusade,* pp. 114–16.

32. Ibid., pp. 118–19.

33. Ibid., p. 119.

34. Ibid., p. 121.

35. Ibid., p. 126.

36. Ibid.

37. Ibid., p. 131.

38. Ibid., p. 136.

39. Ibid.

40. Ibid., p. 147.

41. Ibid., p. 151.

42. Ibid., p. 159.
43. Ibid., p. 168.
44. Ibid.
45. Ibid., p. 174.
46. Ibid., p. 181.
47. Ibid., p. 176.
48. Ibid., p. 191.
49. Ibid., p. 209.
50. Ibid., p. 210.
51. Ibid.
52. Ibid., pp. 210–11.
53. Ibid., p. 239.
54. Ibid., p. 268.
55. Ibid., p. 274.
56. Ibid., p. 300.
57. Ibid., p. 316.
58. Ibid., pp. 316–17.
59. Ibid., p. 316.
60. Ibid., p. 318.
61. Ibid.
62. Ibid.
63. Acocella. Holy Smoke, p. 96.
64. Phillips. *The fourth crusade and the sack of Constantinople.* p. 78.
65. Ibid., p. 295.
66. Ibid., p. 299.
67. Ibid., p. 302.
68. Ibid.
69. Ibid., p. 303.
70. Asbridge. *The first crusade,* p. 35.
71. Phillips, K. *American theocracy,* p. 106.
72. Panksepp, J. (1998). *Affective neuroscience: The foundations of human and animal emotions.* New York: Oxford.
73. Chang, I. (1997). *The rape of Nanking.* New York: Penguin.

CHAPTER 2

1. Amos. *The Holy Bible (Old Testament),* 1:6–8.
2. Asbridge, T. (2004). *The first crusade: A new history.* Oxford: Oxford University Press. Phillips, J. (2003). *The fourth crusade and the sack of Constantinople.* London: Jonathan Cape.
3. Weatherford, J. (2004). *Genghis Khan and the making of the modern world.* New York: Crown.
4. Mann, C.C. (2005). *1491.* New York: Knopf.
5. Sweeney, E.R. (1991). *Cochise: Chiricahua Apache Chief.* Norman: University of Oklahoma Press.
6. Ibid.
7. Rowe, F. (1977). *Extinction—The Beothucks of Newfoundland.* Toronto: McGraw-Hill Ryerson.

8. Brown, D. (1970). *Bury my heart at Wounded Knee.* New York: Holt. Rummel, R.J. (2004). *Death by government.* New Brunswick, NJ: Transaction Publishers.

9. Rummel. *Death by government.*

10. Ibid.

11. Charney, I.W. (1999). *The encyclopedia of genocide* (Vols. 1 and 2). Santa Barbara: ABC-Clio. Power, S. (2002). *A problem from hell: America and the age of genocide.* New York: Harper Collins Perennial. Brown, *Bury my heart at Wounded Knee.* Tuchman, B. (1979). *A distant mirror: The calamitous 14th century.* New York: Knopf.

12. Jewitt, J.R. (1815/1994). *White slaves of the Nootka.* Surrey, B.C.: Heritage House.

13. Ibid., p. 13.

14. Mozino, J.M. (1792/1970). *Noticias De Nutka.* Seattle: University of Washington Press.

15. Mann. *1491,* p. 275.

16. Brown. *Bury my heart at Wounded Knee.*

17. Hochschild, A. (1999). *King Leopold's Ghost.* Boston: Houghton Mifflin.

18. Ibid., p. 165.

19. Ibid., p. 166.

20. Ibid., p. 174.

21. Rummel. *Death by government.*

22. Ibid., p. 390.

23. Gilbert, M. (1994). *The First World War: A complete history.* New York: Henry Holt.

24. Power. *A problem from hell: America and the age of genocide.*

25. Conquest, R. (2000). *Reflections on a Ravaged Century.* New York: Norton.

26. Ibid.

27. Power. *A problem from hell: America and the age of genocide.*

28. Ibid. Also, Dallaire, R. (2003). *Shake hands with the devil.* Toronto: Random House of Canada.

29. Suedfeld, P. (1999). Toward a taxonomy of ethnopolitical violence: Is collective killing by any other name still the same? *Peace and Conflict: Journal of Peace Psychology, 5*(94).

30. Rummel. *Death by government.*

31. Charney. *The encyclopedia of genocide.*

32. Wynne-Edwards, V.C. (1962). *Animal dispersion in relation to social behavior.* Edinburgh and London: Oliver and Boyd.

33. Chirot, D. (1998). Conference on ethnopolitical warfare: Causes and solutions, Londonderry, Northern Ireland.

34. Suedfeld. Toward a taxonomy of ethnopolitical violence.

35. Wynne-Edwards. *Animal dispersion in relation to social behavior.*

36. Becker, E. (1973). *The denial of death* (p. 150). New York: The Free Press.

37. Brown. *Bury my heart at wounded knee.*

38. Asbridge. *The first crusade: A new history.*

39. Conquest, R. (1986). *The harvest of sorrow.* New York: Oxford University Press.

40. Greenberg, J., et al. (1992). Terror management and tolerance: Does mortality salience always intensify negative self reactions to others who threaten one's worldview? *Journal of Personality and Social Psychology, 63.*

41. Kadri, S. (2005). *The trial: A history, from Socrates to O.J. Simpson.* New York: Random House.

42. Milgram, S. (1974). *Obedience to authority.* New York: Harper & Rowe.

43. Janis, I. (1982). *Victims of groupthink,* 2nd ed. (Boston: Houghton Mifflin.

44. Power. *A problem from hell: America and the age of genocide.*

45. Chang, I. (1997). *The rape of Nanking.* New York: Penguin.

46. Ibid.

47. Hersh, S. (1970). *My Lai 4: A report on the massacre and its aftermath.* (New York: Vintage Books. Kadri. *The trial: A history, from Socrates to O.J. Simpson.* Kelman, H.C., and Hamilton, V.L. (1989). *Crimes of obedience.* New Haven: Yale University Press.

48. Danner, M. (1994). *The massacre at El Mozote.* New York: Vintage Books.

49. Dutton, D.G., & Kerry, G. (1999). Modus operandi and personality disorder in incarcerated spousal killers. *International Journal of Law and Psychiatry, 22*(3–4). Wolfgang, M. (1958). *Patterns of criminal homicide.* Philadelphia: Pennsylvania Press.

50. Dallaire. *Shake hands with the devil.*

51. Power. *A problem from hell: America and the age of genocide.*

52. Darley, J. (1999). Methods for the study of evil doing actions. *Personality and Social Psychology Review, 3*(3). Darley, J., and Latane, B. (1968). Bystander intervention emergencies: Diffustion of responsibility. *Journal of Personality and Social Psychology, 8.*

53. Suedfeld, P. (2001). Theories of the Holocaust: Trying to explain the unimaginable. In D. Chirot and M.E. Seligman (Eds.), *Ethnopolitical warfare: Causes, consequences and possible solutions* Washington, DC: APA Press.

54. Chang. *The rape of Nanking.*

55. Takemoto, T., and Ohara, Y. (2000). *The alleged "Nanking Massacre": Japans rebuttal to China's Forged claims.* Tokyo: Meishei-sha.

56. Woods, J.E. (1998). *The good man of Nanking: John Rabe.* New York: Vintage Books.

57. Danner. *The massacre at El Mozote.*

58. Dallaire. *Shake hands with the devil.*

59. Le Bon, G. (1895).*La psychologie des foules.* Paris: F. Olean.

60. Ibid., p. 35.

61. Ibid., p. 37

62. Freud, S. (1921). *Group psychology and the analysis of the ego.* London: International Psycholanalytic Press.

63. Ibid.

64. Becker. *The denial of death.* Becker, E. (1975). *Escape from evil.* New York: The Free Press.

65. Becker. *Escape from evil,* p. 5.

66. Ibid., p. 111.

67. Ibid., p. 105.

68. Nell, V. (2006). Cruelty's rewards: The gratifications of perpetrators and spectators. *Behavioral and Brain Sciences, 29.*

69. Masson, J., and McCarthy, S. (1995). *When elephants weep: The emotional lives of animals.* New York: Dell Publishing.

CHAPTER 3

1. Power, S. (2002). *A problem from hell: America and the age of genocide.* New York: Harper Collins Perennial.

2. Ferguson, N. (2006). *The war of the world.* New York: Penguin.

3. Power. *A problem from hell: America and the age of genocide.*

4. Ferguson. *The war of the world,* p. 176.

5. Ibid.

6. Ibid.

7. Power. *A problem from hell: America and the age of genocide,* p. 8.

8. Million Armenians killed or in exile. (1915, December 15). *New York Times* (p. 3).

9. Power. *A problem from hell: America and the age of genocide,* p. 517.

10. Ferguson. *The war of the world,* p. 177.

11. Power. *A problem from hell: America and the age of genocide,* p. 5.

12. Ibid., p. 6.

13. Ibid., p. 7.

14. Ferguson. *The war of the world,* p. 182.

15. Ibid., p. 183.

16. Ibid., p. 177.

17. Dolot, M. (1987). *Execution by hunger. The hidden holocaust.* New York: Norton.

18. Ulam, A. (1987). Introduction. In M. Dolot (Ed.), *Execution by hunger. The hidden holocaust.* New York: Norton.

19. Conquest, R. (1986). *The harvest of sorrow.* New York: Oxford University Press.

20. Ferguson. *The war of the world,* p. 216.

21. Conquest. *The harvest of sorrow.*

22. Ferguson. *The war of the world,* p. 216.

23. Dolot. *Execution by hunger. The hidden holocaust,* p. 140.

24. Ibid., p. 158.

25. Ferguson. *The war of the world,* p. 217.

26. Conquest. *The harvest of sorrow,* p. 126.

27. Ferguson. *The war of the world,* p. 217.

28. Ibid., p. 220.

29. Rummel, R.J. (2004). *Death by government* (p. 36). New Brunswick, NJ: Transaction Publishers.

30. Ibid., p. 37.

31. Ferguson. *The war of the world,* p. 623.

32. Power. *A problem from hell: America and the age of genocide,* p. 96.

33. Bergner, D. (2003). The most unconventional weapon. *New York Times Magazine,* pp. 48–53.

34. Chang, I. (1997). *The rape of Nanking* (p. 88). New York: Penguin.

35. Power. *A problem from hell: America and the age of genocide,* p. 119.

36. Ibid.

37. Janis, I. (1982). *Victims of groupthink* (2nd ed.). Boston: Houghton Mifflin.

38. Power. *A problem from hell: America and the age of genocide,* pp. 143 and 488.

39. Ibid., p. 144.

40. Ferguson. *The war of the world,* p. 624.

41. Ibid., p. 622.

42. Power. *A problem from hell: America and the age of genocide,* p. 120.

43. Ibid., p. 129.

44. Ibid., p. 489.

45. Ibid.

46. Ibid., p. 129.

47. Ibid., p. 91.

48. Becker, E. (1975). *Escape from evil.* New York: The Free Press.

49. Staub, E. (1996). Cultural-societal roots of violence. *American Psychologist,* pp. 117–33.

50. Human Rights. (1999). *Leave none to tell the tale: Genocide in Rwanda.* New York: Human Rights Watch. Power. *A problem from hell: America and the age of genocide,* p. 336.

51. Dallaire, R. (2003). *Shake hands with the devil* (p. 123). Toronto: Random House of Canada.

52. Power. *A problem from hell: America and the age of genocide,* pp. 337-340.

53. Dallaire. (2004). Speech given at the University of British Columbia.

54. Human Rights. *Leave none to tell the tale: Genocide in Rwanda.*

55. Dallaire. *Shake hands with the devil.*

56. Ibid.

57. Ressler, R.K., et al. (1992). *Sexual homicide: Patterns and motives.* New York: Free Press.

58. Chang. *The rape of Nanking,* p. 94.

59. Dallaire. *Shake hands with the devil.*

60. Ferguson. *The war of the world,* p. 627.

61. Human Rights Watch. (1992–1993). *War crimes in Bosnia-Hercegovina.* New York: Human Rights Watch.

62. Power. *A problem from hell: America and the age of genocide,* p. 249.

63. Ibid., p. 254.

64. Ferguson. *The war of the world,* p. 629.

65. Power. *A problem from hell: America and the age of genocide,* pp. 287 and 295.

66. Ibid., pp. 412–13.

67. Ferguson. *The war of the world,* p. 630.

68. Power. *A problem from hell: America and the age of genocide,* p. 47.

69. Ferguson. *The war of the world,* p. 628.

70. Ibid., p. 630.

71. Phillips. (2003). *The fourth crusade and the sack of Constantinople.* London: Jonathan Cape.

CHAPTER 4

1. Ferguson, N. (2006). *The war of the world: Twentieth century conflict and the descent of the West* (pp. 245–269). New York: Penguin.

2. Gilbert, M. (1994). *The First World War: A complete history* (p. 30). New York: H. Holt. (Gilbert 1 henceforth.)

3. Ibid., p. 30

4. Snyder, L.L. (1981). *Hitler's Third Reich: A documentary history* (p. 23). New York: Nelson-Hall Inc.

5. Goldhagen, D.J. (1996). *Hitler's willing executioners: Ordinary Germans and the Holocaust* (p. 49). New York: Alfred A. Knopf, Inc.

6. Schachter, S. (1951). Deviation, rejection and communication. *Journal of Abnormal and Social Psychology, 46,* pp. 190–207. Festinger, L. (1954). *A theory of social comparison processes* (pp. 117–40). *Human Relations, 7.*

7. Goldhagen. *Hitler's willing executioners: Ordinary Germans and the Holocaust,* p. 49.

8. Ibid., p. 50.

9. Cited in Goldhagen, *Hitler's willing executioners: Ordinary Germans and the Holocaust,* p. 50. For an account of the elaborate Christian demonology of the Jews and the endless ills attributed to their doing, see Trachtenberg, J. (1986). *The Devil and the Jews: The Medieval Conception of the Jew and its relation to Modern Anti-Semitism* (Philadelphia: Jewish Publication Society).

10. Goldhagen. *Hitler's willing executioners: Ordinary Germans and the Holocaust,* p. 54.

11. Ferguson, *The war of the world,* p. 31.

12. Ibid., p. 32.

13. Ibid., p. 33.

14. Goldhagen. *Hitler's willing executioners: Ordinary Germans and the Holocaust,* p. 55.

15. Ibid., p. 55.

16. Eley, G. (2000). Ordinary Germans, Nazism, and Judeocide. In Geoff Eley (Ed.), *The "Goldhagen Effect:" History, memory, Nazism-facing the German past* (p. 5). Ann Arbor: University of Michigan Press.

17. Ibid., p. 6.

18. Ibid., p. 6.

19. Ferguson. *The war of the world,* pp. 60–65.

20. Ibid., p. 60.

21. Ibid., pp. 60–63.

22. Ibid., p. 65.

23. Snyder. *Hitler's Third Reich: A documentary history,* pp. 24–25.

24. Ibid., p. 249.

25. Ibid., p. 249.

26. Macmillan, M. (2003). *Paris 1919: Six months that changed the world.* New York: Random House.

27. Gellately, R. *The Gestapo and German society: Enforcing racial policy 1933–1945* (p. 140). Oxford: Clarendon Press (Gellately 1 henceforth).

28. Snyder. *Hitler's Third Reich: A documentary history,* p. 16.

29. Burleigh, M. (2000). *The Third Reich: A new history* (p. 49). New York: Hill and Wang.

30. Snyder. *Hitler's Third Reich: A documentary history,* p. 16.

31. Macmillan. *Paris 1919: Six months that changed the world* (Chapter 15). Snyder. *Hitler's Third Reich: A documentary history,* p. 16.

32. Snyder. *Hitler's Third Reich: A documentary history,* p. 17.

33. Ibid., p. 18.

34. Ibid., p. 18.

35. Ibid., p. 18.

36. Ibid., p. 57.

37. Ibid., p. 56.

38. Ibid., pp. 56–57.

39. Ibid., p. 20.

40. Ibid., p. 3.

41. Ibid., p. 4.

42. Ibid., p. 23.

43. Ibid., p. 70.

44. Ibid., p. 70.

45. Ibid., p. 70.

46. Ibid., p. 80.

47. Ibid., p. 80.
48. Ibid., p. 81.
49. Ibid., p. 93.
50. Ibid., p. 95.
51. Ibid., p. 95.
52. Ibid., pp. 21 and 96.
53. Ibid., pp. 95–96.
54. Ibid., p. 131.
55. Ibid., p. 152.
56. The Waffen-SS ("Armed SS") was the combat arm of the Schutzstaffel. Headed by Reichsführer-SS Heinrich Himmler, the Waffen-SS saw action throughout the Second World War, and many members were found guilty of war crimes during the Nuremberg Trials.

After humble beginnings as a protection unit for the NSDAP leadership, the Waffen-SS eventually grew into a force of 38 combat divisions comprising over 950,000 men and including a number of elite units. In the Nuremberg Trials, the Waffen-SS was condemned as part of a criminal organization due to their involvement with the National Socialist Party (NSDAP), and Waffen-SS veterans were denied many of the rights afforded other German combat veterans who had served in the Wehrmacht, Luftwaffe, or Kriegsmarine. Conscripts, however, were exempted from that judgment, as many of them were forced to join the organization by German authorities. The origins of the Waffen-SS (Armed SS) can be traced back to the creation of a select group of 200 men who were to act as Hitler's bodyguard. This bodyguard was created by Hitler in reaction to his unease at the size and strength of the SA (Sturmabteilung or Storm Troopers). The SA had grown so large that Hitler felt he needed an armed escort that was totally dedicated to him. Thus the Schutzstaffel (SS) or protection squad was created. After Hitler's imprisonment (and subsequent release) in the wake of the failed Munich Putsch in 1923, Hitler saw even further need for a body guard, and the place of the SS was solidified in the Nazi hierarchy.

Until 1929—the SA was still the dominant force in the Nazi Party, however—the SS was growing in strength and importance. In January 1929, Hitler appointed Heinrich Himmler to lead the SS (his rank was Reichsführer), and it was Himmler's goal to create an elite corps of armed soldiers within the party. However, the SS was still a very small organization, and Hitler wanted an effective force by 1933. Himmler set out to recruit men who represented the elite of German society, both in physical abilities and political beliefs. Through his active recruitment, Himmler was able to increase the size of the SS to about 52,000 by the end of 1933.

Although the SS was growing exponentially, the SA mirrored the growth of Hitler's private army. The SA had over 2 million members at the end of 1933. Led by one of Hitler's old comrades, Ernst Röhm, the SA represented a threat to Hitler's attempts to win favor with the German army. As well, the SA threatened to sour Hitler's relations with the conservative elements of the country, whose support Hitler needed to solidify his position in the German government. Hitler decided to act against the SA, and the SS was put in charge of eliminating Röhm and several other high ranking officers in the SA. The Night of the Long Knives on June 30, 1934, also saw the execution of thousands of SA men and effectively ended the power of the SA.

Source: Wikipedia
57. Gellately, R. (2001). *Backing Hitler: Consent and coercion in Nazi Germany* (p. 69). Oxford: Oxford University Press (Gellately 2 henceforth).

58. Ibid., p. 69.

59. Snyder. *Hitler's Third Reich: A documentary history*, p. 15.

60. Gellately, R. (2003). The Third Reich, the Holocaust, and visions of serial genocide. In R. Gellately and B. Kiernan (Eds.), *Specter of genocide: Mass murder in historical perspective* (p. 253). New York: Cambridge University Press (Gellately 3 henceforth).

61. Ibid., p. 253.

62. Ibid., p. 253.

63. Ibid., p. 253.

64. Browning, C. (2000). *Nazi policy, Jewish workers, German killers* (p. 5). New York: Cambridge University Press (Browning 1 henceforth).

65. Gellately 1, p. 137.

66. Ibid., p. 172.

67. Goldhagen. *Hitler's willing executioners: Ordinary Germans and the Holocaust,* p. 136.

68. Browning 1, pp. 31–32.

69. Ibid., p. 117.

70. Ibid., p. 117.

71. Ibid., p. 117.

72. Ibid., pp. 125–126.

73. Ibid., pp. 125–126. Burleigh. *The Third Reich: A new history,* p. 181.

74. Browning 1, p. 126.

75. Ibid., p. 126.

76. Ibid., p. 126.

77. Gellately 2, p. 34.

78. Ibid., p. 34.

79. Ibid., p. 51.

80. Ibid., pp. 52–53.

81. Ibid., p. 35.

82. Ibid., p. 38.

83. Ibid., p. 38. Snyder. *Hitler's Third Reich: A documentary history,* p. 219.

84. Gellately 2, p. 38.

85. Ibid., p. 38.

86. See Ross, L. (1988). Review of Arthur Miller: The obedience experiments. *Contemporary Psychology, 33*(2), pp. 101–4.

87. Gellately 3, p. 243.

88. Snyder. *Hitler's Third Reich: A documentary history,* p. 85.

89. Ibid., p. 85.

90. Gellately 2, p. 35.

91. Gellately 3, p. 243.

92. Gellately 2, p. 36.

93. Ibid., p. 49.

94. Ibid., p. 49.

95. Ibid., p. 64.

96. Goldhagen. *Hitler's willing executioners: Ordinary Germans and the Holocaust,* p. 394.

97. Ibid., p. 136.

98. Ibid., p. 394.

99. Ibid., p. 136.

100. Gellately 1, p. 102.

101. Ibid., p. 104.
102. Ibid., p. 104.
103. Ibid., p. 104.
104. Ibid., pp. 105–106.
105. Ibid., pp. 105–106.
106. Ibid., p. 106.
107. Gellately 3, p. 243.
108. Ibid., p. 244.
109. Ibid., p. 244.
110. Ibid., p. 244.
111. Goldhagen. *Hitler's willing executioners: Ordinary Germans and the Holocaust*, pp. 136–137.
112. Ibid., p. 137.
113. Gellately 2, p. 81.
114. Ibid., p. 82.
115. Ibid., p. 82.
116. Ibid., p. 36.
117. Ibid., p. 36.
118. Ibid., p. 43.
119. Ibid., p. 37.
120. Ibid., p. 37.
121. Ibid., p. 92.
122. Ibid., p. 93.
123. Ibid., p. 35.
124. Ibid., p. 35.
125. Ibid., p. 35.
126. Ibid., p. 63.
127. Ibid., p. 63.
128. Burleigh. *The Third Reich: A new history*, p. 158.
129. Ibid., p. 158.
130. Ibid., p. 284.
131. Gellately 2, p. 75.
132. Ibid., p. 75.
133. Ibid., p. 69.
134. Burleigh. *The Third Reich: A new history*, p. 173.
135. Gellately 2, p. 75.
136. Ibid., p. 113.
137. Ibid., p. 113.
138. Ibid., p. 114.
139. For a detailed examination of the power politics between the Vatican, the Nazis, and Mussolini, see John Cornwell's *Hitler's Pope: The secret history of Pius XII* (New York: Viking Press, 1999). Cornwell, a Catholic and Senior Research Fellow at Jesus College, Cambridge, was appalled by the power politics (that allowed the Vatican to be spared) and Pius's "personal antipathy toward the Jews" he discovered in previously classified Vatican archives. As Cornwell concludes (p. 384), "I am convinced that the cumulative verdict of history shows him (Pius XII) to be not a saintly exemplar for future generations, but a deeply flawed human being, from who Catholics, and our relations with other religions, can best profit by expressing our

sincerest regret." Nazis, such as Adolph Eichman, escaped to South America with Vatican passports before they were found hiding out, using aliases by the Mossad. [Thomas, G. (1999). *Gideon's Spies: The secret history of the Mossad.* New York: St. Martin's Press.]

140. Burleigh. *The Third Reich: A new history,* p. 234.
141. Ibid., p. 233.
142. Gellately 2, pp. 111–12.
143. Ibid., p. 113. Burleigh. *The Third Reich: A new history,* p. 233.
144. Gellately 2, p. 114.
145. Ibid., p. 114.
146. Ibid., p. 114.
147. Ibid., p. 114.
148. Ibid., p. 115.
149. Ibid., p. 115.
150. Ibid., p. 115.
151. Ibid., p. 115.
152. Ibid., p. 116.
153. Ibid., p. 116.
154. Goldhagen. *Hitler's willing executioners: Ordinary Germans and the Holocaust,* p. 117.
155. Gellately 2, p. 38.
156. Ibid., pp. 38–39.
157. Ibid., pp.47–48.
158. Ibid., p. 48.
159. Ibid., pp. 48–49.
160. Ibid., p. 49.
161. Ibid., pp. 38–39.
162. Ibid., p. 39.
163. Ibid., p. 39.
164. Snyder. *Hitler's Third Reich: A documentary history,* p. 211.
165. Ibid., p. 211.
166. Burleigh. *The Third Reich: A new history,* p. 294.
167. Goldhagen. *Hitler's willing executioners: Ordinary Germans and the Holocaust,* p. 138.
168. Gellately 1, pp. 106–7 and 160. Burleigh. *The Third Reich: A new history,* p. 294.
169. Gellately 1, pp. 106–8. Burleigh. *The Third Reich: A new history,* p. 294.
170. Gellately 1, pp. 106–7.
171. Ibid., p. 188.
172. Ibid., p. 111.
173. Ibid., p. 111.
174. Ibid., p. 112.
175. Ibid., p. 112.
176. Ibid., pp. 131–32.
177. Ibid., pp. 131–32.
178. Ibid., p. 138.
179. Ibid., p. 138.
180. Gellately 2, p. 39.
181. Ibid., p. 39.
182. Ibid., p. 40.
183. Ibid., p. 40.

184. Ibid., p. 40.
185. Ibid., p. 43.
186. Ibid., p. 43.
187. Ibid., p. 43.
188. Ibid., p. 43.
189. Ibid., p. 43.
190. Ibid., pp. 40–41.
191. Ibid., p. 45.
192. Ibid., p. 45.
193. Ibid., p. 46.
194. Ibid., p. 80.
195. Ibid., p. 80.
196. Gellately 1, pp. 190 and 233.
197. Goldhagen. *Hitler's willing executioners: Ordinary Germans and the Holocaust,* p. 138.
198. Gellately 1, p. 251. Gellately 2, p. 116.
199. Gellately 1, p. 182.
200. Ibid., p. 182.
201. Ibid., p. 73.
202. Ibid., p. 73.
203. Ibid., p. 73.
204. Gellately 1, p. 140.
205. Ibid., p. 140.
206. Gellately 2, p. 74.
207. Ibid., p. 106.
208. Gellately 2, p. 109. Gellately 3, p. 252.
209. Gellately 2, p. 109.
210. Gellately 3, p. 252.
211. Gellately 2, p. 109.
212. Gellately 3, p. 252.
213. Ibid., p. 109.
214. Ibid., p. 78.
215. Ibid., p. 78.
216. Ibid., p. 104.
217. Ibid., p. 104.
218. Ibid., p. 105.
219. Ibid., p. 105.
220. Goldhagen. *Hitler's willing executioners: Ordinary Germans and the Holocaust,* p. 139.
221. Ibid., p. 139.
222. Gellately 2, pp. 2–3.
223. Ibid., p. 58.
224. Ibid., p. 58.
225. Ibid., p. 59.
226. Ibid., p. 62.
227. Ibid., p. 62.
228. Ibid., p. 62.
229. Gellately 1, p. 112.

230. Gilbert, M. (1986). *The Holocaust: The Jewish tragedy* (p. 69). Suffolk: St Edmundsbury Press (Gilbert 2 henceforth).

231. Gilbert 2, p. 69. Snyder. *Hitler's Third Reich: A documentary history,* p. 219.

232. Gellately 1, pp. 113 and 117.

233. Gilbert 2, p. 70.

234. Ibid., p. 71.

235. Gellately 1, p. 114.

236. Ibid., p. 116.

237. Gilbert 2, p. 71.

238. Ibid., p. 71.

239. Ibid., p. 71.

240. Gellately 1, p. 119.

241. Gilbert 2, p. 73.

242. Gellately 1, p. 119.

243. Ibid., pp. 122–23.

244. Ibid., p. 120.

245. Gellately 3, p. 248.

246. Ibid., p. 246.

247. Ibid., p. 247.

248. Ibid., p. 247.

249. Browning 1, p. 3.

250. Burleigh. *The Third Reich: A new history,* p. 647.

251. Gellately 2, p. 101. Goldhagen. *Hitler's willing executioners: Ordinary Germans and the Holocaust,* p. 143.

252. Gellately 2, p. 101.

253. Ibid., p. 102.

254. Ibid., p. 102.

255. Gellately 2, p. 103. Gellately 3, p. 246.

256. Gellately 2, p. 103. Burleigh. *The Third Reich: A new history,* pp. 393–99.

257. Cited in Eley. Ordinary Germans, Nazism, and Judeocide, p. 16.

258. Ibid., p. 16.

259. Gellately 2, p. 103.

260. Goldhagen. *Hitler's willing executioners: Ordinary Germans and the Holocaust,* p. 145.

261. Browning 1, p. 5.

262. Ibid., p. 6.

263. Ibid., p. 6.

264. Snyder. *Hitler's Third Reich: A documentary history,* pp. 426 and 428.

265. Snyder. *Hitler's Third Reich: A documentary history,* pp. 428–29.

266. Gellately 3, p. 259.

267. Ibid., p. 259.

268. Browning, C. (1998). *Ordinary men: Reserve Police Battalion 101 and the final solution in Poland* (p. 9). New York: HarperPerennial (Browning 2 henceforth).

269. Browning 2, pp. 11.

270. Wright, E. (2004). *Generation kill: Devil Dogs, Iceman, Captain America and the new face of American war.* New York: G. P. Putnam's Son.

271. Browning 2, p. 11.

272. Ibid., p. 11.

273. Browning 1, pp. 24–25.
274. Ibid., pp. 24–25. Gilbert, M. (2006). *Kristallnacht: Prelude to destruction* (p. 159). New York: Harper Collins.
275. Gilbert 2, p. 154.
276. Browning 1, p. 25.
277. Goldhagen. *Hitler's willing executioners: Ordinary Germans and the Holocaust,* p. 149.
278. Ibid., p. 149.
279. Browning 2, p. xvii.
280. Ibid., p. 5.
281. Ibid., p. 11.
282. Ibid., p. 12.
283. Ibid., p. 12.
284. Ibid., p. 12.
285. Ibid., p. 12.
286. Ibid., p. 12.
287. Ibid., p. 12.
288. Ibid., pp. 12–14.
289. Ibid., pp. 12–14.
290. Ibid., p. 14.
291. Ibid., p. 14.
292. Ibid., p. 14.
293. Ibid., pp. 16–17.
294. Ibid., p. 18.
295. Ibid., p. 18.
296. Ibid., p. 18.
297. Ibid., p. 18.
298. Ibid., p. 19.
299. Ibid., p. 19.
300. Ibid., pp. 19–20.
301. Ibid., pp. 21–22.
302. Goldhagen. *Hitler's willing executioners: Ordinary Germans and the Holocaust,* p. 149.
303. Browning 2, pp. 24–25.
304. Goldhagen. *Hitler's willing executioners: Ordinary Germans and the Holocaust,* p. 149.
305. Ibid., p. 151.
306. Ibid., p. 149.
307. Ibid., p. 149.
308. Gellately 3, p. 261.
309. Browning 1, p. 118.
310. Ibid., p. 118.
311. Ibid., p. 118.
312. Ibid., p. 121.
313. Ibid., p. 139.
314. Ibid., p. 28.
315. Burleigh. *The Third Reich: A new history,* p. 649.
316. Browning 1, p. 29.
317. Ibid., p. 30.
318. Ibid., p. 127.

319. Browning 2, p. 26.
320. Ibid., p. 27.
321. Browning 1, p. 127.
322. Goldhagen. *Hitler's willing executioners: Ordinary Germans and the Holocaust,* p. 154.
323. Browning 1, pp. 1–2.
324. Ibid., p. 36.
325. Browning 2, pp. 49–50.
326. Ibid., pp. 49–50. Goldhagen. *Hitler's willing executioners: Ordinary Germans and the Holocaust,* p. 157.
327. Gilbert 2, p. 121.
328. Browning 2, pp. 49–50.
329. Ibid., pp. 122–23.
330. Ibid., pp. 122–23.
331. Ibid., p. 124.
332. Ibid., p. 124.
333. Browning 1, p. 39.
334. Ibid., p. 45.
335. Ibid., pp. 45–46.
336. Ibid., p. 65.
337. Ibid., p. 65.
338. Ibid., p. 67.
339. Ibid., p. 76.
340. Ibid., p. 76.
341. Ibid., p. 50.
342. Burleigh. *The Third Reich: A new history,* p. 647.
343. Ibid., p. 648.
344. Ibid., p. 649.
345. Ibid., p. 650.
346. Browning 1, p. 50. Goldhagen. *Hitler's willing executioners: Ordinary Germans and the Holocaust,* p. 158.
347. Gilbert 2, pp. 283–84.
348. Browning 2, p. 27.
349. Ibid., p. 27.
350. Ibid., p. 30.
351. Ibid., p. 32.
352. Ibid., p. 32.
353. Ibid., p. 35.
354. Ibid., p. 36.
355. Gellately 3, p. 251.
356. Browning 2, p. xv.
357. Ibid., p. xv.
358. Browning 1, p. 55.
359. Ibid., p. 31.
360. Burleigh. *The Third Reich: A new history,* p. 417.
361. Browning 1, p. 56.
362. Ibid., p. 40.
363. Ibid., p. 40.

364. Browning 2, pp. 133–134.
365. Ibid., pp. 133–34.
366. Ibid., pp. 133–34.
367. Browning 1, p. 97.
368. Browning 2, p. 137.
369. Ibid., p. 137.
370. Ibid., pp. 138–39.
371. Ibid., pp. 138–39.
372. Ibid., p. 94.
373. Ibid., p. 95.
374. Ibid., p. 95.
375. Ibid., p. 115.
376. Ibid., p. 115.
377. Ibid., pp. 115–17.
378. Ibid., p. 124.
379. Ibid., p. 124.
380. Ibid., p. 126.
381. Ibid., p. 126.
382. Ibid., p. 126.
383. Ibid., p. 131.
384. Ibid., p. 132.
385. Browning 1, p. 86.
386. Ibid., p. 87.
387. Gellately 2, p. 68.
388. Ibid., p. 68.
389. Ibid., p. 68.
390. Ibid., pp. 68–69.
391. Ibid., p. 69.
392. Goldhagen. *Hitler's willing executioners: Ordinary Germans and the Holocaust,* p. 160.
393. Ibid., p. 160.
394. Ibid., p. 160.
395. Ibid., p. 160.
396. Browning 1, p. 101.
397. Ibid., p. 101.
398. Goldhagen. *Hitler's willing executioners: Ordinary Germans and the Holocaust,* pp. 327–29.
399. Ibid., p. 330.
400. Ibid., p. 330.
401. Ibid., p. 330.
402. Ibid., p. 333.
403. Ibid., p. 334.
404. Ibid., p. 334.
405. Ibid., p. 351.
406. Ibid., p. 351.
407. Gellately 3, p. 253.
408. Ibid., p. 253.
409. Goldhagen. *Hitler's willing executioners: Ordinary Germans and the Holocaust,* p. 413.

410. Ibid., p. 413.
411. Browning 2, pp. 49–50.
412. Beevor, A. (2002). *The fall of Berlin 1945.* New York: Penguin.
413. Ibid., p. 176.
414. Ibid., p. 247.
415. Ibid., p. 246.

CHAPTER 5

1. Weatherford, J. (2004). *Genghis Khan and the making of the modern world.* New York: Crown.
2. Chang, I. (1997). *The rape of Nanking.* New York: Penguin.
3. Danner, M. (1994). *The massacre at El Mozote.* New York: Vintage Books.
4. Chang. *The rape of Nanking,* p. 187. Woods, J.E. (1998). *The good man of Nanking: John Rabe.* New York: Vintage Books.
5. Woods. *The good man of Nanking: John Rabe.*
6. Lipstadt, D.E. (1998). *Denying the Holocaust.* New York: Penguin.
7. Chang. *The rape of Nanking,* p. 40.
8. Ibid., p. 47.
9. Ibid., p. 50.
10. Ibid., p. 95.
11. Ibid., p. 109.
12. Ibid., p. 121.
13. Ibid., p. 57.
14. Browning, C. (1998). *Ordinary men: Reserve Police Battalion 101 and the final solution in Poland.* New York: Harper Collins.
15. Chang. *The rape of Nanking,* p. 59.
16. Ibid.
17. Ibid., p. 58.
18. Stout, C. (2004). *Psychology of Terrorism.* Westport, CT: Praeger.
19. Chang. *The rape of Nanking,* p. 148. Kahn, D. (1991). Roosevelt, MAGIC, and ULTRA. In G.O. Kent (Ed.), *Historians and archivists.* Fairfax, VA: George Mason University Press.
20. Chang. *The rape of Nanking,* p. 217.
21. Ibid., p. 55.
22. Triandis, H.C. (1995). *Individualism and collectivism.* Boulder, CO: Westview.
23. Chang. *The rape of Nanking,* p. 54.
24. Ibid., pp. 57–58.
25. Ibid., p. 54.
26. Ibid., p. 55.
27. Kelman, H.C., & Hamilton, V.L. (1989). *Crimes of obedience.* New Haven: Yale University Press.
28. Hersh, S.M. (1970). *My Lai 4: A report on the massacre and its aftermath.* New York: Vintage Books.
29. Kadri, S. (2005). *The trial: A history, from Socrates to O.J. Simpson.* New York: Random House.

30. Hersh. *My Lai 4: A report on the massacre and its aftermath,* p. 72. Brownmiller, S. (1975). *Against our will: Men, women and rape* (pp. 86–113). New York: Fawcett, Columbine.

31. Lifton, R. J. (1973). *Home from the war—Neither victims nor executioners.* New York: Simon and Schuster.

32. Kelman & Hamilton. *Crimes of obedience,* p. 9.

33. Ibid., p. 3.

34. Wright, E. (2004). *Generation Kill.* New York: G. P. Putnam.

35. Hersh. *My Lai 4: A report on the massacre and its aftermath.*

36. Brownmiller. *Against our will: Men, women and rape,* pp. 101–9.

37. Kadri. *The trial: A history, from Socrates to O. J. Simpson,* p. 244.

38. Ibid., p. 246.

39. Ibid., p. 247.

40. Ibid., p. 248.

41. Kelman & Hamilton. *Crimes of obedience,* pp. 7–8.

42. Kadri. *The trial: A history, from Socrates to O. J. Simpson,* p. 248.

43. Kelman & Hamilton. *Crimes of obedience.*

44. Kadri. *The trial: A history, from Socrates to O. J. Simpson,* p. 251.

45. Ibid., p. 253.

46. Ibid., p. 250.

47. Ibid.

48. Danner. *The massacre at El Mozote.*

49. Ibid., p. 67.

50. Ibid., p. 75.

51. Ibid., p. 203.

52. Ibid., p. 152.

53. Ibid., p. 158.

54. Ibid., pp. 159–60.

55. Ibid., p. 189.

56. Brown, D. (1970). *Bury my heart at Wounded Knee* (pp. 88–102). New York: Holt.

57. Waller, J. (2002). *Becoming evil: How ordinary people commit genocide and mass killing* (p. 29). New York: Oxford University Press.

58. Ibid., p. 49.

59. Ferguson, N. (2006). *The war of the world* (p. 124). New York: Penguin.

60. Boswell,R. (2006). A dark chapter in Canada's. *Vancouver Sun,* pp. A10.

61. Chang. *The rape of Nanking,* p. 173.

62. Ibid., p. 38.

63. Kelman & Hamilton. *Crimes of obedience.*

64. Ibid., p. 223.

CHAPTER 6

1. Clarke, J. W. (1998). Without fear or shame: lynching, capital punishment and the subculture of violence in the American south. *British Journal of Political Science, 28,* 269–89.

2. Raper, A. F. (1933). *The tragedy of lynching.* Chapel Hill: University of North Carolina Press.

3. Ibid., p. 87.

4. Brundage, W. F. (1993). *Lynching in the New South.* Chicago: University of Illinois Press.

5. Ibid., p. 32.

6. Wells-Barnett, I. B. (1899). Lynch law in Georgia. Wells-Barnett, I. B. (2002). *On lynchings* (p. 34). New York: Humanity Books.

7. Wells-Barnett. *On lynchings,* p. 37.

8. Ibid., p. 33.

9. Brundage, W. F. (1997). *Under sentence of death: Lynching in the South* (p. 48). Chapel Hill: University of North Carolina Press.

10. Schlesinger, L. B. (2004). *Sexual murder: Catathymic and compulsive homicides* (p. 199). Boca Raton: CRC Press.

11. Ibid.

12. Wells-Barnett. *On lynchings,* p. 29.

13. Beck, E. M., & Tolnay, S. E. (1990). *A festival of violence.* Chicago: University of Illinois Press.

14. Ibid., p. 44.

15. Raper. *The tragedy of lynching,* p. 67.

16. Beck & Tolnay. *A festival of violence.*

17. Cantril, H. (1941). *The psychology of social movements.* New York: Chapman and Hall, Ltd.

18. Ibid.

19. Ibid., p. 84.

20. Ibid.

21. Milton, G. F. (1931). *Lynchings and what they mean.* Atlanta: The Commission Publishing.

22. Raper. *The tragedy of lynching,* p. 52.

23. Ibid., p. 54

24. Clarke. Without fear or shame.

25. Beck & Tolnay. *A festival of violence,* p. 66.

26. Ibid., p. 68.

27. Ibid.

28. Clarke. Without fear or shame, p. 73.

29. Howard, W. (1995). *Lynchings.* London: Associated University Press.

30. Ibid., p. 87.

31. Ibid., p. 88.

32. Ibid., p. 60.

33. Ibid., p. 36.

34. Ibid., pp. 39–44.

35. Ibid., p. 51.

36. Ibid., p. 63.

37. Ibid., p. 64.

38. Ibid., p. 54.

39. Ibid., p. 55.

40. Ibid., p. 55.

41. Staub, E. (1999). The roots of evil: Social conditions, culture, personality and basic human needs. *Personality and Social Psychology Review, 3*(3), 179–92.

42. Beck & Tolnay. *A festival of violence,* p. 47.

43. Brundage, W. F. *Lynching in the New South.*

44. Becker, E. (1973). *The denial of death.* New York: The Free Press.

45. Wright, G.G. (1990). *Racial violence in Kentucky: Lynchings, mob rule and "legal lynchings."* London: Louisiana State University Press.

46. Smead, H. (1986). *Blood justice.* New York: Oxford University Press.

47. Howard. *Lynchings,* p. 92.

48. Browning, C.R.. (1998). *Ordinary men: Reserve Police Battalion 101 and the final solution in Poland.* New York: Harper Collins.

49. Haritos-Fatouros, M. (2003). *The psychological origins of institutionalized torture.* London: Routledge.

50. Wells-Barnett. *On lynchings,* p. 122.

51. Cantril. *The psychology of social movements,* p. 11.

52. Ibid., p. 115.

53. Raper. *The tragedy of lynching,* p. 86.

54. Beck & Tolnay. *A festival of violence,* p. 85.

CHAPTER 7

1. Useem, B., and Kimball, P. (1989). *States of siege: U.S. Prison riots 1971–1986.* New York: Oxford University Press.

2. McKay, R. (1972). *New York State Special Commission on Attica.* New York: Bantam Books.

3. Useem and Kimball. *States of siege: U.S. Prison riots 1971–1986,* p. 27.

4. Ibid., p. 37.

5. Ibid.

6. Wolfgang, M. (1958). *Patterns of criminal homicide.* Philadelphia: Pennsylvania Press.

7. Useem and Kimball. *States of siege: U.S. Prison riots 1971–1986,* p. 50.

8. Ibid., p. 56.

9. Brownmiller, S. (1975). *Against our will: Men, women and rape* (p. 49). New York: Fawcett, Columbine.

10. Zimbardo, P., et al. (1972). A Pirandellian prison: The mind is a formidable jailer. *New York Times Magazine,* pp. 26–43.

11. Brickman, P. (1978). Is it real? In *Advances in Experimental Social Psychology.* New York: Wiley.

12. Lifton, R.J. (1986). *The Nazi doctors: Medical killings and the psychology of genocide.* New York: Basic Books.

13. Ibid., p. 343.

14. Ibid., p. 347.

CHAPTER 8

1. Turnbull, C. (1972). *The mountain people* (p. 11). New York: Simon and Schuster.

2. Ibid., pp. 232–33.

3. Beevor, A. (2002). *The fall of Berlin 1945* (pp. 310–11). New York: Penguin.

4. Suedfeld, P. (2001). Theories of the Holocaust: Trying to explain the unimaginable. In D. Chirot and M.E.P. Seligman (Eds.), *Ethnopolitical warfare: Causes, consequences and possible solutions.* Washington, DC: APA Press.

5. Fein, H. (1979). *Accounting for genocide: National responses and Jewish victimization during the Holocaust.* New York: Free Press.

6. Davenport and Stam. (2004). genodynamics.org

7. Gourevitch, P. (1998). *We wish to inform you that tomorrow you will be killed with your families: Stories from Rwanda.* New York: Picador. Human Rights. (1999). *Leave none to tell the tale: Genocide in Rwanda.* New York: Human Rights Watch. Mamdani, M. (2001). *When victims become killers: Colonialism, nativism, and the genocide in Rwanda.* Oxford: James Currey.

8. Gourevitch. *We wish to inform you that tomorrow you will be killed with your families: Stories from Rwanda.* Human Rights. *Leave none to tell the tale: Genocide in Rwanda.*

9. Mamdani. *When victims become killers: Colonialism, nativism, and the genocide in Rwanda.*

10. Davenport and Stam.

11. Human Rights. *Leave none to tell the tale: Genocide in Rwanda.*

12. Staub, E. (1999). The roots of evil: Social conditions, culture, personality and basic human needs. *Personality and Social Psychology Review, 3*(3), 179–92. Staub. (2000). Genocide and mass killings: Origins, prevention, healing and reconciliation. *Political Psychology, 21*(2), 367–82.

13. Staub. The roots of evil: Social conditions, culture, personality and basic human needs, p. 181.

14. Waller, J. (2002). *Genocide and mass killing.* New York: Oxford University Press.

15. Dawkins, R. (1976). *The selfish gene.* London: Oxford University Press. Tajfel, H., & Turner, J.C. (1986). The social identity theory of intergroup behavior. In S. Worchel and W. Austin (Eds.), *Psychology of intergroup relations.* Chicago: Nelson-Hall.

16. Conquest, R. (1986). *The harvest of sorrow.* New York: Oxford University Press. Dolot, M. (1987). *Execution by hunger. The hidden holocaust.* New York: Norton.

17. Janis, I. (1982). *Victims of groupthink* (2nd ed.). Boston: Houghton Mifflin.

18. Ibid., p. 11.

19. Hatzfeld, J. (2003). *Machete Season: The killers in Rwanda speak* (p. 121). New York: Farrar, Straus and Giroux.

20. Ibid.

21. Ibid.

22. Ibid., p. 119.

23. Ibid.

24. Ibid., p. 120.

25. Ibid.

26. Ibid., p. 120.

27. Gourevitch. *We wish to inform you that tomorrow you will be killed with your families: Stories from Rwanda.*

28. Cohen, P. (Director). (1989). *The architecture of doom* (119 minutes). Sweden.

29. Staub. The roots of evil: Social conditions, culture, personality and basic human needs. Staub. Genocide and mass killings: Origins, prevention, healing and reconciliation.

30. Power, S. (2002). *A problem from hell: America and the age of genocide* (p. 145). New York: Harper Collins Perennial.

31. Human Rights. *Leave none to tell the tale: Genocide in Rwanda.*

32. Hatzfeld. *Machete Season: The killers in Rwanda speak,* p. 121.

33. Staub. The roots of evil: Social conditions, culture, personality and basic human needs.

34. Ibid., p. 182. Waller. p. 134.

35. Bandura, A. (1979). The social learning perspective: Mechanisms of aggression. In H. Toch (Ed.), *Psychology of crime and criminal justice* (pp. 298–336). New York: Holt, Rinehart & Winston. Bandura, A. (1988). Social cognitive theory of moral thought and action. In W.M. Kutines and J.L. Gewirtz (Eds.), *Moral development: Advances in theory.* Hillsdale, NJ: Erlbaum

36. Bandura, A. (1987). Mechanisms of moral disengagement. *International Security Studies Program* (p. 3). Washington, DC: Woodrow Wilson Center for Scholars.

37. Osofsky, M., et al. (2005). The role of moral disengagement in the execution process. *Law and Human Behavior, 29*(4), 371–93.

38. Ghigilieri, M. (1999). *The dark side of man: Tracing the origins of male violence.* Reading, MA: Perseus Books.

39. Hatzfeld. *Machete Season: The killers in Rwanda speak,* p. 122.

40. Sherif, M., et al. (1961). *Intergroup cooperation and competition: The robbers cave experiment.* Norman, OK: University Books Exchange.

41. Tajfel and Turner. The social identity theory of intergroup behavior.

42. Simmel, G. (1950). *The sociology of George Simmel.* Glencoe, IL: Free Press.

43. Pepitone, A., & Kleiner, R. (1957). The effects of threat and frustration on group cohesiveness. *Journal of Abnormal and Social Psychology, 54,* 192–99.

44. Chang, I. (1997). *The rape of Nanking* (p. 41). New York: Penguin.

45. Kadri, S. (2005). *The trial: A history, from Socrates to O.J. Simpson* (p. 225). New York: Random House.

46. Cohen, P. (1989). *The architecture of doom.* Sweden.

47. Danner, M. (1994). *The massacre at El Mozote* (p. 75). New York: Vintage Books.

48. Bandura. The social learning perspective: Mechanisms of aggression.

49. Le Bon, G. (1895). *La psychologie des foules.* Paris: F. Olean.

50. Loewenberg, P. (1983). *Decoding the past: the psychohistorical approach.* New York: Knopf.

51. Hatzfeld. *Machete Season: The killers in Rwanda speak.*

52. Staub, E. (1996). Cultural-societal roots of violence. *American Psychologist,* 117–33, p. 120.

CHAPTER 9

1. Browning, C. (1998). *Ordinary men: Reserve police battalion 101 and the final solution in Poland.* New York: Harper Collins.

2. Ibid., p. 53.

3. Ibid., p. 57.

4. Ibid., p. 58.

5. Ibid., p. 59.

6. Ibid.

7. Ibid., p. 73.

8. Ibid.

9. Ibid., p. 62.

10. Ibid.

11. Ibid., p. 64.

12. Ibid., p. 66.

13. Ibid., p. 67.

14. Ibid., p. 68.

15. Ibid.

16. Ibid., p. 69.

17. Ibid.

18. Ibid., p. 72.

19. Grossman, D. (1995). *On killing: The psychological costs of learning to kill in war and society.* Boston: Little, Brown and Company.

20. Ibid., p. 4.

21. Baumeister, R.F., & Campbell, W.K. (1999). The intrinsic appeal of evil: Sadism, sensational thrills, and threatened egotism. *Personality and Social Psychology Review, 3*(3), 210–21.

22. Solomon, R.L. (1980). The opponent-process theory of acquired motivations: The costs of pleasure and benefits of pain. *American Psychologist, 35,* 691–712.

23. Dutton, D.G., & Painter, S.L. (1980). Traumatic bonding: The development of emotional attachments in battered women and other relationships of intermittent abuse. *Victimology: An International Journal, 6*(1–4), 139–55.

24. Solomon. The opponent-process theory of acquired motivations, p. 693.

25. Baumeister & Campbell. The intrinsic appeal of evil.

26. Browning. *Ordinary men: Reserve police battalion 101 and the final solution in Poland,* p. 77.

27. Ibid.

28. Hersh, S.M. (1970). *My Lai 4: A report on the massacre and its aftermath.* New York: Vintage Books.

29. Brownmiller, S. (1975). *Against our will: Men, women and rape* (pp. 101–9). New York: Fawcett, Columbine.

30. Kadri, S. (2005). *The trial: A history, from Socrates to O.J. Simpson* (p. 244). New York: Random House.

31. Kelman, H.C., & Hamilton, V.L. (1989). *Crimes of obedience* (p. 6). New Haven: Yale University Press.

32. Hersh. *My Lai 4: A report on the massacre and its aftermath.*

33. Ibid., p. 7.

34. Kelman and Hamilton. *Crimes of obedience,* p. 7.

35. Ibid., p. 8.

36. Kadri. *The trial: A history, from Socrates to O.J. Simpson.*

37. Sallah, M., & Weiss, M. (2005). *Tiger force: A true story of men and war.* New York: Little, Brown and Company.

38. Ibid., p. 315.

39. Ibid., p. 203.

40. Dutton, D.G., & Kerry, G. (1999). Modus operandi and personality disorder in incarcerated spousal killers. *International Journal of Law and Psychiatry, 22*(3–4), 287–300.

41. Staub, E.. (1999). The roots of evil: Social conditions, culture, personality and basic human needs. *Personality and Social Psychology Review, 3*(3), 179–92.

42. Le Bon, G.. (1895). *La psychologie des foules.* Paris: F. Olean.

43. Ibid., p. 15.

44. Fromm, E. (1973). *The anatomy of human destructiveness* (p. 323). New York: Fawcett Crest.

45. Zimbardo, P.G., et al. (1972). A Pirandellian prison: The mind is a formidable jailer. *New York Times Magazine,* pp. 26–43.

46. Danner. (1993). The Massacre at El Mozote. *The New Yorker,* p. 88.

47. Ibid.

48. Freud, S. (1921). *Group psychology and the analysis of the ego.* London: International Psycholanalytic Press.

49. Redl, F. (1942). Group emotion and leadership. *Psychiatry,* 573–82.

50. Zimbardo, P.G. (1969). The human choice: Individuation, reason and order vs. deindividuation, impulse and chaos. *Nebraska Symposium on Motivation.* Lincoln, NE: University of Nebraska Press.

51. Lifton, R.J. (1973). *Home from the war—Neither victims nor executioners.* New York: Simon and Schuster.

52. Zimbardo. The human choice: Individuation, reason and order vs. deindividuation, impulse and chaos.

53. Ibid.

54. Mawson, A.R. (1987). *Transient criminality: A model of stress induced crime.* New York: Praeger.

55. Ibid., p. 61.

56. Bowlby, J. (1969). *Attachment and Loss. Attachment* (2nd ed., Vol. 1). New York: Basic Books. Bowlby, J. (1973). *Attachment and Loss. Separation* (Vol. 2). New York: Basic Books.

57. Baumeister, R.F. (1990). Suicide as an escape from self. *Psychological Review, 97*(1), 90–113.

58. Dutton, D.G., and Yamini, S. (1995). Cognitive deconstruction and projective-introjective cycling in cases of adolescent parricide. *American Journal of Orthopsychiatry, 65* (1), 39–47.

59. Baumeister. Suicide as an escape from self.

60. Dutton and Yamini. Cognitive deconstruction and projective-introjective cycling in cases of adolescent parricide, p. 43.

61. Gurvitz, T., et al. (1995). *Reduced hippocampal volume on magnetic resonance imaging in chronic post traumatic stress disorder.* Miami, FL: International Society for Stress Studies.

62. Dutton and Yamini, Cognitive deconstruction and projective-introjective cycling in cases of adolescent parricide, p 46

63. Gurvitz et al. *Reduced hippocampal volume on magnetic resonance imaging in chronic post traumatic stress disorder.*

CHAPTER 10

1. Hickey, E.W. (2002). *Serial murderers and their victims* (p. 70). Belmont, CA: Wadsworth.

2. Staub, E. (1999). The roots of evil: Social conditions, culture, personality and basic human needs. *Personality and Social Psychology Review, 3*(3), 179–92.

3. Chang, I. (1997). *The rape of Nanking* (p. 50). New York: Penguin.

4. Baumeister, R.F., et al. (1990). Victim and perpetrator accounts of interpersonal conflict: Autobiographical narratives about anger. *Personality Processes and Individual Differences, 59*(5), 994–1005.

5. Ressler, R.K., et al. (1992). *Sexual homicide: Patterns and motives.* New York: Free Press, Ressler, R.K., et al. (1986). Sexual killers and their victims. *Journal of Interpersonal Violence, 1* (3), 288–308.

6. Ressler, R.K., et al. (1986). Murderers who rape and mutilate. *Journal of Interpersonal Violence, 1*(3), 273–287, p. 273.

7. Brownmiller, S. (1975). *Against our will: Men, women and rape* (p. 109). New York: Fawcett, Columbine.

8. Malamuth, N. (1981). Rape proclivity as a function of exposure to violent sexual stimuli. *Archives of Sexual Behavior, 10,* 33–47. Malamuth, N., et al. (1980). The sexual responsiveness of college students to rape depiction: Inhibitory and disinhibitory effects. *Journal of Personality and Social Psychology, 38,* 399–408.

9. Malamuth, N. (1981b). Rape proclivity amongst males. *Journal of Social Issues, 1981*(37 (4)), 138–154.

10. Bader, M.J. (2002). *Arousal: The secret logic of sexual fantasies.* New York: St. Martin's Press.

11. Brownmiller. *Against our will: Men, women and rape.*

12. Sallah, M., & Weiss, M. (2005). *Tiger force: A true story of men and war* (pp. 201–2). New York: Little, Brown and Company.

13. Brownmiller. *Against our will: Men, women and rape.*

14. Ibid., p. 49.

15. Ibid., p. 51.

16. Ibid., p. 53.

17. Ibid., p. 55.

18. Ibid., p. 56.

19. Woods, J.E. (1998). *The good man of Nanking: John Rabe.* New York: Vintage Books.

20. Beevor, A. (2002). *The fall of Berlin 1945.* New York: Penguin.

21. Ibid., p. 29.

22. Ibid., p. 29.

23. Ibid., p. 107.

24. Ibid., p. 107.

25. Ibid., p. 107–198.

26. Ibid., p. 326.

27. Ibid., p. 326.

28. Ibid., p. 326.

29. Ibid., p. 409.

30. Ibid., p. 414.

31. Ibid., p. 414.

32. Ibid., p. 414–415.

33. Simon, R.I. (2005). *Bad men do what good men dream.* Washington, DC: American Psychiatric Press, Inc.

34. Ibid., p. 75.

35. Ibid., p. 78.

36. Ressler et al. *Sexual homicide: Patterns and motives,* p. 54.

37. Hickey. *Serial murderers and their victims.*

38. Ressler et al. *Sexual homicide: Patterns and motives.*

39. Ibid., p. 54.

40. Brownmiller. *Against our will: Men, women and rape.*

41. Ghigilieri, M. (1999). *The dark side of man: Tracing the origins of male violence.* Reading, MA: Perseus Books.

42. Brownmiller. *Against our will: Men, women and rape.* Sallah & Weiss. *Tiger force: A true story of men and war.*

43. Brownmiller. *Against our will: Men, women and rape.*

44. Ghigilieri. *The dark side of man: Tracing the origins of male violence.*

45. Palmer, C. (1988). Twelve reasons why rape is not sexually motivated: A skeptical examination. *The Journal of Sex Research, 25*(4), 512–30.

46. Ibid., p. 518.

47. Beevor, *The fall of Berlin 1945,* p. 107

48. Power, S. (2002). *A problem from hell: America and the age of genocide.* New York: Harper Collins Perennial.

49. Hickey. *Serial murderers and their victims.*

50. Hartwich, A. (1959). New York: Capricorn Books.

51. Ibid., p. 94.

52. Malamuth et al. The sexual responsiveness of college students to rape depiction: Inhibitory and disinhibitory effects.

53. Chang. *The rape of Nanking.*

54. Schlesinger, L. B. (2004). *Sexual murder: Catathymic and compulsive homicides* (p. 198). Boca Raton: CRC Press.

55. Ibid., p. 199.

56. Ibid.

57. Ibid.

58. Holmes, R. M. (1988). *Serial Murder.* Newbury Park, CA: Sage.

59. McClelland, D. C. (1975). *Power: The Inner Experience.* New York: Halstead.

60. Harden, B. (2003). The banality of Gary: A Green River chiller, *Washington Post,* p. 1.

61. Ibid.

62. Hickey. *Serial murderers and their victims.*

63. Ibid., p. 106.

64. Ressler et al. Murderers who rape and mutilate.

65. Hickey. *Serial murderers and their victims.*

66. Marshal, W. L., & Kennedy, P. (2003). Sexual sadism in sexual offenders: An elusive diagnosis. *Aggression and Violent Behavior, 8*(1), 1–22.

67. Hickey. *Serial murderers and their victims,* p. 17.

68. Hersh, S. M. (1970). *My Lai 4: A report on the massacre and its aftermath.* New York: Vintage Books. Lifton, R. J. (1973). *Home from the war—Neither victims nor executioners.* New York: Simon and Schuster.

69. Hickey. *Serial murderers and their victims,* p. 70.

70. Ibid., p. 176.

71. Becker, E. (1975). *Escape from evil.* New York: The Free Press.

72. Waller, J. (2002). *Becoming evil: How ordinary people commit genocide and mass killing.* New York: Oxford University Press.

73. Gilbert, N. (1993). Advocacy research overstates the incidence of rape and acquaintance rape. In R. J. Gelles and D. R. Loseke (Eds.), *Current controversies on family violence* (p. 128). Newbury Park: Sage.

CHAPTER 11

1. Browning, C. R. (1998). *Ordinary men: Reserve Police Battalion 101 and the final solution in Poland.* New York: Harper Collins.

2. Baumeister, R. F., and Campbell, W. K. (1999). The intrinsic appeal of evil: Sadism, sensational thrills, and threatened egotism. *Personality and Social Psychology Review, 3*(3), 210–21.

3. Conroy, J. (2000). *Unspeakable acts: Ordinary people: The dynamics of torture.* New York: Alfred A. Knopf.

4. Haritos-Fatouros, M. (2003). *The psychological origins of institutionalized torture.* London: Routledge.

5. Conroy. *Unspeakable acts: Ordinary people: The dynamics of torture,* p. 285.

6. Ibid., p. 285–86.

7. Ibid., p. 88.

8. Zimbardo, P. (2006). *The Lucifer effect: Understanding how good people turn evil.* New York: Random House.

9. Milgram, S. (1974). *Obedience to authority.* New York: Harper & Row.

10. Kadri, S. (2005). *The trial: A history, from Socrates to O.J. Simpson* (pp. 245–46). New York: Random House.

11. Lifton, R. J. (1986). *The Nazi doctors: Medical killings and the psychology of genocide.* New York: Basic Books.

12. Ibid., p. 341.

13. Ibid., p. 343.

14. Ibid., p. 341.

15. Arendt, H. (1964). *Eichmann in Jerusalem: A report on the banality of evil.* New York: Viking Press.

16. Kelman, H.C., and Hamilton, V.L. (1989). *Crimes of obedience.* New Haven: Yale University Press.

17. Ibid.

18. Ibid., Table 9.1, p. 215.

19. Ibid.

20. Lifton. *The Nazi doctors: Medical killings and the psychology of genocide,* p. 338.

21. Brickman, P. (1978). Is it real? In *Advances in Experimental Social Psychology.* New York: Wiley.

22. Arendt. *Eichmann in Jerusalem: A report on the banality of evil,* p. 105.

23. Lifton. *The Nazi doctors: Medical killings and the psychology of genocide.*

24. Waller, J. (2002). *Becoming evil: How ordinary people commit genocide and mass killing.* New York: Oxford University Press.

25. Ibid., p. 5.

26. Ibid., p. 7.

27. Kadri. *The trial: A history, from Socrates to O.J. Simpson.*

28. Browning. *Ordinary men: Reserve Police Battalion 101 and the final solution in Poland,* p. 122.

29. Lifton. *The Nazi doctors: Medical killings and the psychology of genocide,* p. 187.

30. Baumeister and Campbell. The intrinsic appeal of evil, p. 212.

31. Waller, p. 123

32. Baumeister and Campbell. The intrinsic appeal of evil.

33. Toch, H. (1969/1993). *Violent men: An inquiry into the psychology of violence.* Washington, DC: American Psychological Association.

34. Groth, A.N. (1979). *Men who rape: The psychology of the offender.* New York: Plenum.

35. MacNair, R.M. (2002). *Perpetration-induced truamatic stress: The psychological consequences of killing.* Westport, CT: Praeger.

NOTES 187

36. Ibid.

37. Solomon, Z., et al. (1996). Acute posttraumatic reactions in soldiers and civilians. In B.A. van der Kolk, A.C. McFarlane, and L. Weisaeth (Eds.), *Traumatic Stress: The effects of overwhelming experience on mind, body and society.* New York: Guilford Press.

38. Herba, C.M., et al. (2007). The Neurobiology of Psychopathy: A Focus on Emotion Processing. In H. Herve and J.C. Yuille (Eds.), *The Psychopath: Theory, research and practice.*. Mahwah, NJ: Lawrence Erlbaum and Associates.

39. Mawson, A.W. (1987). *Transient criminality: A model of stress induced crime.* New York: Praeger.

40. Zimbardo, P. (1969). The human choice: Individuation, reason and order vs. deindividuation, impulse and chaos. *Nebraska Symposium on Motivation.* Lincoln, NE: University of Nebraska Press.

41. Baumeister, R. (1990). Suicide as an escape from self. *Psychological Review, 97*(1), 90–113.

42. Van der Kolk, B.A., et al. (1996). *Traumatic stress: The effects of overwhelming experience on mind, body and society.* New York: Guilford.

43. MacNair. *Perpetration-induced traumatic stress: The psychological consequences of killing.*

44. Baumeister and Campbell. The intrinsic appeal of evil: Sadism, sensational thrills, and threatened egotism.

45. Zimbardo, P., et al. (1972). A Pirandellian prison: The mind is a formidable jailer. *New York Times Magazine,* pp. 26–43.

46. Bandura, A. (1987). Mechanisms of moral disengagement. *International Security Studies Program.* Washington, DC: Woodrow Wilson Center for Scholars.

47. Ferguson, N. (2006). *The war of the world* (p. 124). New York: Penguin.

48. Ibid., p. 124.

49. Ibid.

50. Mawson. *Transient criminality: A model of stress induced crime,* p. 182.

51. Brownmiller, S. (1975). *Against our will: Men, women and rape.* New York: Fawcett, Columbine. Chang, I. (1997). *The rape of Nanking.* New York: Penguin. *Frontline.* (2004). "Ghosts of Rwanda." New York and Washington, DC: Public Broadcasting System.

52. Conroy. *Unspeakable acts: Ordinary people: The dynamics of torture,* p. 262.

53. Brownmiller. *Against our will: Men, women and rape,* p. 109.

54. Suedfeld, P. (2000). Reverberations of the Holocaust fifty years later: Psychology's contributions to understanding persecution and genocide. *Canadian Psychology, 41,* 1–9.

55. Conroy. *Unspeakable acts: Ordinary people: The dynamics of torture,* p. 285.

56. Staub, E. (1990). *Psychology and torture.* New York: Hemisphere.

CHAPTER 12

1. Le Bon, G. (1895). *La psychologie des foules.* Paris: F. Olean.

2. Waller, J. (2002). *Becoming evil: How ordinary people commit genocide and mass killing.* New York: Oxford University Press.

3. Ibid., p. 155.

4. Ibid.

5. Tajfel, H., and Turner, J.C. (1986). The social identity theory of intergroup behavior. In S. Worchel and W. Austin (Eds.), *Psychology of intergroup relations* (p. 22). Chicago: Nelson-Hall.

6. Bowlby, J. (1973). *Attachment and Loss. Separation* (Vol. 2). New York: Basic Books.

7. Nell, V. (2006). Cruelty's rewards: The gratifications of perpetrators and spectators. *Behavioral and Brain Sciences, 29,* 211–57.

8. Ibid., p. 216.

9. Lee, R.B. (1979). *!Kung San: Men, women and work in a foraging society.* Cambridge: Cambridge University Press.

10. Nell. Cruelty's rewards, p. 223.

11. Wrangham, R., and Peterson, D. (1996). *Demonic males: Apes and the origins of human violence* (p. 216). Boston: Houghton Mifflin.

12. Panksepp, J. (1998). *Affective neuroscience: The foundations of human and animal emotions* (p. 147). New York: Oxford.

13. Nell. Cruelty's rewards, p. 9.

14. Ibid.

15. Ibid., p. 220.

16. Ibid., p. 219.

17. Davidson, R.J., et al. (2000). Emotion, plasticity, context, and regulation: Perspectives from affective neuroscience. *Psychological Bulletin, 126*(6), 890–909.

18. Jackson, D.C., et al. (2000). Suppression and enhancement of emotional responses to unpleasant pictures. *Psychophysiology, 37*(4), 515–22.

19. Pietrini, G., et al. (2000). Neural correlates of imaginal aggressive behavior assessed by positron emission tomography in healthy subjects. *American Journal of Psychiatry, 162*(11), 1771–1781.

20. Raine, A., et al. (1998). Reduced prefrontal and increased subcortical functioning assessed using poistron emmision tomography in predatory and affective murderers. *Behavioral Sciences and the Law, 16*(3), 319–32.

21. Ibid.

22. Miller, L. (2000). The predator's brain: Neurodynamics of serial killers. In L.B. Schlesinger (Ed.), *Serial offenders: Current thought, recent findings, and unusual syndromes.* Boca Raton, FL: CRC Press.

23. Ibid., p. 79.

24. Money, J. (1990). Forensic sexology: Paraphilic serial rape (blastophilia) and lust murder (erotophilia). *American Journal of Psychotherapy, 44,* 26–36.

25. Davidson, R.J., et al. (2000). Dysfunction in the neural circuitry of emotion regulation —a possible prelude to violence. *Science, 289,* 591–94, p. 591.

26. Ibid. Pietrini et al. Neural correlates of imaginal aggressive behavior assessed by positron emission tomography in healthy subjects.

27. Dutton, D.G. (2002). The neurobiology of abandonment homicide. *Aggression and Violent Behavior*(7), 407–21.

28. Stein, D. (2000). The neurobiology of evil: Psychiatric perspectives on perpetrators. *Ethnicity and Health, 5*(3/4), 303–15.

29. Nino, C.S. (1996). *Radical Evil on Trial.* New Haven: Yale University Press.

30. Ibid., p. 9.

31. Kadri, S. (2005). *The trial: A history, from Socrates to O.J. Simpson.* New York: Random House. Nino. *Radical Evil on Trial.*

32. Nino. *Radical Evil on Trial,* p. 9.

33. Agence-France-Presse. (2006). Family "buried alive" by Saddam regime. *Vancouver Sun,* pp. A10.

34. Fisher, M. (2006). Does Iraq need another Saddam? *Vancouver Sun.*

35. Ibid.

36. Chang, I. (1997). *The rape of Nanking* (p. 102). New York: Penguin.

37. Ibid., p. 175.

38. Brackman, A. (1987). *The other Nuremberg: The untold story of the Tokyo War Crimes trial* (p. 173). New York: Morrow. Chang. *The rape of Nanking.*

39. Sallah, M., and Weiss, M. (2005). *Tiger force: A true story of men and war.* New York: Little, Brown and Company.

40. Arendt, H. (1964). *Eichmann in Jerusalem: A report on the banality of evil.* New York: Viking Press.

41. Kadri. *The trial: A history, from Socrates to O.J. Simpson.*

42. Goldhagen, D. (1996). *Hitler's willing executioners: Ordinary Germans and the Holocaust.* New York: Knopf.

43. Browning, C.R. (1998). *Ordinary men: Reserve Police Battalion 101 and the final solution in Poland.* New York: Harper Collins.

44. Eley, G. (2000). *The "Goldhagen effect": History, memory, nazism-facing the German past.* Ann Arbor: University of Michigan Press.

45. Chang. *The rape of Nanking.*

46. Chang. *The rape of Nanking,* pp. 174–75.

47. Kadri. *The trial: A history, from Socrates to O.J. Simpson.*

48. Ibid., p. 219.

49. Ibid., p. 220.

50. Ibid.

51. Ibid., p. 223.

52. Ibid., pp. 224–35.

53. Ibid., p. 227.

54. Ibid., p. 228.

55. Ibid., pp. 228–29.

56. Ibid., p. 229.

57. Ibid., p. 230.

CHAPTER 13

1. Baumeister, R., and Campbell, W.K. (1999). The intrinsic appeal of evil: Sadism, sensational thrills, and threatened egotism. *Personality and Social Psychology Review, 3*(3), 210–21. Browning, C. (2000). *Nazi policy, Jewish workers, German killers.* New York: Cambridge University Press. Browning, C. (1998). *Ordinary men: Reserve Police Battalion 101 and the final solution in Poland.* New York: Harper Collins. Goldhagen, D. (1996). *Hitler's willing executioners: Ordinary Germans and the Holocaust.* New York: Knopf. Zimbardo, P. (1969). The human choice: Individuation, reason and order vs. deindividuation, impulse and chaos. *Nebraska Symposium on Motivation.* Lincoln, NE: University of Nebraska Press.

2. Zimbardo, P., et al. (1972). A Pirandellian prison: The mind is a formidable jailer. *New York Times Magazine,* pp. 26–43.

3. Baumeister and Campbell. The intrinsic appeal of evil.

4. Kadri, S. (2005). *The trial: A history, from Socrates to O.J. Simpson.* New York: Random House.

5. Zimbardo. The human choice: Individuation, reason and order vs. deindividuation, impulse and chaos.

6. Stout, C. (2004). *Psychology of terrorism.* Westport, CT: Praeger.

7. Feldman, N. (2006). Islam, terror and the second nuclear age. *New York Times Magazine,* pp. 72–79.

8. Conroy, J. (2000). *Unspeakable acts: Ordinary people: The dynamics of torture* (p. 286). New York: Alfred A. Knopf.

9. Brownmiller, S. (1975). *Against our will: Men, women and rape.* New York: Fawcett, Columbine. Chang, I. (1997). *The rape of Nanking.* New York: Penguin. Loewenberg, P. (1983). *Decoding the past: The psychohistorical approach.* New York: Knopf. Suedfeld, P. (2001). Theories of the Holocaust: Trying to explain the unimaginable. In D. Chirot and M.E.P. Seligman (Eds.), *Ethnopolitical warfare: Causes, consequences and possible solutions.* Washington, DC: APA Press.

10. Dietz, P., et al. (1991). Threatening and otherwise inappropriate letters to Hollywood celebrities. *Journal of Forensic Sciences, 36,* 185–209.

11. Darley, J. (1999). Methods for the study of evil doing actions. *Personality and Social Psychology Review, 3*(3), 269–75, p. 269.

12. Wright, E. (2004). *Generation Kill.* New York: G.P. Putnam.

13. McConnell, S. (2005). The logic of terrorism. *The American Conservative.*

INDEX

ABOUT THE AUTHOR

DONALD G. DUTTON is Professor of Psychology at the University of British Columbia. A Licensed Clinical Psychologist, Dutton has researched violence in forensic and domestic situations across 30 years. He has led court-mandated treatment groups for violent offenders, interviewed spousal killers, and authored four books plus more than 100 articles on the psychological mechanisms of violence perpetrators. Dutton has appeared on *Dateline NBC, Larry King Live,* National Public Radio, and *Good Morning America.*